FIGHTING FOR
SURVIVAL

FIGHTING FOR
SURVIVAL

My Journey through Boxing Fame, Abuse,
Murder, and Resurrection

CHRISTY MARTIN
AND
RON BORGES

ROWMAN & LITTLEFIELD
Lanham • Boulder • New York • London

Published by Rowman & Littlefield
An imprint of The Rowman & Littlefield Publishing Group, Inc.
4501 Forbes Boulevard, Suite 200, Lanham, Maryland 20706
www.rowman.com

86-90 Paul Street, London EC2A 4NE, United Kingdom

British Library Cataloguing in Publication Information Available

Library of Congress Cataloging-in-Publication Data Available

ISBN 9781538153581 (cloth : alk. paper)
ISBN 9781538153598 (electronic)

♾™ The paper used in this publication meets the minimum requirements of
American National Standard for Information Sciences—Permanence of Paper for
Printed Library Materials, ANSI/NISO Z39.48-1992.

To my wife, Lisa, for her unwavering support and encouragement, and to all the underdogs the world has ever counted out and every victim of domestic abuse still longing to become a survivor.

—*Christy Martin*

To Nina, the one person always in my corner with sound advice and an enswell when I need it, and to Laura and Jack, my reasons to keep on fighting.

—*Ron Borges*

CONTENTS

FOREWORD

Don King

It is never easy to be a pioneer. I know, because I was one in the world of boxing promotion. It is one of the many reasons I have such respect and admiration for Christy Martin.

The pioneer has no trail to follow, no role model to emulate. The pioneer must blaze her own trail, as Christy did in the world of female prize fighting. Such an endeavor did not even exist as a legitimate sport until she and I combined to create it. I gave her the platform when I made her the first female fighter I ever promoted, but all that did was open a door. It was Christy who had to fight her way through it to the top by facing down the naysayers and the wayfarers and standing up to the challenges, the setbacks, the disappointments, and the difficulties to turn a dream into a reality. In the end, she proved she had the physical attributes to respond and the mental aptitude to carry on.

The thing I first saw in her was that she was a fighter. She was aggressive, but she had more than aggression. She had skill, and she had will, but it takes more than skill and will. It takes attitude, and this young lady had that in abundance. She was a rare commodity in boxing and in life—she could fight, and she had an "I-don't-give-a-damn-what-you-think" attitude toward her critics and those who kept insisting her dream was an impossibility.

The naysayers and the dream slayers could not stop her, because she refused to listen. She marched to the beat of her own drummer, and that drummer could punch.

From the first time I saw her fight, it was clear to me she was not afraid. She was not afraid to fight anybody, not afraid to accept any challenge, and damn sure not afraid of the skeptics and the haters who said women couldn't fight. It has been really great for me to watch her stand up for women in the sport of boxing, and now she is doing the same for women facing the even bigger scourge of domestic violence.

Christy is someone who deals with what is real. In the boxing world that meant dealing with a harsh reality. Although boxing is a sport, it is also known as the "hurt business" for a reason. You must be willing to endure great sacrifice and pain to win fame and acclaim inside a boxing ring. Christy Martin did the former and achieved the latter like no other woman in sports history.

In boxing we can argue all night long over who is the greatest of all time, but in her case, no one can argue that if the International Boxing Hall of Fame had not recognized her in its first class of female fighter inductees in 2020, it would have been a terrible injustice. When she became a prizefighter, there was no such thing as women's boxing. The few women trying to make it in the hurt business were viewed by most of society as a sideshow or female invaders in a man's world. How wrong those skeptics were.

Christy Martin was battling against custom and tradition. She was fighting against perception and prejudice. She was squaring off against the very notion that women can't fight, or should not fight. She had to fight not just her opponents, but also the system. She beat them both time and again until she was finally recognized as the GOAT of her sport.

To this day, if I go anywhere in the sports world and mention women's boxing, the first name I hear is Christy Martin. That will never change, because she blazed the trail for all the young women fighting today. They all owe her a debt of gratitude.

Some may say, "If it hadn't been Christy Martin, it would have been someone else." To them I say, well, it WAS Christy Martin. She is the one who left a mark. She is the reason women like Laila Ali and Clarissa Shields began to box. She showed all women it could be done, even in the face of a system massed against her. She did what only trailblazers can do. She made a way out of no way.

Promoters and television executives didn't want to put her on. They wanted nothing to do with women in boxing. But I had Mike Tyson, the great heavyweight champion, and I told those men if they wanted Tyson, then they had to have Christy, too. But opportunity is not fulfillment. She had to do something with those opportunities, and she did. That's why I'm so very proud of her and all that she has accomplished.

Christy fought for me for nearly a decade, and we set records and broke barriers. From her first knockout win, I knew she had something special. She fulfilled my prophecy. She wanted to be big. She wanted to be a star. She wanted success. The difference with her was she also wanted to work for it. Christy Martin never asked for anything easy.

She would fight anyone. She would fight anywhere, any time. She was a fighter in the ring but a charmer outside the ring. She had personality to go with ability. She cared about the fans and understood what I meant when I would say, "My power lies with my people ties." Fans loved to see her fight, because they knew what they were going to get. She had integrity and a commitment to the sport and to the fans who pay the bills, and she gave those fans what they wanted. Every time she stepped into the ring she came with bad intentions.

If you want to sell a steak, you can't just have the sizzle. You have to have the sauce, too. Christy Martin understood that. That's what made her special. She was more than just a great fighter. She was a great saleswoman for women and for what they could accomplish if someone was just willing to give them an opportunity.

I admire her courage and her steadfastness in a sport filled with duplicitous individuals who will do you harm to do themselves good. Devil be damned was always her attitude. That's part of what helped to make Christy great.

Even after her own husband masterminded her from existence almost to nonexistence, she refused to quit. When she announced her comeback after he shot and stabbed her and left her for dead, I wasn't surprised. I was apprehensive for her but not surprised that she was fighting back. That was her essence. That's who she was the first day I met her and signed her to a contract. It's who she is today. Christy Martin is a winner.

That's why this book, *Fighting for Survival*, is a revelation. It's a story filled with the ups and downs of life, the very highs and the abysmal lows of her fight against the longest of odds to become a champion. Most of all, it's a story filled with the power that comes from refusing to lose.

Christy Martin is providing in these pages a roadmap for anyone facing difficulty and adversity in life by telling her story unfiltered and unambiguous. It's an inspiring story of a woman I greatly respect and admire, a woman who understood you must believe the unbelievable to snatch the possible out of the impossible.

Dead on the Floor

I could hear my husband sharpening a knife in the front room. Because he was also my longtime abuser, I knew he wasn't doing it to carve up a turkey. He was doing it to carve up his wife.

Long after he left me for dead on my bedroom floor, that day turned out to be a day of thanksgiving. True, it was the day I nearly died like so many other battered and abused women do each year in America at the hands of their domestic partners, but for me it became the day I finally came to life.

Like all the battles that would make me the first woman fighter inducted into the International Boxing Hall of Fame, it would be a bloody victory over myself as much as my opponent. I'm Christy Martin, the fighter who legitimized combat sports for women. I've been called the Jackie Robinson of female boxing, because I was the one who transformed it into a legitimate athletic contest, not a circus act. For more than 20 years, it was a great ride. The only problem was that I nearly died in the process of helping create a new sporting venue for women, because for all of that time, and for most of my life really, I was hiding the fact that there was much more to my life than championship fights and the biggest paydays any female fighter ever earned. You see, I was also a closeted gay woman athlete in a sport, and a world, where homosexuality was never going to sell. Not in the 1980s. Not in the 1990s. Not so much even today, frankly.

You may believe otherwise, and I certainly understand it's a different world now than the one I knew coming up as a woman in what is a male-dominated sport. But if it's so different, where are all the other gay women boxers? Where are all the gay women cage fighters? Why are the biggest female stars in most sports still sold as much in high heels and short skirts as in sneakers or cleats?

We all know there are plenty of gay men and women in professional sports. There always have been, and there always will be. A few, like the American soccer star Megan Rapinoe, proudly proclaim it. That's great, but the truth is it's a lot easier to do that with an Olympic gold medal around your neck and a

World Cup in your arms. For most of the rest of us, it's a public declaration not so easily made and one that can make for a difficult life.

How would I know? Well, you see, I'm also Christy Salters, a coal miner's daughter from Itmann, West Virginia, long locked in a fight with myself and with what I came to believe was a family and a society that demanded I live in the shadows. It was a fight more real and more damaging to me than anything I faced in the 59 professional boxing matches in which I became the biggest name on the women's side of the sport and the only one to make millions in the process. That was true the day I retired in 2012, and I believe it's basically still true today.

I had celebrity and fame, which frankly aren't always the same thing, even though they come with a lot of the same baggage. When I first got into boxing in 1989, female fighters were viewed as little more than a titillation for half-drunk male spectators before the real boxing began. Female boxing was not seen by most fans as a true sporting event until I was fortunate enough to make it one.

Female boxing was banned in most of the world when I first climbed into the ring on September 9, 1989. It remained that way for many years. It was neither a recognized Olympic sport nor a professional one. The few places where it was legal, it was ridiculed. Critics would ask, why would women want to fight? Why would anyone want to watch them if they did? Maybe for the same reasons that men did? That last question was something no one ever thought to ask.

As for mixed martial arts, which would later become the financial colossus now known as Ultimate Fighting Championship (more familiarly called simply UFC), there was no place for a woman inside its caged octagon either.

Yet by the late afternoon of November 23, 2010, Christy Martin was the most famous female fighter in the world. By then people had come to accept women in boxing and MMA as legitimate athletes. Unfortunately for me, on that day I would be making headlines in a far different arena.

Before nightfall I would be stabbed a half dozen times, have one of my calves sheared off like it was a pot roast, end up with one ear dangling off the side of my head from being pistol whipped, and finally left on the floor with a 9 mm bullet hole in my chest. I was still the World Boxing Council women's super-welterweight champion and the highest earning female fighter in boxing history, but I was a lot of other things, too, and one was nearly dead. Dead on the inside as well as the outside.

I had been sexually abused at the age of six but kept it a dark secret for nearly 40 years. I was domestically abused for two decades but kept that a secret, too. All that time I'd also been hiding from the world the fact that I was a lesbian locked in a sham marriage designed to protect me from a sporting world I'd come to believe would never accept me as I was. Why should it? My own mother hadn't.

Although I appeared to be one person on the outside, the truth was I was at this point nearly broke, a cocaine addict, and bleeding out on my carpet. Where once I would have done anything to avoid being knocked to the ground, I was ready to just lie there and let myself be counted out.

But it's funny what goes through your mind when your husband has just shot you in the chest. Only minutes before Jim Martin pulled the trigger and finally ended 19 years of domestically abusing me in every way possible—mentally, physically, and emotionally—I thought I wanted to die.

I'd told my friends that for several days and, truth be told, Jim had told me he'd kill me for more than 20 years if I ever tried to leave him. So it wasn't like I didn't know what was coming. In my mind, when that day began, I was fine with it. Anything to end the life I'd been living. But even though I was willing to die, I wasn't willing to die without a fight.

Boxers, one of which I was for 23 years, say that all the time. We all say we're willing to die in the ring. For a lot of us, it is true, unbelievable as that may sound. We think of ourselves as warriors, because that is what we are trained to become. I'd been paid millions of dollars to knock people out and accept a simple truth—fighters would rather die in a boxing ring than quit on their stool or have someone throw in the white towel of surrender.

That's not true in MMA and the UFC, where they let you tap out. If you get yourself into too much trouble in the octagon and don't think you can get out, you're allowed to quit. There's no stigma to it. Just tap out, and it's over. You walk out of the cage, take a shower, and go have a few beers. Not a problem.

Technically, you can do the same thing in boxing, but the culture won't accept it, even when it's really the only logical thing to do. In the boxing ring, you don't tap out. You get carried out on your shield, or you walk off in shame. That may be nuts in the opinion of a lot of people, but it is how boxers view their world. Too often they die in the ring because of it. That's why they call it the hurt business. Because it hurts.

I believed in that code from the first time I stepped into the ring, and I fought that way. It was the main reason I became so popular. I came to fight, and too much of the time I came to bleed, and every fan knew it. Because I was willing to do both, I didn't lose a fight for nearly a decade. That's why people paid a lot of money to watch me fight. They knew what they'd get. Blood and somebody on the floor.

So, it came as no surprise to me on November 23, 2010, that I'd made the decision I'd made. I was ready to die in the last fight of my life—the fight to free myself from a life that had gone bat shit crazy, to be honest.

I was ready to fight my own husband, who was also my boxing trainer and manager, to win back what he'd taken from me. He took my identity, although to be fair he wasn't alone. As my promoter, Don King, used to say, I'd been a coconspirator in my own demise. So had my family.

I was finally ready to fight to win control of what was left of my life, but if I died trying, that was OK, too. Or so I thought until I saw my pink-handled, 9 mm Glock in my husband's fingers. Just like that, I wasn't quite so willing to give up my life just to find myself.

When you're lying there dying on the floor, your whole thinking process changes. Do you really want to die *today*? Maybe not.

By that point in my life, not many things surprised me, but my reaction to seeing my own handgun pointed at me did. It surprised the fighter in me, and it sure surprised the woman in me that the world called "the coal miner's daughter." That woman had once been a lost little girl, growing up scared of who she was in a little West Virginia coal mining town the world didn't even know existed, just like it didn't know I existed. Much had changed about that little girl by then, but not enough to save me from being abused, one way or another, for most of my life.

So, the shocking reality that I wasn't as ready to quit on life as I thought stunned me like a punch in the face, which by then I had had a lot of experience coping with. I wasn't willing to die after all. I could feel myself mustering the will to fight back one more time.

Jim was my first trainer in boxing but only the latest in a long line of people who had abused me in so many ways. Few people knew about all that until the day came when my secret life played out on national newscasts and later on *Court TV*. "Murder Trial of the Year!" they called it then, and I guess maybe it was, although like most everything else that has happened in my life, that took a while to become clear. Just like what led me to be staring up at that gun in the first place.

By that day, my husband and I knew my boxing career was nearly over, and our relationship was, too. We'd talked about it many times. At one point,

I'd even drawn up a contract that would allow him to still train me, and I'd be responsible for all of our joint expenses, like insurance and training costs, if he'd agree to a divorce. He wanted no part of it.

So, I'd decided I'd try to fight a few more times even though I was well past my prime just to make us some money before we split up for good. Despite the millions I'd made boxing, we were nearly broke, and that way we could go our separate ways and at least have something to show for 20 years in boxing beyond the memories and the big fights and all the hiding I'd done in between them.

It wasn't like he didn't know who I really was. The truth is in a lot of ways he knew me better than anybody, even better than my parents. They should have tried to understand who I was, but they didn't. Or they couldn't. Jim knew that, and he used it to control me. To this day, I'm not sure which was worse.

Jim understood I was gay pretty much from the start of our relationship. Maybe he convinced himself for a while that I was bisexual, but he knew the truth. For a time, I convinced myself maybe that's who I was, too, but deep inside I knew otherwise. We were just two lonely people thrust together in a hard world. The one thing I was sure of back then was that not many people in the world I knew wanted to hear anything about a gay female boxer.

Around this time, I'd reconnected with my first love, Sherry Lusk, a girl I'd had a relationship with when we were in high school. That lasted until a year or so after we went off to college, but then we both found other women, as is usually the case with first loves. You go your separate ways, but you never do forget them.

We'd had some contact off and on over the years, but not much, really. She had sent me a message once congratulating me on my boxing success. And around 1994 or 1995, I was supposed to fight in Raleigh, North Carolina, and she was living nearby, so she came over to watch me train. She'd also sent me a *Sports Illustrated* cover I was on to autograph for her, which I did. But there really wasn't much of anything happening between us for years.

Then in early 2010, as my life and my marriage were unraveling, I began talking with her on Facebook. Jim knew it, because he knew everything I did. He had cameras all over our house, filming me 24/7. He'd follow me everywhere, just showing up at places where I'd gone. He'd walk into a nail salon or come into my hairdresser's shop for no reason but to let me know he knew every step I took. It made me uncomfortable. It was like I was always under surveillance, but I never thought there was much I could do about it without risking someone finding out the truth about me.

Once I got back in touch with Sherry, one thing led to another. She wasn't in a relationship. She was living in Charlotte and recovering from her own cocaine issues, which I found out later. So, she was alone. In my mind, so was I. Up to that point in my life, I always had been alone, even when it looked like I wasn't. I didn't totally realize that then, or understand what that can do to you, but I do now.

Sherry and I started playful flirting, but the truth was I wasn't leaving Jim Martin for her. Maybe he thought I was, but that was not going to happen. I wasn't leaving him for someone else, but the week before Jim tried to murder me, I did finally go to see Sherry.

I was supposed to be in Tampa that Saturday night to work as a commentator on an amateur boxing show, but I told him on Thursday I was going to drive up to St. Augustine first to visit with her. He knew who she was and what she had once been in my life but didn't seem bothered by it. In fact, he asked if he could come along, even though he knew the answer.

Before I left, he reminded me of something I'd heard many times by then. He said, "If you leave me, I'll kill you." I'm sure that sounds pretty chilling, but he'd been saying it to me for so long it didn't really register any more in the way that it should have. You hear the words, but you don't totally believe them anymore, which is how a lot of abused women end up dead.

The crazier things got, and the more controlling he became, the more I started to wonder, though, and this time something seemed different. The words were the same, but there was an edge to them I hadn't really felt before. Maybe it was his tone. Maybe I sensed desperation or a different sort of irritation in his voice. I'm not sure what it was, but the truth was that at that point I didn't care what he said to me or what he did to me. In my mind, I was already dead.

It's hard for people to understand why I would stay in that kind of a relationship for nearly 20 years, especially when I was the one supporting us with my purses from boxing. I was a world champion. I had become a well-known athlete. I'd had a million dollars in the bank. So why would a successful gay woman athlete stay in an abusive relationship for 20 years with a man 25 years older than she was? If you've ever been in one, you probably understand. If not, maybe by the end of this book you will.

That's the kind of emotional control someone can have over you. You know you should leave, but you're ashamed of the situation you're in and afraid of the consequences if you go. In my case, I was also hiding a secret I felt he would expose if I walked away before my boxing career was over. I had gotten to the point where I was legit, afraid he might kill me, but I was more afraid he would ruin my career. I thought he could take away everything I'd worked all my life to build.

By this time, I'd been doing cocaine almost daily for nearly four years. It had gotten to the point where I was doing it every day just to get through the nightmare my life had become. I did it in my house. I did it on the way to the gym. I did it on the way home. I did it in the gym. I did it to escape, because I didn't have the courage to just walk away and start over. How do you do that as a fading, 42-year-old prize fighter? Start over doing what? So, instead, you look for one more fight. Or maybe two. At that point, fighting was all I really knew how to do.

You don't get yourself in that kind of situation overnight. It doesn't happen in a day or a week or a year. It takes a lifetime to slide that far down, but there I was. Down but not quite out.

So, I stayed with him, but we pretty much were living separate lives. We were in the same house, but we didn't sleep together or do much together but train on the days I was able to do it. Train and get high. Sleep and wake up. Repeat.

Jim was the one who had introduced drugs into my life, although if I'm honest about it, he didn't make me do them. That was my choice, one of many I regret. All he did was leave them around the house. I think he knew eventually I would use, and he was right. It was another way to keep control over someone he could sense was starting to slip away.

The funny thing is the day I went off to see Sherry, I didn't intend to spend the night with her. We were just going to meet and talk like old high-school friends do, and then I was going to drive to Tampa to get ready to broadcast those fights. But I did stay, and that's how things came to a head.

There's a famous old boxing trainer named Cus D'Amato. He was a big name in boxing in the 1960s because he stood up to the Mob when it was running the sport and refused to let his fighters fight for them. Near the end of his life, he was the guy who discovered Mike Tyson in a juvenile detention center in Upstate New York and set him on the road to becoming the youngest heavyweight champion in boxing history. He was a mysterious legend of the sport.

I never met him, but people say he was like an old mystic or something. He used to say a lot of things about human nature and the power of the mind. He understood people, which is probably why he was a successful trainer. One thing he used to say was, "What you do in the end is what you were going to do all along."

I don't know if that's true, but it's probably exactly what happened with me and Sherry. We did in St. Augustine what we were going to do all along. We slept together. Not that I particularly cared.

I didn't realize it then, but I can see now I was going back to look for that innocent kind of love I felt for her when I was just a girl in middle school. That crazy kind of love Patsy Cline sang about. The blind love that makes you think you can do anything. Maybe I was a piece of shit, but it didn't matter to me if I fucked up her life. At the time, I didn't give any credence to her life. That's a terrible thing to say, but it's the truth. I just wanted that feeling of blind love back.

The problem for me was it wasn't like high school anymore. She was still pretty much the same, but Christy Salters wasn't. That Christy was gone. Christy Martin was much different from the girl from Mullens who just wanted to be free to be with the person I'd fallen in love with but knew I had to keep well hidden. I was still hiding from all that, but things had gotten to the point where the hiding had to end, one way or another.

Jim called Thursday night and told me he knew where I was and what we were doing. He was threatening me without saying anything threatening. There was something in his voice. You learn to sense trouble when you fight for a living. You sense it before it happens. That's one way you survive in a boxing ring. Same thing in life.

That night I just felt my life had become a slow death sentence, and if there is one thing that was true about me, it's that I didn't do anything slow for very long. I always went for broke, win or lose, so I stayed the night with Sherry. It was the Thursday before Thanksgiving.

We had breakfast the next day, and then I drove back home. Jim didn't say anything about where I'd been, and the next day, which was Saturday, I drove to Tampa to work the show. On the way Jim called and told me the promoter had a hotel room for me if I wanted to spend the night. I decided I'd do that.

Once I got there, people said they hadn't seen me this happy in a long time. I told some of them that I was about to leave Jim, but it was all going to be fine. I thought it was, no matter how I left. Upright or on my shield, I would be leaving the way I'd lived. I'd be leaving like a fighter.

Then I called Sherry, and she agreed to meet me in Altamonte Springs after the show, and we stayed together again before I drove home on Sunday night. I didn't expect to see her any time soon, or maybe ever again, but she called on Monday, and I agreed to meet her in Daytona Beach.

I told Jim I was leaving again, but I didn't tell him where I was going. I got to Daytona first and checked us into our room. She showed up on her motorcycle a little later, and the minute she walked in my phone rang. It was Jim.

"I'm so close I could touch you," is what he said, cold as you can imagine. "I saw the way you greeted her." Then he hung up.

That freaked me out, because I was afraid that he might show up and kill me right there. When we finally went to get something to eat, my phone rang again.

"You're in my sights," is all he said. Then he hung up. We got up and went back to the room and never moved all night. The next day was November 23, the day that changed my life.

Sherry and I went to Denny's for breakfast, and I told her I was going back home. She told me not to. She said I could just disappear, but I told her Christy Martin couldn't just disappear. Not anymore.

I'm pretty stubborn about most things. I was going back, and whatever happened was going to happen. She knew me well enough to understand that. So, she made me memorize her cell phone number. I remember her saying, "Nobody knows anyone's number anymore." I thought it was a funny thing to say, but I knew it was true, so I memorized it. Then I headed back home.

I was certain he was going to try to kill me, but like a fight against a big-name opponent, I knew I had to face it, or I would have to run for the rest of my life. When I was boxing, I never ran. That was part of my appeal with the public. The fans knew Christy Martin came to fight. I always came forward, even when I shouldn't have. This was probably one of those times I shouldn't have, but it was all I knew. I didn't see any other option. It was like my approach to a fight: I'd get her, or she'd get me. Frankly, I was pretty sure he'd get me, but I didn't give a shit. In boxing, that's a good attitude to have and a necessary evil. In a domestic abuse situation like I was in, it probably isn't the smartest approach.

When I got back, I was driving toward the house and saw Jim outside with a friend of his named Scott Selkirk, who lived down the street. They were in the driveway, and the two of them together made me uncomfortable. I was afraid they were going to kill me, so I drove on by and went to my hairdresser to say goodbye and called one of my closest friends to tell her what I was doing. She told me not to go back, too. Of course, I didn't listen.

When I finally got home, what was crazy is I went into my bathroom and looked at three little specks of dried blood that were on the wall near the mirror. I'd left them there, just three little drops, from one of the other times a couple years before when Jim had hit me so hard, he knocked a tooth through my lip.

It kept bleeding all over the place, and when I finally cleaned up, I left those three spots on the wall. They were like a reminder. I guess they should have been a warning, too, but instead of listening, I just told a friend of mine who worked for my promoter that if I ever disappeared, she should take the cops to those three specks of blood.

Jim walked in, and I told him I was tired and needed to lie down and then I wanted to go to the gym to work out. My head was pounding. As I was lying there, I could hear him sharpening that knife, which wasn't all that unusual. He always had a lot of knives around, and he'd sharpen them there, but then I heard him on the phone, and I knew something was different this time. He was talking to one of my relatives, and I heard him say I was a lesbian and I was leaving him for a woman. I'd never said that. I said I was leaving, but I wasn't leaving him for a woman. I was leaving him for my own sanity, what little was left of it.

For some reason, I sat up and put on one shoe. That's when he walked back in. He had his hands behind his back and he said, "I got something I want to show you."

I thought maybe it was a contract for a fight. I hadn't fought in 14 months. I was barely training, and it seemed like maybe my career was over, but we both needed a payday, and I thought maybe he'd come up with one. On paper I was still the WBC super-welterweight champion. I knew what I really was, which was a mess, but I also knew if you had a reputation and a championship belt, you could still get paid for that, even if you were only getting paid this time to take a beating and lose that belt.

That's when Jim turned his back, and I saw the knife tucked in the back of his waistband. To be honest, I never thought he'd stab me. Shoot me? Sure. But stab me? I didn't really believe he would do that, so I just looked at him and said, "What are you going to do? Kill me?"

Just like that he was on me. Stabbing me. He stabbed me deep three times on my left side and then one good time into my left breast. I started kicking and trying to fight back, and that's when he started slashing me and cut my calf half off.

He pulled out my gun and started to hit me with it. He pistol-whipped me so bad they had to sew my right ear back on after I got to the hospital. I was bleeding all over the place as he kept walking in and out of the room like a wild animal. Prowling. I didn't know it then, but he'd cut his hand, which they told me later is pretty common when someone is trying to stab another person multiple times.

I started pleading with him to stop. I even told him I still loved him. At one point I remember saying, "Don't make my parents bury another child!" I don't remember him saying anything. Just walking in and out of the room.

I begged him to call 9-1-1. Instead, he took the battery out of my Blackberry and threw it across the room. We had a wall phone in the bathroom that he unplugged. Then he walked into the bedroom holding it with the wire dangling from it and said, "Oh, this phone's not working either." Every time he pushed the buttons of that disconnected phone, he was smiling.

At some point, it finally hit me. You'd think I would have already realized it, but all of a sudden, I understood he couldn't let me live. He was slamming my head into the dresser and pistol-whipping me, and that's when the switch flipped. A lot of people say they're ready to die, like I'd done all that week. You might think that, too, if you're beaten down and as lost as I was at the time. But what I learned that day is what you're really feeling at that point isn't that you want to die. It's that you don't know how to live anymore.

This is the web you can get caught up in with domestic violence. Domestic abuse isn't just about bruises. It is an emotional beatdown. That's often how it goes. They batter you emotionally until they feel they may be losing control of you. That's when it turns physical.

So, there he was now, standing over me holding my own pink-handled 9 mm Glock in his hand. We started fighting over it, and as we wrestled with each other, I got my hand on the release button for the magazine near the trigger and pressed it. The magazine kicked out, but he still had the gun in his hand. Unfortunately, my 9 mm handgun held 6+1, meaning six bullets in the clip and one in the chamber. You can't "kick" that last one out.

Jim aimed it at me again, and I just lost it. I remember screaming, "Motherfucker, you cannot kill me! I hate you! You don't have the balls to shoot me."

Like everything else I'd thought about Jim Martin, I was wrong about that, too.

The man who had trained me, managed me, taught me everything I knew about boxing and who was supposed to protect me shot me right in the chest. Right in the same hole where he'd stabbed me in the breast. The bullet went clean through me and would have come out my back, but it stopped because I was lying on a cement floor. The doctors told me later that three inches made the difference—I would have been dead right there. Then he walked into the bathroom, got in the shower, and started washing the blood off his hands.

I grabbed some shirts and tried to hold the blood in against my chest. My lung was punctured from the stab wounds, and it started making gurgling noises and spurting blood all over the place. I fell back and was looking up at the ceiling, waiting to die, and right at that moment I saw an air vent register in the ceiling. It was like it was a portal to God.

Now, I'm not a particularly religious person. Nothing like that. It's just what I felt at the moment. I remember saying, "Please help me get out of here." That's when I heard the shower running. I don't know how, but somehow I got up, grabbed my car keys and the gun, and stumbled out the door, but when I got to my car I realized I had the wrong keys.

I knew I couldn't go back inside, so I just went into the street and kind of tried to carjack anyone who came by. The first guy was in a pickup truck, and he just swerved around me and was gone. Can't imagine why.

As it turned out, the guy in the truck drove a block up and turned around to come back, but by then a car had stopped. The man driving was named Rick Cole. Never met him before, but he was my angel. He told me later I looked at him and just said, "Please don't let me die."

That still strikes me as funny, because I'd been so ready to die all week until I was finally faced with it. I can't even tell you why I was fighting so hard. Maybe it's just my nature. Maybe it was instinct. Or maybe it was because I knew that if I did, I might get one last chance to be who I really was born to be in this world.

Rick put me in the backseat of his car, and we were gone. The whole ordeal had lasted just under an hour . . . or 19 years, depending on how you care to look at it. Later the guy in the pickup got in touch with me to let me know he had come back for me. He told me that by the time he'd turned around and driven back by the house, he saw Jim standing in the front yard in his underwear. Just standing there staring. I never saw him. By then I was gone. The next time I saw Jim Martin, he was in handcuffs.

After Rick got me in his car, he drove to the hospital, which thankfully was only about five minutes away. All I could think to do was apologize for bleeding all over his backseat. He told me later I said it over and over.

How had my life come to this? To know that we have to go all the way back to where things started. Back to a little coal mining town in southern West Virginia and a confused little girl who couldn't tell her family she was gay or about what someone had done to her when she was only six.

My dream had been to become a successful boxer, and I'd lived that dream. I fell in love with the sport, but the truth is I was fighting long before I started boxing. Fighting sexual abuse, domestic abuse, and my fear that the world I'd created would come crashing down around me one day if the fact that I was not just a successful woman athlete but a gay woman athlete ever came out to a world not ready to deal with it. Living life in the closet is stifling. It's as deadly to your soul as Jim Martin was standing over me with that gun in his hand.

Like a lot of abused women, my life had become a web of lies, deceits, and violence. The difference with me was that from the outside it looked like I was immune from the kind of trouble I had been facing all those years. I'd been the first woman to fight on national television. The first to fight on pay-per-view shows with Mike Tyson. I was on the cover of *Sports Illustrated*. I was supposed to be rich. So how could I be someone bleeding on the floor of my bedroom with a bullet in my chest? The simple answer is because it can happen to anyone, but no one's story is ever quite that simple.

That's the story I'm here to tell. The rest of my story. The real story that I believe millions of abused and closeted people suffering in the shadows like I once did need to hear, because it's a story about hope. As I was riding in the back of that car, bleeding on the man's upholstery and not sure if I was going to wake up the next morning, hope was all I had left. What is hope, really? It's the possibility for change. That's all hope is, but sometimes it's enough to keep you going.

But let's be clear about one thing before we go too far down that road. Trust and believe when I tell you: this is not a victim's story. Although a lot of folks might see it that way, it is not a victim's story at all.

It's a survivor's story. A hope-filled story. It's my story.

Honestly it is.

Coal Miner's Daughter

All you need to know to understand the limits of Itmann, West Virginia, is this: your cell phone won't work there.

Itmann is a coal camp that sits along a one-mile strip of West Virginia Route 16 with the Appalachian Mountains pressing down hard against it on one side and the Guyandotte River squeezing it tightly on the other. If you cross the river, the railroad tracks lie only a few feet away, so when it comes to housing there isn't much open space. Not that there needs to be. The last census said Itmann had 283 people living there, earning a median income of $23,932. It is not a place where people dream big, if they feel free to dream at all. Mostly they work hard just to survive.

That's where I grew up. In a coal camp once owned by the man who ran the biggest coal mine in our area, I.T. Mann. To make it easy to understand the size of the place, it is exactly one mile in a straight line between "Welcome to Itmann" and "Thanks for Coming."

The mine owners controlled economic life in Itmann, not only with the jobs buried deep inside those mountains that surrounded us, but also with the biggest building in town—the company store. That's where you bought your groceries and nearly everything else you needed to live and work there. You were buying from the same company that was helping you pay for those goods, so some weeks there were men, and families, who never saw a dollar because their pay had already been spent before they picked up their check.

The company store is gone now, and by the time I was born, on June 12, 1968, my family didn't do its shopping there, but the shell of the place still towers over our little town. It's in sad disrepair, just like the coal industry, but it's listed as a historic landmark and is still the biggest building in Itmann. It's a reminder of what places like Itmann were and what they are today.

In 1916 the Pocahontas Fuel Company constructed 120 buildings along the creek and two years later opened the first Itmann mine. During the 1950s and 1960s, Pocahontas was the most productive mine in West Virginia, and the coal seam they found in Pocahontas Mine No. 3 was said to be one of the purest in the world. When John F. Kennedy ran for president in 1960, he visited Mullens, where I was born, and went down into one of the three Itmann mines that were open then. Everybody knows what room he stayed in at the Wyoming Hotel. The hotel is closed now, but as late as the early 1980s those mines were still open and employed more than 500 people making good union wages.

Nearly everybody I knew growing up was either a miner, a railroad worker, or a teacher. My grandmother's house overlooked the Elmore Yard, which was the railroad repair yard. Once the Virginian Railway was called the richest little railroad in the world, because it connected coal country to Roanoke, Virginia. The terrain was so steep and rugged up through the hollers between the Elmore Yard and Clarks Gap that they used some of the largest locomotives in the world to climb that grade until they electrified the railroad line between Mullens and Roanoke in 1925.

For many years the coal that miners like my dad dug out of those mountains fueled half the naval ships in the world. In the 1920s, 862,000 mining jobs existed. That had fallen to 135,000 by 1990, and it was down to 42,000 in April 2020, when the coronavirus and growing concerns over carbon emissions and climate change shut down most of the mines. Things change, but boom or bust, coal country remains a place where people work hard to scratch out a living. For a long time, the living was good, until it wasn't. Either way, the work was the same. Hard.

Most of the mines in the area are closed today, and most of the jobs that gave our little community life are gone, but my family is still there. All of them but me. I love West Virginia and the people back home, but I can't remember a single day I didn't think I was going to leave for something bigger, even though I had no idea what that might be.

My parents and my mom's mother wanted me to be a teacher. My grandmother wanted to become a teacher, but she couldn't go to college, so that was her dream for me. I could already write my name in cursive in kindergarten, because she taught me how and practiced with me. She made up flash cards for me in math. She became a teacher in that way. West Virginians are resourceful.

Although I had no idea what I was going to do, I knew my dream was different. I wanted to do my thing. Knowing I was gay was part of it. I wanted to be open and live free. and I knew if I were to live that life back home, my family would not be welcoming. That had to be part of the reason I always felt I'd leave. Why else at a young age was I already thinking like that?

I certainly never thought I'd become a boxer. But wherever I went and whatever I was doing, I understood it was in that southern West Virginia cocoon where I grew up that I learned what it meant to work hard, play hard, and realize that the world is not always what you hope it will be or need it to be, so deal with it and move on.

West Virginia is where I learned to compete with a passion and an aggressive streak that was unsettling to some and a lifesaver for me. That aggression didn't always make life easy for Christy Salters, but it made possible a life I could have never imagined and the fulfillment of a dream that first took shape on the basketball court my dad poured for me in our backyard.

When you come from a coal camp so small there's no stoplight and no need for one, any town is big in your mind. So Mullens seemed like the big city to me even though it was right up the road a few miles and only had about 1,500 people. That's where I went to high school and where I had my first success in sports as a girl playing on boys' Little League and basketball teams. It's where I first learned to dream.

What's important when you grow up in a small place is to not let the rest of the world become so big to you that it eliminates the faith to dream of your own possibilities. The world is kind of restricted in a place like Itmann. I'm not putting it down, but it can be a hard place to dream big dreams, though that was never the case for me because of my parents, Johnny and Joyce Salters.

I was their first born and always felt that gave me a special place in our family, especially with my dad. My mom told me the day I was born, my dad made sure nobody but her held me until he could get home from the mine. He was in his work clothes the first day we laid eyes on each other, and that's how I guess I'll always think of him. A loving man in work clothes, which he's still wearing today. He turned 75 in 2020 and went to work on his birthday. He never had to lecture me about working hard. All I had to do was watch him.

Both of my grandfathers worked in the mines and ended up with black lung disease to prove it. My uncles worked in the mines. So did my younger brother, Randy. They entered those mines from the side rather than going straight down, riding in on a tram line, not down in an elevator. There were some areas inside where they could stand and work, but in other parts they had to lie on their back or their side, digging the coal out of the side of the mountain. That's like having a 12-hour MRI with coal dust falling in your face the whole time.

The expression "fire in the hole" came out of those mines. To knock the coal free, sometimes a miner would have to drill a hole in the wall and pack it with black powder and a fuse. When they lit the fuse, they'd holler "fire in the hole" to warn the other miners that a charge had been set so they could take cover. "Boom!" Out came the coal. Then you'd bend over and start gathering it up.

My dad was luckier than most. He was a union welder for Maben Energy, so he didn't have to go down in the mines every day. He was in there a lot repairing machinery, though, and every night he'd come home covered in soot. So did most every other working man in town. They made a good living doing it, but at the end of the day the miners all knew the company really didn't care about them. Your worth was based on how strong your back was and how much coal you could pull out of those mountains. Which meant, in the long run, you weren't worth much in the company's eyes, and you knew it.

One of my grandfathers worked in what was called the preparation plant. He cleaned the coal before it was shipped. He was breathing in coal dust all day long. When they finally diagnosed him with black lung disease, I can't say anyone was surprised. You just accepted it and then fought the company for disability. You dealt with it and moved on.

Those of us outside the mines were luckier. We only had to combat the fine black dust that seemed to seep unseen into your house. It covered everything, but you were never sure how it got there. You were always polishing the furniture because if you didn't, you'd get up with a black smudge mark on your arm.

I wanted to be like my dad, but I didn't want to go down in those dark holes. My dad and brother said it never bothered them, but it sure would have bothered me. Randy told me many times he enjoyed it even though he got electrocuted once in the mine and severely injured on several other occasions. He started when he was around 19 and saw some good years until he got hurt so bad he had to stop. I think he'd go back down there tomorrow if he could, but he passed away in 2020. Working in the mines had a lot to do with that, too.

Coal mining is a world not unlike boxing in that the people inside have to work together as a group, and they have to have each other's back, because a lot of things can go wrong down there. They have to rely on each other the way I learned to rely on the people in my corner. Everyone has an important job inside the ropes and inside the mines, and you all have to do your job well to survive and be successful. Randy liked that aspect of it. I felt the same way inside a boxing ring. We both felt comfortable in an uncomfortable environment. Coal mining's not for everybody, I'll tell you that, and neither is boxing.

Growing up I was always with my dad. I threw baseballs with my dad. I played basketball with my dad. I threw footballs with my dad. He was going to let me play midget football until they said they wouldn't let a girl play. Sports became his way of connecting with me.

I can't even remember a time I didn't like sports. It came natural to me. If I hadn't liked it, I wouldn't have put the time into it that I did, but around fourth grade I began to see I was better than most of the girls and a lot of the guys. At 12 I made the Little League All-Star team as a catcher, and I was starting on the boys' basketball team, so I knew pretty early that I was a good athlete. I had no idea where that might lead me, but I loved everything about it. Especially the winning.

My dad was always demanding. He used to run me through basketball drills after he'd get home from work, and it was hard to get a positive word out of him. When I'd miss a shot, he'd throw the ball back a little harder than after I made one, letting me know without saying it that I needed to do better.

That's where I got my work ethic. He taught me you had to do everything you could to get better every day, because if you didn't there was someone somewhere who was doing what you didn't want to do. They were getting better. Were you?

I really came to believe in that, and I still do. Are you doing all you can to get better? That doesn't apply just in sports. It's true in the rest of your life, too. No matter your circumstances, are you doing something to get better, or to make your circumstances better? If not, you're cheating yourself.

One time when I was a freshman in high school, I missed 11 free throws. After the game, he didn't get all over me the way you hear some parents do with their kids, but there was no arm around my shoulder either. He just said, "If you made a few of those shots, you'd have won the game. But you didn't." He didn't have to say anything more. I went home and shot free throws that night. I never missed that many free throws again.

My dad always told me, "You can do anything you want to do, be anything you want to be." I should have had a poster on my bedroom wall that said, "I Can Be President!" I did have a Smurfette poster that said, "Girls Can Do Anything!" That's what my dad always said. I can't tell you how many times he told me, but it was often enough that I really did believe it.

Later I learned he never thought that would include boxing. I also came to understand as I grew older that it also didn't include being gay. I could be anything, it turned out, but who I was. Anything but a girl who liked girls. Anything but that.

Growing up, the hollers and the mountains seemed to always be pressing on me in a way that was beautiful but also limiting. I didn't totally understand what that meant yet, but what I did get was that my dad thought I could compete against anyone and be as good as they were, boy or girl. Maybe better if I worked at it. And so, I did. Not just at sports. At everything.

I was never afraid of competing. For me it's always been about the competition. If you just want to perfect the skill, OK, but I want to win. Just throwing a left hook perfectly, the art of doing that, is fine, but I wanted to throw a left hook that knocked you out.

I think you have to teach kids what winning and losing mean. Teach them what it takes to win, like my dad did for me. There's a huge price you pay for trying to be the best. You give up things, especially time. What you learn in sports is not just applicable to the games. What you're learning is not just about winning games. It's about winning in life.

How do you win in life? You have to be willing to compete. You have to be willing to get up when you get knocked down and get back in the game, because you are going to get knocked down. Who doesn't? So, you have to learn to believe in yourself, even when no one else does.

Why did I get up early in the morning and run all those miles for more than 25 years? So that I could tell myself I was running while everyone else was sleeping. I was always willing to pay whatever the price was to win. Everybody wants to win when they ring the bell, but did they want to win all those weeks in the gym or out running before dawn? That's when the fight is actually decided. Everybody wants to win for sure, but not everybody wants to prepare to win.

That's what I learned from my dad, from high school and college sports and, finally, from boxing. Winning isn't simple, and it definitely isn't easy. It doesn't just happen. You have to prepare to win, and someone has to teach you how to do that. My dad was the first who did.

It's no different in life. If you want to be a winner, you have to be willing to pay the price over and over and over again. You have to be relentless. That doesn't mean you'll always win, because you won't, no matter how well prepared you are. We all lose sometimes, but if you did all you could, you always know you gave yourself the best chance to win, no matter whether its sports or learning how to speak properly.

In the fourth grade, there was a boy in my class that I became friends with. He was from a wealthy family in Mullens, at least wealthy as far as I was concerned. One day we were talking about grades and he laughed at the way I said "readin', writin', and 'rithmetic." He said I didn't say those words right.

I never forgot that. I went home and practiced saying reading, writing, and arithmetic. In later years, when I found myself speaking in public, I always tried very hard not to let my West Virginia accent be so pronounced. I worked on how I said certain words. Ever since that day, I've been very conscious about how I sound.

Wherever my dad went, I went. When he sat down to dinner, I sat right next to him. Still to this day that's how it is when I go back home to visit. When I'm not home, that chair next to my dad stays empty.

I got a lot of love from my dad, but I got my aggressiveness from both of my parents. My mom could get fired up in a minute. Because my dad loved sports, she was always involved, too. She was the one driving kids to practice or games. The mom doing whatever had to be done to help our team. She was always supportive that way.

She also could get HOT! Once, at a high school softball game against our big rivals over in Pineville, she heard that the other school's new coach had said some unkind things about me being too aggressive. After the game she got in that coach's face. My coach ran over to get between them, and all of a sudden, an arm came flying over my coach's head and hit the other coach right in the lip. I think Mom bloodied her a little bit. I can be the same way, and I saw that day where I got it from. But it was really my dad who gave me the will to be great. When he'd throw that basketball back to me harder when I missed than after I made a shot, it was a message he didn't have to state. Work harder. Do better. Be better. Don't miss. Attack. That's what I became.

I was an athlete who always attacked. I was only 5-foot-4 in high school, but I had a chip on my shoulder the size of those mountains around me. That's another thing my dad taught me. You're out there to win, so never back down from a challenge. Embrace it.

By fifth grade, they'd combined the elementary schools in Itmann and Mullens, but I was still playing on the boys' teams. Back then that was unusual. Now you see it all the time, and I think it's great for the girls and great for the boys, too. It's great for all of them to see a girl can be an athlete and a competitor. I was on the border of that change in society's thinking. In the 1970s and 1980s, girls in sports was just starting. For the most part, the goal was still to be a cheerleader, not an athlete, but that was never my goal. If I had even a little bit to do with legitimizing that change, I'm proud of it.

I was an All-Star catcher in Little League, loved football and was doing well in basketball, which was really what I liked best. In fifth grade I made the boys' basketball team, but a girl in my class claimed I only made it because someone told the coach they had to have a girl and someone from Itmann on the team. Since I fit both descriptions, she said it was the only reason they picked me.

I remember thinking that seemed pretty strange, because I was playing all the time, not just sitting on the end of the bench. If I was the token Itmann "girl," isn't that where they'd have put me?

That was the start of me never wanting to get anything because I was a girl, or later a woman. I didn't want any part of getting anything because of my race or my sex or any of that. I wanted to be there because I was the best. I still feel that's the way it should be. The best candidate, the best athlete, the best student. That's who should get whatever there is to get.

Of course, to get it you have to be given the opportunity, and for a long time that didn't happen if you were a woman or a person of color. Certainly not if you were gay. And if you were a gay woman, your chances were even worse.

That's begun to change quite a lot, but none of it is changing as fast as it should. It was only in 2015 that same-sex marriage was finally legalized around the country by the Supreme Court. It took decades of legal battles and nine judges to legalize love, and some people are still fighting it. Really?

All you can hope for in that regard is continued progress. Certainly, that's my hope for women athletes, gay and straight. Just judge us on our ability and give us all a chance to show what that is. You can't ask for more than that. If you're good enough, you won't need more than that. But you need a fair chance first, which in my case was a long time coming in boxing and even longer in my personal life.

Until fourth grade, I remember having boyfriends, but I always felt different inside. I never felt like I truly fit. I knew from the time I was very young that I was different than the other girls. I wasn't interested in dresses and a lot of the things my mom wanted me to get involved with. I felt I was gay long before I knew what that meant.

So many lesbians my age will tell you they were in love with Buddy, the character played by Kristy McNichol on the TV show "Family." I know I was. I was 8 when that show first came on, and I never missed it. I was maybe 10 or so when I knew I was attracted to her. She was a tomboyish kind of teenage girl, and I was the same way, but I was never really comfortable with who I was, except when I was playing sports. That was especially true on the basketball court.

I remember once we were playing basketball with some girls, and I knocked one of them down. My gym teacher really scolded me. She said I was playing too rough. I told her, "But that's the way you play." What she was really telling me was I wasn't playing like a girl. That didn't mean a thing to me. I couldn't understand that thinking. I played hard. Didn't matter who it was against.

After seventh grade, my mother wouldn't let me play with the boys any more. For her that was the cutoff where boys and girls didn't play together. If she was concerned about the sexual side of it, she didn't have much to worry about. Maybe it was just the difference in size and strength as the boys started to move into puberty. I never bothered to ask her why, because at that point it didn't really matter. There were girls' teams in Mullens I could play on by then.

In eighth grade, we had a woman coach who had no clue about basketball. It got to the point I'd tell her to just sit down during a time out. "I got this," was something I said a lot then. She should have sat my ass on the bench, but she didn't. She let me go. What I didn't realize then was she was doing us all a favor. If we didn't have a teacher or another adult coaching, we couldn't have had a team. So even though she didn't know what she was doing, what she was really doing was giving me a chance to play. I should go back and thank her, frankly.

One reason I loved basketball was that I could play hard and free. When the games were over, I had to go back to following the rules of society. But on the court I could play like a man, even though that was never how I looked at it. In my mind, I was just playing to win. That's just one example of what became a fact of life for me. My life has always been divided between how I saw things and how the world saw things.

By the time I got to Mullens High School, the coaches knew who I was. I was on the softball team and the girls' basketball team from the start. I liked softball, but I got myself thrown off the team twice by my coach, Barry Smith. All the years I spent in sports, he was really the only coach who ever said no to me. Maybe if a few more had, I might have been better off. I didn't like it at the time, but Coach Smith was good for me.

He told me once that he saw from the start I was aggressive and kind of headstrong. He said I was the kind of player who he'd give the take sign to, and if I thought I could get a hit, I'd swing anyway.

If I had to slide, I was going to go into you. I guess I could be hard on my teammates sometimes, too, because not every girl played the way I did. Barry told me years later, "You were our best player, and you were our hardest working player. You never slacked off. But you weren't always our best teammate. You just wanted to win so damn bad."

Coach Smith was right about that. He was right about something else he said once, too. He said I played angry, like I felt I had to get back at anyone who hurt me or held me back. He said he thought I picked the right sport when I ended up boxing, because I played like a warrior, and in boxing I didn't have to rely on any teammates to be successful. I had to do it alone. He also told me he never quite knew what I was angry about. For a long time neither did I.

I had a pent-up rage inside about having to hide that I was gay from the world as I knew it. You're so angry that you can't be who you want to be, and you can't change who you are. You're trapped, and it makes you mad without understanding what you're really mad about. In sports, it's acceptable to be overly aggressive, so you can let out some of those emotions in a safe place. At times it even gets rewarded. It's not acceptable to be overly aggressive in the rest of your life, though, especially if you're a girl, but it had to come out; and sports became the vehicle that allowed that for me, which was a blessing.

It was important to me to be the best just to feel OK about myself. If I had to run you over to win, I would. Once, in Little League, I did just that to a male cousin who was playing on a rival team. I was at second base, and I caught a fly. He was on base and had to scramble back to the bag before I tagged him for a double play. I lowered my shoulder and flipped him over my back and tagged him out. People were mad at me, but I figured he was going to try to run me over, so I ran him over first. I think my dad liked it, frankly. I know I did.

A lot of that anger had to do with feeling I had to hide who I was from almost everybody I knew. I fought my sexual identity for a long time, and that takes a toll. I'd say through high school I identified more as being bisexual than a lesbian, even though I knew better. I knew who I really was, but at that point I was hiding even from myself.

I had a boyfriend, off and on, all through high school. I had an affair with one of my male teachers in high school, too. I really had a thing for him for a little while. I know he was definitely supposed to say no, but I really pressured him. He was married, but I didn't care. I don't think I was sleeping with him to try to convince myself or anyone else that I wasn't gay. I think it was the whole student-teacher thing, like you read about. But even at that, all through high school, whether I was sleeping with my boyfriend or my teacher, I always had a girlfriend, and she took precedence. I never had a question in my mind about that.

In towns as small as Itmann and Mullens, people talk. I knew they wondered about me. It is exhausting hiding who you are from your family and your friends and the world around you. You're always afraid someone knows the truth. You may tell yourself you don't care, but if you really didn't care, you wouldn't be hiding what you're doing or what you're feeling, now would you?

Looking back, I spent nearly my whole life hiding. My relationship with my mother is very strained because of it. I wish we could have had a closer relationship when I was growing up, but we couldn't because I was always hiding my sexuality from her. I wish I could have just gone to her when I was 12 or 13 and said, "Mom, I like girls, not boys." But I knew I couldn't. She would never have accepted that.

I have a lot of guilt about not being the kind of daughter my parents wanted in that way. If I could have been what they wanted, I would have done it, but I couldn't, and that caused a lot of tension between us for a long time. In my heart I felt so much guilt for not being the daughter my mom wanted. I didn't go to my senior prom. My mom wanted that. I didn't. I wasn't ever the daughter she wanted, I don't believe. Not really. That's been a heavy load to carry for both of us.

It's hard to always feel like you have to hide in plain sight. Hiding how you feel. Hiding who you are. Hiding who you love. Eventually hiding what you're doing. You wonder sometimes, "Why can't they just love me for who I am? Why can't everyone just accept me for me?"

It's better now than it was back in the '80s and '90s. A lot better in some places. But don't kid yourself. Is it better for a little girl growing up in a small town, up a holler in West Virginia, or out in some farm town in the Midwest or in the Bible Belt? I'm not so sure it's as different as we want to believe. I hope it is, but I meet a lot of kids and parents who approach me when I'm speaking at functions asking how to cope with being gay or with having a gay child. That makes we wish things were changing faster, but I learned long ago that change takes time. So does winning the fight to be free to be yourself.

People often ask me how did you even know you had to hide the fact you were gay when you were a kid? That is a good question. It's subtle the ways you first get the messages about how people think. You hear the jokes or the insulting remarks adults make about gay people. You sense deep inside you that a lot of people don't think it is right to be gay. How do you know they feel that way? Some people tell you. I had an aunt tell me once after they knew I was gay that I'd burn in hell for it. She told me that on the way into a family dinner. Thanks for sharing.

From the time you're a little girl, people are always asking if you have a boyfriend. Nobody ever asked, "Do you have a girlfriend?" There's a very clear message there that comes through when you don't feel the way they think you should. It lets you know you're different, and it makes you feel uneasy.

You see your mom and dad. Your aunts and uncles. Your friends' parents. You know that's the way society thinks things should be. It was how the church says it should be. No one talks to their child about being attracted to another girl when your parents have "the talk" about sex. It never comes up. I guess it's because parents don't want to think of their child as not normal, but what's "normal?" At 10, I didn't know what normal was, but I knew I wasn't it. Even today, I know I'm not normal, because if I were, I wouldn't have become a boxer!

When you're a teenager, you're wrestling with a lot of things. That's true whether you're gay or straight, but if you were a gay teenager back in the '80s, like I was, it was pretty difficult. Put it this way. You weren't coming out in Itmann, West Virginia. Not unless you were planning on leaving the same day.

Today, most everyone accepts me back home just the way I am, and if someone doesn't, I don't really give a damn. It's great when I go back now and see old friends and their families. Everybody is glad to see me, and I'm just as glad to see them. It wasn't always that way, but at least I always had sports to give me shelter.

In high school basketball, I was really excelling. I was a good shooter and quicker than a lot of girls, so even though I was only 5-foot-4, I could score, and I was ruthless about it. There was no shot I wouldn't take. As far as I was concerned, I was open as soon as I walked into the gym.

My senior year I averaged 27 points, 6 rebounds, and 2 steals a game. I was named first team All-State my junior and senior seasons, I made the state tournament All-Star team, and I was named all-area all four years of high school. Now, you have to remember this was West Virginia, not a huge state like New York or California, but it was enough to get me what I wanted most: a chance to go to college.

Aubrey Nuckols was my high school coach, but it was his brother, Don, who had the most influence on me. He was the boys' team coach and a legend in that part of West Virginia. He coached Mike D'Antoni and his brother, and they won everything. Don was a winner.

They have a sign outside Mullens now that says "Home of Christy Martin," and there's also one that says "Home of Mike D'Antoni." Mike was an NBA player and twice NBA coach of the year. I think he's a little more famous than I am because the state paid for his sign. Don Nuckols paid for mine, and I'm grateful to him for it.

I'd say I got a little of my brashness from Don. My parents and other people in town would talk about the "Don Nuckols strut." When he came into an opposing team's gym with his team, he let them know he was there by the way he strutted around. My mom said I had that, too. When his team won, he wanted everyone to know it. I got that part of my sportsmanship, or maybe lack of it, from Don. He was some character. I learned a lot about the attitude you need to be a winner from him, no question.

As successful as I'd become as an athlete, the older I got, the more I felt the pressure of hiding who I was and how I felt. To escape that feeling, I became a pretty wild child. I drank a lot. I got arrested in eighth grade for underage drinking, and they hauled me to the local jail. My parents came to get me, and I got the strap that night, but it was already too late. At 13, I thought I was 30. I was grown in my mind.

That led to some problems, because I always wanted to please people, and I started associating drinking with popularity. I was running around with 30-year-olds when I was still a teenager. I sold speed to friends of my parents. I was a bad kid doing things I shouldn't have done.

There were people in town who never thought I'd amount to anything, and considering some of the things I was doing, I can understand their reservations. It was all part of dealing with the consequences of my sexual identity. I didn't feel like I could stand up for myself with my parents and just tell them I was gay, so I rebelled in other ways. I knew there were people in town who talked about me in private, but no one ever said anything to my face, so I kept hiding. What no one knew was that being gay wasn't the only thing I was hiding.

The Thing We Carry, the Things We Hide

had no idea what was happening. I just knew it shouldn't be happening in the way a six-year-old knows something is wrong, but she has no ability to stop it or make it right.

I was in the basement rec room of my house in Itmann when a 15-year-old cousin who was up visiting from North Carolina started to do things to me that made me feel trapped and uncomfortable. My parents were both upstairs, but they might as well have been a million miles away. Down in that dark place, I was alone, and someone was forcing me to do something to them that didn't feel right. At the same time, he was doing something to me that felt awfully wrong. I was scared to do what he said, and I was scared not to. I didn't have any understanding about sex, but even at six I knew I wanted someone to come down to make him stop. But I was also scared that if they did and caught us, they might blame me.

Then I heard my dad's boots coming down the stairs. Whenever the memory of what happened that day comes back, that's what I hear first. The sudden sound of boots on the stairs, coming loud and fast. Like he knew something was happening, and he wanted you to know he was on the way.

That's when the boy stopped. He zipped up his pants, and I just sat there. My dad never asked what was going on. He didn't ask me later if my cousin had touched me. He didn't ask either of us anything. He just came down those stairs awfully fast, and that made it stop. My cousin never came back to our house in West Virginia again.

To be six years old and forced to be involved in oral sex with a teenage boy was a terrible thing, but not feeling safe to tell my dad or mom what had happened was worse. I never said a word about it to my parents until Jim's murder trial was about to begin. I was 43 years old by then and had been carrying that memory inside me all those years. I only told them then because I was afraid

Jim's lawyers might bring it out in court. Jim was the only person I ever talked to about it, which turned out to be a serious mistake in judgment on my part, because he often used it against me in terrible ways.

When I finally explained what had happened to me 37 years earlier, my parents didn't say a word. My dad's eyes teared up a little bit when I told them, but he remained silent. So did my mom. It was never brought up again.

How do you hear that someone has molested your daughter when she was six and have no other reaction than that? They had no words for me, which may be why I had no words for them the day it happened. I didn't say anything then because I was afraid to tell them. I was afraid what my dad might do to my cousin, and I was afraid my mom would be angry with me because she was close to his grandmother, and she was still alive.

I wasn't sure if they would believe me. If my dad did, and he did something to my cousin, that wouldn't be good; and if they didn't, or they blamed me for it, that would be terrible. It's strange to me now why I would care what happened to my cousin, but I guess it was that I didn't want my dad to lose his temper and get in trouble for something he might have done in anger. So, I kept silent all those years.

I didn't know how to feel about it. It confused me. You want your cousin to like you. You want to do things that make people like you. But not that!

As I got older, I began to understand how wrong it was. I came to believe my dad knew something happened downstairs that wasn't right. There had to be a look on my face when he first saw me that told him something, didn't there?

I do believe it confused me about sex. It got sex very twisted for me for a long time. It's certainly not why I'm gay. That day had nothing to do with my sexuality, but it was something that changed my life.

From the age of six, I've had to live with the question: Why? Why did he do that to me? Why didn't I tell my parents? Why did I protect this guy who was molesting me instead of protecting myself? Why? Why? Why?

I've asked myself that question so many times and never come up with a satisfactory answer. Shame, of course, was part of it, but why didn't I feel like I could tell my parents what he'd done? I'll never know the answer for sure, but I know my trust issues with people started that day. Part of trust is believing I can tell you anything, and you'll take care of me. Obviously, I didn't feel that way. Looking back, that's the day when my hiding started.

Sugar Ray Leonard, the Hall of Fame boxer and Olympic champion, talked about that in his autobiography. He said he was sexually abused twice when he was a teenager, once by one of his national team coaches and once by a man who used to support him financially while he was an amateur trying to make the 1976 Olympic team. He said in his book that the only people who knew until he made it public were his two wives, and both had the same reaction. They told him not to go there. To keep it hidden. He says he paid for that, and so did they. I paid for making the same choice when it came to my own problems with sexual abuse and later domestic abuse. Silence is not the answer to violence, abuse, or emotional trauma like that, but at six you have no idea what the answer is. All you know is you're scared because something very bad just happened to you.

You're embarrassed and ashamed, and your abuser convinces you that no one will believe you. There's a stigma attached to having been a victim of sexual abuse. The same is true of domestic abuse. Some people think you're weak. You think you're weak. But the real weakness comes from not talking about it. From not cleaning out the wound and cauterizing it. The weakness comes from trying to bury it when there is no hole deep enough. Not even at the bottom of a coal mine.

You can try, but it's a secret that will come out one way or another. A lot of times it's the way you handle other situations, situations you don't even think are related. It can come out as addiction or anger issues, uncontrolled aggression or total acquiescence. Or all of them. I'd have to say that was me. At different times in my life, I've dealt with all those things, and often not very well.

You keep wondering if somehow it was your fault, this thing that was done to you. You know at six that's impossible, but still you wonder, so you hide it, and you stay silent. Silence becomes your coping mechanism, like a fighter covering up when you're hurt and being heavily attacked.

That was what I did, and it's what a lot of other people I've spoken with did who had similar experiences. But when you're silent, the secrets eat away at you. It's like having poison inside you. It's corroding your self-esteem and clouding your judgment, even though you don't necessarily realize it for a long time.

If there's one thing I'm sure about that incident, it is that it became the first dark hiding place I needed to find. It wouldn't be the last. Seven years later, I had sex with a girl for the first time. I kept that secret for as long as I could, too. I kept all those years of emotional and physical abuse by Jim secret. Keeping secrets and searching for dark places to hide them became a part of my life. They were how I coped, but that doesn't really work very well for very long. Not without other consequences, even if you don't realize that until years later.

From six years old, I internalized my feelings about who I was and what was really going on in my life. If telling my whole story now can help someone not live the messed-up life I lived for so long, that's the only goal I really have. If telling it all can give someone else some strength when they need it, it's worth the telling.

Leonard spoke about that once during a lecture he gave at Penn State after that school's football program was rocked by allegations of widespread child abuse done by one of their longtime assistant coaches. Ray said the killer is silence, and he was right. Kids need the confidence to be able to talk with their parents about anything. I didn't feel I could safely do that, and we all paid a high price for that in my family that we're still trying to heal from.

I don't know to this day how that experience shaped me because I can't remember how I felt prior to being molested. Did it totally change who I became, or was I already on the road I followed, no matter what? I'll never know, and that created doubts deep inside me about who I really was, or who I might have become. It undermined my sense of self and my faith in my own judgment for a very long time. It also left me full of a quiet rage that found a safe outlet in the boxing ring.

I don't believe for a minute that incident changed my sexual identity. Not at all. I have found there's a common thread among some women in the lesbian community of abuse at a young age, but the truth is it's in a lot of straight people's lives, too. It didn't make me a man hater. I never felt like that. But I do wonder who I was before it happened. How much of a role did it play in some of the bad choices I made, or the anger I've carried inside for so long? I don't know the answer, but I do know it screwed me up for the rest of my life in some ways. It certainly damaged my sense of self-worth for a long time, even after I became the most famous woman fighter in the world.

My way of coping with it was I put that memory in a box and tried to lock it up, but I revisited that box a lot in my teen years. I became much more aware of my little cousins and what people were around them, what situations they were in. I felt I needed to try to be there to protect them if they needed it.

I kept waiting for his grandmother to die, but before she did, I finally had to come clean just before Jim's trial in 2011. A few years after that trial was over, my mom told me she'd seen that cousin, and he'd asked how I was doing. I couldn't believe she would even speak to him. Why would she even bring up his name to me? I don't know, but when she did, all the anger was still there, boiling just below the surface.

What I realize now is I did with that memory the same thing she did with the knowledge that her daughter was gay and later was maltreated by her husband. She stuck her head in the sand. Frankly, I'm guilty of that, too. I stuck my head in the sand for a lot of years, so who am I to judge?

It still comes into my mind sometimes. It always arrives unexpectedly, like the first chilly wind in the fall. When it does, it's like it just happened all over again. I hear my dad's footsteps on the stairs and feel the same fear and shame. Then I find a way to push the memory away. Stuff it back in the box, because that's the only way you can be a survivor and not someone's victim. You move on the best you can.

I got good at putting different parts of my life in boxes. I compartmentalized things all my life so I could function. That's how I lived for many years. As long as I stayed within certain parameters, things were fine. As long as I could keep the locks on all those boxes, I could keep hiding right in plain sight. It's how I survived. Surviving is not living, but it's not dying either. It's holding on until you can find a way to start living again. For me, sports were the way I held on until I found that other way. I found a girl named Sherry Lusk when I was turning 13, and we fell in love.

My relationship with Sherry started when I was in eighth grade. She was a junior in high school and the top female athlete in our town. I met her playing basketball, and there was a natural gravitation because she was "it" in Mullens as an athlete, and that's what I wanted to become. I looked up to her. I wanted to be just like her—the best player.

She started coming by my house on weekends to get me to play basketball, which I thought was the coolest thing ever. She was 16 and wanted to be my friend. At the beginning it was like, "Wow! She's taking the time to play ball with me?"

I didn't think anything more about it at first. There was never really a time we weren't together from that time until my sophomore year in high school, when she went off to college up in Morgantown at West Virginia University.

At first it was just about sports and drinking and having fun with a close friend. It didn't get sexual until Christmas break of my eighth-grade year. I was over at her family's house, and it was just one of those things where we kissed each other and then sort of jumped back like, "Oh that was an accident!" Then the accidents kept happening.

At first, neither of us were sure what we wanted. She was hiding. I was hiding. It's what you do at that point. You're kids who aren't sure yet who you are. We both had boyfriends at the time, in my case Chris Caldwell, who had been my sort of boyfriend since we were in the fifth grade. He was my first love, really. Then Sherry came along, and everything changed.

I was her first girlfriend, and obviously she was my first, too. We covered up what was going on with basketball. We were both good players trying to get better, so it was logical that we'd often be together. On the surface it all made sense to people, because I was seen as the next player who was supposed to be good so, of course, we would practice a lot, and that meant we'd be together a lot. Sherry and I were on the same page from the moment we met. We were totally comfortable together. It just felt right.

By the time I got to ninth grade, I was so crazy about her I didn't even care anymore what people thought, but we still kept it a secret. I didn't care if people thought I was gay at that time, but Sherry wasn't ready for that, so we hid it the best we could. We played it off like two close friends who love sports and having fun together.

When you're living that way, you're always anxious. In the back of your mind, you're waiting for the moment someone outs you, and your whole life crashes down on you. I was too young to understand what that might mean, but I could feel the tension of it. Tension between me, my family, and my secret life was always in the background.

On one level at that age, you don't really care what people think, but that doesn't include what your parents think. You want to be free, but there are constraints because we both knew there were people we loved who could never accept what we were doing. You don't want to hurt them, but you don't want to live life in the shadows, always hiding who you are and who you love, either. It creates a constant balancing act that is exhausting.

Sherry's parents were getting divorced at the time, so there was some turmoil in Sherry's life, and I had my own baggage, so we had that in common. Knowing I was gay and having to hide it made me feel like I never quite fit in anywhere. I didn't fit in with the girls, because they were interested in the boys, and I was interested in the girls. I didn't fit in with the boys anymore because I was a girl. So being the life of the party became one of my coping mechanisms.

I have an addictive personality, so when you added alcohol, and later drugs, to the equation along with my self-esteem issues, coming to grips with being gay, having been molested as a kid, and living this life of hiding, it was a pretty toxic mix for a teenager. Or for an adult, for that matter. Probably one way to build a fighter is a mix like that. It certainly turned me into one.

I was a bold kid who wanted people to like me. One way to hide my secrets was to be the life of the party. I did some crazy things to try to be accepted and to keep people thinking I wasn't who I really was. That's one of the dangers of being a young person trapped in the closet, sexually and emotionally. You can make a lot of mistakes and do a lot of dangerous things just trying to be accepted by somebody. Some group. Any group really.

Being a good athlete helped in that regard. That automatically gave me a group to be a part of. Having Sherry alongside made it easier, but it only took about a year or so before people started to talk. Or I should say whisper. Back then nobody talked about something like whether they had two lesbian high school basketball players in town. They just judged you without even knowing you. And then they whispered to each other.

Around this time, Sherry's mother had back surgery and couldn't get out of bed. She'd just gotten home and was flat on her back in her bedroom. We knew she was there, but we thought she'd never hear us in Sherry's room having sex. I don't know what we were thinking. Maybe we weren't thinking at all, which is kind of common at that age and most likely the truth.

Regardless, she knew what was going on. She couldn't get out of bed, but the next day she told Sherry she was never to see me again. She never contacted my parents about it that I know of, and she never spoke to me about it. Not long after that Sherry moved in with her dad.

She told me it was so we could be together. I believed her, but her mom told me not long after I'd been shot by Jim that that wasn't the case. Sherry had actually moved to her dad's because she could live the way she wanted with no rules. With her dad she had total freedom. Not just freedom to be with me. Total freedom to do whatever she wanted. He had no idea what was going on in her life or in the life the two of us had together. So, Sherry became the first person in a lifetime of people who controlled me by lying to me and telling me what I wanted to hear.

My freshman year we became high school teammates. She was a senior, and by that point a lot of people were talking. Our coach that year was a lesbian, and even she said some stuff about us being a "couple." Try that today, and you get fired, but not back in 1983. I was so crazy in love I didn't really care what anyone was saying.

When Sherry went off to college, I was crushed even though I knew that was coming. The first year we were apart, she would send me cards all the time, and I'd go up to Morgantown for football games and things on the weekends to see her. We kept that up until I graduated from high school, but she had other girlfriends at college I didn't find out about until later. We were growing apart, but it wasn't until I left for college myself that everything changed completely.

With time and distance, we drifted apart the way you often do when you're young. When we finally broke up, it was the last time I would see her for a long time.

My senior year of high school I developed a friendship with a girl from a rival high school I'd played basketball against. I was attracted to her, and she happened to come to my graduation party. One thing led to another, and we got together. She was already going to Concord College up in Athens, West Virginia, but I'd accepted a basketball scholarship to Salem University to try to be close to Sherry in Morgantown, so it didn't seem like this new relationship was going anywhere.

As it got nearer to the time to leave for Salem, though, I began to have second thoughts. I started thinking it wouldn't be a good move for me to go to college so close to Sherry. I was afraid I'd waste all my time trying to keep us together rather than actually going to school, and I didn't want to put myself in a situation where I didn't get my education because I was chasing a relationship I knew was over. So, I called the coach at Salem and told him I wasn't coming and enrolled at Concord. I went from having college paid for by basketball to announcing to my parents I was going to Concord, and they would have to pay for it.

It wasn't like I had a discussion about it with them. I just told them I'd given up my basketball scholarship and wasn't going to Salem. Looking back on it, that made no sense, but that was how I thought at the time. Not only was I giving up a free education, but I had no reason to think I'd play basketball at Concord because they never recruited me even though I lived barely an hour from campus.

When I got there, it was the first time I felt totally free. I was far enough away from home to be openly gay, and that was such a relief. My relationship with Sherry was falling apart, but soon I got together with the girl I'd played basketball against in high school, and we were a couple for several years. I was enjoying my freedom of living on my own as a gay woman for the first time. But one big part of my life was missing.

I didn't play basketball my freshman year and had kind of given up on it. But I took a PE class, and the football coach saw me and told the women's basketball coach he should take a look at me. I was in the gym a lot because I was majoring in physical education, and I still loved to play, even if now it was just pickup ball.

One day he came by, and I guess he liked what he saw. I didn't know Russell Hill at all, except that he was fairly new as the women's coach. The year before he'd led the team to an 18-13 record, which was the first winning season ever for the Lady Lions (can you believe that name?), so people were excited about the team's prospects.

He introduced himself and told me he'd heard of me but didn't know I was on campus. He asked if I wanted to try out. I said sure and went to some spring scrimmages, and he put me on the team and started to let me play a little bit.

He already had a good point guard, which I'd played in high school even though I was mostly a shooter, so I started off as kind of the sixth player my sophomore year. But a girl got injured, and he put me in the three spot, which is like a small forward. Considering that I was only 5-foot-4, that was an understatement.

I knew I had to come up with a new way to compete and decided it was playing like that crazy man on Michael Jordan's Chicago Bulls' teams—Dennis Rodman. He was a guy who made himself an NBA All-Star because he was scrappy on defense and always got into the right position to rebound. He had a sixth sense about where the ball was going and where the open spots were on the floor, and I decided that's how I had to play to get in the game.

I developed that same kind of court sense. I did the same thing in college basketball I would do later in boxing. I made a place for myself where no place existed. By mid-season my sophomore year, I was starting and playing a lot.

In high school there wasn't a shot I wouldn't take. I could be in the parking lot and still felt I was in my range. College was different. I could still score some, but I wasn't the scorer any more. I was a fighter. I fought for rebounds, I fought for loose balls, and I fought on defense. I did what my dad taught me. I competed.

I knew I wasn't going to be playing professional basketball, but I always dreamed one day I'd be somebody. I used to practice signing my autograph while I was at college. I worked on it until I perfected it, making sure it was so legible anyone seeing it would know who it was. I have no idea why I did that. I didn't know what I was going to be successful at, but I guess I had faith there was something special inside me. I've signed a lot of autographs since. They're all legible.

Coach Hill was a good coach for me to play for. He wasn't a guy to give inspirational speeches, but he understood the game, and he knew how to get the most out of his players. He also knew what business to stay out of. Your lifestyle was not a concern of his.

In those days, I had a significant faithfulness issue. That was a problem in high school, and it didn't change really until I met Jim, which is pretty ironic when you think about it. While I was still in my new relationship, I became attracted to one of my teammates, a girl we all called "P", and I kept trying to figure out how I could go out with her.

"P" was a very pretty girl. Guys were always around her, but I'd heard she had also dated women, so I went for it, and pretty quickly I was into a new relationship, and we started living together off campus. I was living in an apartment, and she was always there, so my parents had to know something was up, but nobody talked about it. She'd been to my parents' house but always as my roommate and my teammate, not my girlfriend. I was still living a lie whenever I went home. I was still trying to make life easier for everyone but me.

Talk about the elephant in the room. In our case, it was the lesbians in the bedroom. It wasn't silent acceptance though. It was just silence, and that's a hard way to exist for everybody involved.

I was 20 years old by then, so why didn't I take the initiative and just tell them? It wasn't like I was wrestling with the idea of being gay. So why didn't I come out to my family? For the same reason so many young gay men and women don't to this day. When's the right time to upset your parents?

At college I wasn't hiding my lifestyle, but I wasn't walking all over campus holding hands with my girlfriend, either. I didn't care if people there knew I was gay, but I didn't feel the need to advertise my sexual identity. I was just trying to live my life the way I wanted.

I had gotten pretty serious about college by then and just wanted to get my degree and start working, so I pretty much stayed at school all year, even in the summer, so I could get through as fast as I could. At the same time, I was having some good moments with the basketball team. I'd found a way to adjust my game and my life to new circumstances, and for the first time that I could remember, most days I felt free.

Then one afternoon, when I least expected it, I was literally given a sign that changed the entire trajectory of the rest of my life.

How'd I Get Myself into a Toughman Contest?

never expected to see a sign in the window of Lowery's shoe and sporting goods store that would open a new world for me, but as soon as I did, I knew what was coming next.

Actually, to tell you the truth, I didn't have any idea what was really coming next, but I was sure of one thing—I was going to be among the first women to fight in the Toughman competition held every year in Beckley, West Virginia, about an hour ride from where I was attending college.

If I hadn't seen that sign, I might never have become a boxer. If I'd never seen that sign, I would never have met Jim Martin. I would never have become a national phenomenon or the face of women's prizefighting or had that face on the cover of *Sports Illustrated*. Of course, I also never would have been living in the closet for nearly 20 years as a gay athlete in hiding, or been shot by my husband after two decades of domestic abuse either. Life is about crossroads, choices, and dealing with the twists and turns you can never see coming. All you can do is make the best choice possible with the information you have at the time, and on that day in 1987, the 19-year-old Christy Salters I was then could make only one choice. Where do I sign up?

Because there were no professional sports in West Virginia, we had to get our sports fix in other places. There was big-time college football and basketball at the University of West Virginia, but other than that it was more fringe sports that appealed to us, and one of them was Toughman, which was kind of a regional boxing tournament for guys who had never boxed but thought they were tough. Mostly the entrants were coal miners, barroom brawlers, and men with a chip on their shoulder who thought they were the baddest asses in town. Some proved they were. A lot of others found out they weren't.

Toughman began in Bay City, Michigan, in 1979 when a guy named Art Dore and his friend, Dean Oswald, got tired of hearing local boxing fans criticize some of the small-time prizefighters they promoted. They were sitting around one night after a fight card with a bunch of people who kept saying they could beat them, and Art got miffed enough to decide to let them try to prove it.

He rented a small arena and opened up his ring to anyone willing to stop talking and step inside those ropes. Not to face professional fighters or even seasoned amateurs, of course, just other weekend warriors with faith in their fists. You couldn't have had more than five sanctioned amateur fights to enter, so these were mostly guys whose experience had come in parking lots, coal yards, or on street corners, yet much to Dore's surprise family and friends stood on line outside that arena for more than an hour in the snow the first night to buy tickets. The event sold out two nights running, and the same thing happened when he set up another card down the road a ways in Marquette, Michigan, not long after. That was the birth of Toughman.

The idea quickly spread throughout the Midwest, and eventually it became a national phenomenon for a while. They televised Toughman contests on Fox, FX, and even Showtime. Championship fights were in Las Vegas. Mr. T, the guy with the Mohawk haircut and hubcap-sized pendants around his neck who became a celebrity bodyguard and then a star on the "A-Team" television show, got his start in Toughman. Some of you may remember him as Clubber Lang in the "Rocky III" movie.

"I don't hate Balboa," Mr. T said before getting ready to fight Rocky. "I pity the fool!" For a while that was the movie line of the year. "I pity the fool!" When I hear it, it still cracks me up.

Mr. T was an actor playing a boxer, but the way he played him was a lesson in salesmanship, and later I'd adopt some of the approach he took in that movie. There was a locker-room scene where he was asked his prediction before his big fight with Rocky. He held a sidelong glance at the camera just long enough to make you uncomfortable, and then he said, "Prediction? PAIN!" That's a form of salesmanship I would later emulate in my own way, sometimes in ways that helped me and other times in ways that made me feel uncomfortable and ashamed. A boxer's job is to win, but it's also to sell tickets, and sometimes your mouth sells those tickets better than your fists ever can.

Mr. T and I weren't the only ones to get our start in Toughman. There was also a decidedly American phenomenon who came along and made it big as well. They called him "Butterbean."

"Butterbean" was a rotund guy from Jasper, Alabama, named Eric Esch—a sweet, really round guy who was laying flooring in a mobile home factory in

Addison, Alabama, when a friend of his dared him to enter a local Toughman contest. Eric was 5-foot-11, but he weighed more than 400 pounds at the time, so he had to go on a diet to get down to the 400-pound superheavyweight limit. He did it, he claimed, by eating only butterbeans, and so a fable was born.

Whatever he was doing worked, because he won that tournament and ended up becoming a five-time Toughman world champion with a 56-5 record. He was just a regular guy who you wanted to root for. He had no real boxing skills, but he kept knocking people out. One thing led to another until eventually one of boxing's biggest promoters, Bob Arum, took a look at Butterbean's bald head, expansive waistline, and red, white, and blue trunks that were as big as a pup tent and saw opportunity knocking. Next thing you knew, Butterbean was fighting on national television as the "King of the Four Rounders."

Sure, it was a gimmick, because four-round fighters aren't the kings of anything, but it made Eric some good money, and he ended up fighting Larry Holmes, one of the greatest heavyweight boxers of all time. Butterbean lost that night to a guy who was 52 years old, but who cared? They call it prizefighting because there's a prize at the end, and it can sometimes be a lot of money, which Butterbean managed to earn in a boxing career that lasted 13 years with only one fight of more than four rounds. That's the insanity of boxing. You never know what will happen, or to whom.

Bean used to say, "In boxing, you've got to have clout." It took a while for me to understand he was talking about more than punching power. Although that helps, the real clout comes from box-office appeal. I never went to Harvard Business School, but here's a loose economic translation of what he meant: "Can you put asses in seats?" If you can, it doesn't matter how you do it; and if you can't, well, it doesn't matter how well you can fight. If you can do both, if you can win in a way people either enjoy or hate, you've got clout. I didn't have it yet, but I was about to get my first lesson in its power.

What Mr. T and Butterbean achieved are the possibilities that exist only in a crazy place like boxing, but I wasn't thinking about any of that happening to me when I saw that sign. I just knew I wanted to try it, because I'd been going to Toughman shows for years with my friends and family and always wondered what I'd do if the bell rang and I found myself standing all alone in one corner of the ring.

By 1987, Toughman was big in southern West Virginia. I'm not sure what that said about entertainment in West Virginia back in those days, but they'd sell out the Raleigh County Armory every year, and I enjoyed going. For some reason, I told the promoter a couple of times that he needed to let women do it. There was no reason for me to say that. I'd never boxed in my life. It wasn't like I'd seen women fighting on television and thought it was cool, or there was a future in it for me. There were no women fighting anywhere that I knew of. I just thought I could do it, and he should give me a chance to try.

As Toughman grew in popularity, Art Dore started looking for partners to expand, and he found one in a West Virginia promoter named Jerry Thomas. Dore contacted Thomas in 1982 about promoting Toughman shows in West Virginia, and eventually Jerry got the franchise rights. The first Toughman he ever ran in Beckley was in 1982. He only had two weight classes and eight fighters, all men. He claims he only had 20 tickets sold the night before the show. However, many people showed up that first night, and Toughman caught on in a hurry.

Originally there were no weight classes for women, but Jerry told me once that he finally added two, not because I kept pestering him to do it, but because of an incident in a grocery store near where he lived in West Virginia. A woman wanted to know why he didn't have women's divisions, and she got a little aggressive about it. She ended up backing him into the canned goods, wagging a finger in his face, and he decided right there, with his back up against No. 9 tomato cans, that maybe it was time to listen to these girls.

But before Jerry had time to open his tournament to women, someone beat him to it. The poster that got me involved in the sport that would become my life was for something called the "Mean Mountaineer" contest. It was the same concept as Toughman, just less well known, if that was even possible.

It didn't matter to me what they called it. I just wanted to see what the experience was like, so I signed up. My mom didn't want me to, because we just naturally didn't agree on much of what I wanted to do or how I wanted to live my life by then. It seemed like our clashes were most often about me not thinking or acting enough like a "lady" to suit her. In this case, she told me it wasn't ladylike to be fighting. Looking back on it, that was probably the attraction for me.

When I signed up, she refused to come, which didn't surprise me. My friends thought I was crazy, but they wanted to see it, so they did come. No surprise there either.

I was ready to go at it, but I had no technique or any idea what I was doing. I told a reporter from the local paper that my plan was to hit them before they had a chance to hit me. Turned out that became my style my whole career, even once I knew what I was doing in the ring. Fans liked it, and so did I. It fit who I was, and not many external things were doing that at the time.

That's how on October 1, 1987, I found myself a college freshman standing in the wings at the Raleigh County Armory wearing a pair of 16-ounce boxing gloves and leather headgear, waiting to try something I knew nothing about but this: it was time to fight.

The event was a two-day deal, if you lasted that long. There were two women's weight classes. The first was up to 150, as I recall, and the second was anything over that. I came in just under 150, so at least I wasn't in with the bigger girls. The way things would turn out later, that wasn't how it usually went during my career, but it did that night.

What you got for winning the first night was a pat on the back and a chance to come back and fight again the next night. If you won twice on Saturday night, you got the $300 prize money and a jacket. If you lost, you got nothing but wounded pride and, in my case, a look from my mother I didn't want to see.

For a college kid, $300 was a lot of money, but I wasn't fighting for the money. I never did that until late in my career, which was a sign that I was done, because you can't fight just for money. The cost is too high for that. At the time I think I felt like I was doing it out of curiosity, but now I understand that somewhere deep inside I understood the boxing ring was a place where it was acceptable to be a tough girl. Maybe that was linked to my sexuality issues and the inner turmoil and anxiety I was living with at the time. I certainly knew in the ring, I could be tough, and I could fight back, and it would all be acceptable. All the rage that had been building inside me for years could come out between those ropes, and they'd give me $300 if I channeled it well enough to win. The only judgment of me would be, can she fight?

Now, I was a pretty aggressive basketball player and a very competitive person, so aggression wasn't an issue, but basketball isn't boxing. You play basketball. Nobody plays boxing, as I was about to find out. I wasn't scared of getting hurt, but that was probably because I didn't realize then how hurt you could get inside a boxing ring. I thought you just show up and fight. I was nervous though, because I didn't want to embarrass myself and get knocked out in 10 seconds. Fear of embarrassment and a hatred of losing are a large part of what drives most high-achieving athletes. They are really one and the same. If fearing pain and injury are your problem, you're done before you start. That's true in boxing, and it's true in life.

Most of the seats at the Armory were on an overhang above the floor, so the fighters gathered under the seats and waited. We fought three one-minute rounds, which may not sound like much, but when someone is throwing hands at you with bad intentions, your anxiety level gets pretty heightened pretty fast, so you can get exhausted in a hurry if you can't find a way to relax. I wasn't too relaxed that night, and I became a lot less so once I climbed into the ring, because I got two shocks the moment I looked around.

The first was that I actually knew my opponent. Her name was Sue McNamara, and we'd had some classes together at Concord College. We weren't friends by any means, but I didn't expect to see a face I recognized staring at me from across the ring, so I was a little startled. But then I saw two faces I recognized a whole lot more than Sue's, and that shocked the hell out of me. Two of the judges were Sherry's mom and stepfather!

I freaked out when I realized they were sitting in the judges' seats at ringside. Sherry's mom hated me, because her daughter and I were in love. My mom believed it was Sherry's fault that I was gay. She blames Sherry for me being gay and for Jim shooting me. It's crazy, but it's what she has convinced herself is true. I guess blaming someone else for something that was nobody's fault but nature's makes it somehow easier on her, but it didn't make it easier on me.

Sherry's mom never felt that way. She knew her daughter was gay, and eventually she came to accept it in a way my mom still hasn't been able to. But none of that mattered at that moment. All that mattered was that those two would be judging my first fight.

When I saw them, I immediately thought, "Oh, shit! I'll have to knock this girl out to win!" This was one of those crossroad moments in my life, and I have to give them both credit. They were very professional. They did their job and just scored what they saw in the fight, not who was doing the fighting.

I didn't see them or talk to them again for nearly 25 years. Not until a few weeks after Jim shot me in 2010. By then, Sherry and I had gotten back together, and they had accepted the situation. By that time, I had become Christy Martin, the famous boxer, to them, not Christy Salters, the kid from Mullens sleeping with their daughter in the next room. I still had the bullet in my back when we went to visit them in North Carolina over Christmas 2010, and we talked about how strange and crazy it was that they had been the judges in the first fight I ever had.

I always respected the fact that they didn't let any personal feelings about me then enter into it when it came to judging a boxing match. They certainly could have. I mean, it was a Toughman contest. It wasn't even like it was a professional fight. Who would have known if they had robbed me and given me a bad decision? Nobody would have cared, but they didn't, and I've always been thankful to them for that. I really do believe they held my future in their hands that night, although none of us knew it at the time. Had I lost that first fight, my whole life path would have been different.

If Sherry's mother and stepdad had held a grudge and given the decision to Sue, I don't think I would have pursued boxing. I didn't know women were trying to make a career out of boxing in 1987, and the real truth is back then, you couldn't do it. I was the first to really manage to do that, and I'm proud I was able to open a lot of doors for other women. But that night I wasn't thinking about blazing a trail. I just wanted to win.

I have my feelings about them, and they're not all positive because of the things they tried to do to break up Sherry and me when we were young and in love. But they were fair that night. To them, I was just another tough girl trying to win, and I'll always be grateful for that because what happened next set me off on a long road that took me all over the world and let me see things I never dreamed of. If I'd lost, I don't know why I would have done it again. It wasn't like I was looking to become a prizefighter. It was just a lark. So, if I hadn't won, why would I have continued?

Sue was tough, and the fight was close, but I did get the decision, which meant I was coming back on Saturday night to do it again. Even though the fight had been exhausting and tougher than I expected, I loved it. I loved how the crowd reacted when I landed a punch and how I reacted when Sue hit me and I had to respond. It challenged your desire and your self-control. It challenged you physically and mentally. You found out in a hurry if you had any determination and any will.

Whenever I fought, I always wanted to get it over with as fast as possible. After I was a professional for a while, I used to say I didn't get paid for overtime, but the real reason was I wanted to knock you out and go home. I didn't just want to beat you by outboxing you. I wanted to dominate the other woman. My thing was knockouts, so if I could get it over with fast, I did, and the next night that's exactly what happened against an unusual opponent.

Her name was Barbara Farley, and she was 41 years old with six kids. They called her "the fighting grandmother," because she also had two grandchildren. She'd beaten a younger girl the first night, but I stopped her, and the place went wild. The next year, as it turned out, I ended up fighting one of her daughters and knocked her out, too. She had wanted to avenge her mother's loss from the year before. It would have been a better story if I'd done it in the same night, but I was just happy to get to the finals.

My last opponent was a big girl who lived about a half hour from where I grew up. She was BIG, maybe 5-foot-9 or 5-foot-10, and I'm barely 5-foot-4. I wasn't even 145, and she must have been right at the 150-pound limit, but if you can fight, size doesn't always matter. I knocked her out with one punch.

Bang!

Down!

Over!

She wasn't staggering around and kind of woozy, she was out, and the crowd went into a frenzy! My god, the reaction was crazy. I can still feel exactly what that did to me. It was awesome. I could feel the adrenaline rush from the crowd, and that was it for me. I was hooked on boxing. That moment when you knock someone out and the crowd reacts is better than any drug. That's why the first thing I thought of when they gave me the champion's jacket and the $300 was, *"When's the next one?"* That jacket is still hanging in my mom's garage.

I didn't have any thoughts that night about having made some sort of feminist statement in the sports world or anything like that. The only thing I thought about was I couldn't wait to do it again next year.

When 1988 came, Jerry Thomas had already been accosted in the canned goods section at the grocery store and by enough girls like me that he'd added two women's divisions to his original Toughman contest, and that's what I entered. No more Mean Mountaineer for me. I was ready to go "big-time."

That year there was a regional Toughman in Beckley and then what was being called "The 9th Annual Toughman World Championships" at the West Virginia Motor Speedway. That's in Parkersburg, West Virginia, so I'm not so sure how big that world was, but it did have fighters from the United States and Canada, not just local fighters, so if I made it there, that would be a step up. I wasn't exactly sure up to what. All I was sure of was that I wanted to win, and I wanted to feel that same rush from the crowd going crazy.

I hadn't done any training since the Mean Mountaineer besides playing college basketball, but that was an edge for me over most of the girls in those tournaments. Many of them were muscular. They looked stronger than me, but I was in better condition, and I was an athlete. Most of them were just tough girls. None of us really knew how to fight, but when the adrenaline started flowing, at least I knew how to move side to side and in and out. I guess I had some punching power, too, which is mostly a natural gift. You can work on technique and form, but you either have punching power, or you don't. You can teach someone how to box, but you can't really teach them how to bring the thunder. Once you understand the mechanics, you either can punch or you can't. That snap is a gift, and I had it, although I had no idea that I did at that point in my life. The edge I knew I had back then was that I had better balance and footwork than most of the other girls, and I had that "I'll show you'" attitude that's worked for me a lot in boxing but not always quite so well in life.

The Toughman format was the same as Mean Mountaineer. Lose and go home. It was sort of like the movie *Hunger Games*. Only one survives.

The first girl I faced that year was the daughter of "the fighting grandmother" I had knocked out the year before. As revenge goes, it didn't work out too well for her, because I knocked her out, too, which got me into the Saturday night fights that would determine who went to the "world" championships. I won both fights that next night, including a decision in the championship match after I knocked down my opponent in the second round and gave her a standing eight count, which is when the referee decides one fighter is hurt bad enough that she needs a break even though she hasn't hit the floor yet. The winner was supposed to get $1,000, but after it was over and they raised my hand, the promoter said he only had $400 and the jacket. I was glad to have it, but that was my first lesson in the economic dark side of prizefighting. It's a world where you don't always get what you expect, but my attitude was "What can you do?" At least I won and had some drinking money.

That July the World Championships were set to be held at the high school football stadium in Parkersburg, not too far down the I-77 highway from Beckley. Thomas had suggested to Al Dore that he add two women's divisions to the world championship tournament he'd been running, and Al said, "Why don't you promote it?" Jerry agreed, and like everything about small-time boxing, it turned into a nightmare.

About a month before the event, the town condemned the bleachers at the high school, so Thomas had to find a new venue. But it couldn't be too far away, because a lot of people from out of town had already made travel plans. The only place big enough was the West Virginia Motor Speedway, which was a 5/8th-mile oval clay track in Mineral Wells, which was right next door to Parkersburg.

Thomas's problem was they'd had a big country music concert there a few weeks earlier, and it backed up traffic for miles down onto I-77. The traffic jam was four or five miles long, and the locals weren't too keen on seeing another event there so soon. But Jerry worked it out, and I headed down there, intending to learn what it felt like to become a champion. I left having learned a different lesson. It was one I didn't like at all.

47

My first fight was against Andrea DeShong, a woman who would end up playing a pretty big role in my life eventually. She was a real fighter, and she was Jerry's fighter, too, which made beating her a little more difficult. I was still just a basketball player in a fight, and this time the basketball player lost a close decision to a trained fighter.

I felt like I won, and she was sure that she had. But it didn't really matter, because she got to go on and win the tournament, and I had to go home, a loser for the first time. The silver lining in it was the next night it poured, and the arena was a mess. The ringside seats were on the clay track, and everyone was slipping and falling down. The ring didn't have a canopy, so the fighters were slipping, too. They were getting soaked, and I was back in my apartment in Athens with a far more serious problem to deal with.

On the surface it seemed like my personal life had sorted itself out. I'd been living with "P" for some time and was still friends with my ex-girlfriend from college as well, although we were no longer together. That was no surprise, because I wasn't totally together myself at the time when it came to being faithful or totally understanding my own sexuality. I'd been with men and women in high school, so I'd say I was bisexual at that time, but to me being in a relationship with a woman was easier. It was always where I was most comfortable. A lot of people would say, are you crazy? Easier? It was for me. I just felt more relaxed in a relationship with a woman.

Unfortunately, that didn't stop me from venturing back and forth. That's how totally confused I still was at times. You naturally struggle with your identity when you're that age, but battling your own sexuality and how your family and others would view you if they knew leaves you lost sometimes. It's like you're in a fog that envelops you. It clouds your judgment. You doubt sometimes the direction you're going. Other times you're totally sure.

Am I truly a gay woman? Is what my parents want for me what I should want, too? Can I be straight if I try? Should I be who I am, or try harder to please everyone else? Who the hell am I, anyway? I asked myself those questions many times. Then, in the midst of all of that I found out who I was, and it left me in shock. I was a 21-year-old gay college athlete with a big problem. I was pregnant.

How on Earth could that happen? Certainly, my girlfriend didn't get me pregnant. But she'd gone home for the summer, and one weekend I was back in Itmann and saw my old boyfriend, Chris. I'll always have a spot in my heart for Chris, I guess. We were boyfriend/girlfriend in fourth, fifth grade, and were off and on all through high school. His mom never wanted that for him. If she'd been accepting of us being together, and we'd become a real couple, who knows what would have happened? Maybe we'd have gone down the road together and been happy, or maybe it would have gone good for a while, and then my true nature would have had to be dealt with. Who knows?

Chris was home for the summer from college, too, and every now and then we'd see each other. One night we went out as friends, had a few drinks, and had drunken sex. I was in love with my girlfriend, so why did that happen? I was selfish, that's why. There's no other explanation.

The next morning, I began thinking *"Oh, my God!"* From that morning until there was no baby, I was sick. I waited four or five weeks and finally took a pregnancy test. The day I did, I was lifting weights with my former girlfriend back in Athens, and I had a test with me I'd bought in the drugstore. I just decided I had to find out, so I went into the bathroom. I knew the answer that was coming. I was positive.

A lot of people would have gotten angry or started crying. I just started drinking. That isn't good for a baby, but I wasn't thinking about that. I didn't want a child, but I personally didn't believe in abortion. I always believed in a woman's right to choose, but my choice, I thought, would never be to have an abortion. Now here I was, thinking about it.

My ex-girlfriend immediately said we should get back together, have the baby, and she'd raise the child. I told her that wasn't happening, so she agreed to drive me down to Johnson City, Tennessee, so I wouldn't be alone when I told "P". I think she was hoping we'd break up over it, and she'd be there to pick up the pieces.

I was afraid how my girlfriend would react, because I knew if it had been me, I would have told her I'm done. But that wasn't what happened. She said she was coming back at the end of the summer, and we'd deal with it. There wasn't much said on the drive back to Athens.

The next day I called Chris, and we met in Mullens. When I told him, the first thing he said was he didn't want a baby, which I understood, because neither did I. The next thing he did was ask if I was sure it was his? What?

I was so angry. It was never a question in my mind whether I'd have the baby. Even if "P" had said we could raise this child together, I doubt that would have changed my mind. I had no money. No job. No idea what the future was and, to be honest, I was about me then. Maybe that's what was wrong in the first place. But how could Chris ask me that? When I think about it today, I can understand why, considering what I'd just done, but I couldn't see that then.

So, here I was about to do something I believed was wrong for me. I guess it was one of those beliefs you have until you're tested. Everyone thinks if a building is on fire, they'll be the one who runs in and grabs the baby, but the truth is 99 percent of us don't. We call 9-1-1 and stand there. I was about to find out that was me when it came to this baby, and that didn't feel very good at all.

I waited a few days, knowing what I was going to do but not able to do it. Finally, I went to the yellow pages, which was the business phone book that no longer even exists. I looked up clinics and found one in Charleston, West Virginia. I only told Chris, those two girlfriends, and one other person. I had to tell my basketball coach, Russell Hill, because I was supposed to be an instructor at his summer basketball camp, and I'd have to miss a couple of days.

He knew I'd dated those two women, so I told him, "You're going to be very shocked that of all the girls on the team, I'm the one coming to you with this."

It was a coach-to-player talk. His first reaction was to look dumbfounded before he said, "Really?" Then he asked if I was OK. He talked to me with a little heart.

I never told my parents. It was just another secret between us. I didn't want the added pressure of them saying they'd raise the baby while I finished school, which I know my mom would have done. The only reason they know today is that I was afraid Jim would make it known during the murder trial, so I called and told them I needed to sit down and have a talk. The two things I told them were about being sexually abused as a kid and the abortion when I was 21.

They told me they already knew about the abortion. They said Jim had told them a couple days before he shot me, but they didn't know whether to believe him. He was frantically calling everyone who knew me at that time, telling them every vile thing he could think of.

He told them that, and they never asked me about it. How do you not ask your daughter if she'd gotten pregnant in college and had an abortion? How do you not do that as a parent? I guess you do it if you don't really want to know, which is how my family too often operated when it came to my life. It hasn't been talked about since.

So, I went off to the clinic, the folks there spoke with me for a little while, and that was it. It wasn't, "Come back in a week after you think it over." I walked in scared, and I walked out in a daze. A friend drove me back to the apartment, and in a couple of days I went to Coach Hill's camp.

When he saw me, he asked if I was all right. I don't think he ever told a soul where I'd been. I told him I was fine. I picked up a basketball and just dribbled off, but the truth is I wasn't OK. I justified my actions in all the ways that you do by saying I wouldn't have been a good mother, and I wasn't in a position to take care of a baby at the time, but I felt guilty. I realized I'd done something I'd always believed was wrong for me. I believe a woman has the right to choose, but I never thought it would be the choice I'd make. Now I had. The truth is I made the selfish choice. I made the choice that was best for me and now, once again, I was hiding who I was and something I'd done.

Every decision you make, good or bad, leads you to where you end up today. I wish I could have had the baby and still had the life I had as far as my boxing career goes, but it's very unlikely that could have happened. How could I have devoted all the time it took to become a boxer if I had had a baby to raise? I made a choice that was best for me, and you can judge me for that however you want. Whatever you think of that choice, I won't quarrel with it. I did what I did, and I have to live with it.

It's one of those things that will always bother me, but it's the decision I made. It was a selfish decision. I have to admit that. I still feel guilty about it, but I had made a choice, and now I had to move forward. When "P" arrived back on campus after the summer break, we never talked about it. I didn't talk to Chris after that for a long time. There was a little bit of just putting my head in the sand and going on. Wonder where I learned how to do that? That was the last time I had sex with a man until Jim, and I went from boxer-trainer to something more.

So, there I was with less than a year to go in college, another basketball season coming up, more guilt feelings inside to lug around, and a growing urge to find my way back into the ring with Andrea DeShong. That ended up taking a little longer than I expected, but in the interim I fought Toughman one more time in 1989, and I won the regionals again. Even though I'd lost in the world championships the year before, I had developed some confidence and felt I could keep doing it for a while longer to make a few dollars and have some fun before I sorted out what I'd do with my life.

I just assumed I'd fight in a few more Toughman contests first because, for whatever reason, getting in the ring against another woman challenged me in a different way than basketball did. It allowed me to release a lot of the frustrations in my life and a lot of the anger that I was carrying inside since I first realized as a little girl that the people I wanted most to love were not the ones my parents or the world were too keen about me falling for.

So, I went back to college knowing I would have enough credits to graduate in December but wanting to finish my senior season of basketball. I registered for enough spring classes to stay eligible, and after I won the regional Toughman tournament in Beckley again I had my mind set on fighting my way back to facing DeShong at the world championships.

Then my phone rang.

I didn't recognize the number, but in those days before cell phones and texting, you actually answered it whether or not you knew who was on the other end. It turned out I didn't know him, but I was blessed to have picked up.

It's kind of ironic that the guy on the other end was named Richard Christmas, because he was bringing me a gift that neither one of us understood. Richard worked for a professional boxing promoter in Bristol, Tennessee, named Larry Carrier, and Carrier wanted to know if I'd come down at the end of September and make my pro boxing debut.

That phone call changed my life forever.

"Want to Box, Girl?"

We've all heard the saying "ignorance is bliss." You've also probably heard someone say at one time or another, "What you don't know won't hurt you." I was about to find out that although maybe the first statement is true, that second one, well, what you don't know certainly can and will hurt you when what you don't know is how to box and what you're about to become is a boxer.

By the time I put down the phone, I'd agreed to drive down to Bristol, which was only about a two-hour ride from Athens, and square off against a girl named Angela Buchanan. Five rounds for $500. One hundred bucks a round, plus a room for the night sounded pretty good to me, especially because I didn't figure it was going to go five rounds judging from my Toughman experiences.

I was close to graduating college and was already looking for a teaching job, even though I knew I really didn't want to spend my life doing that. So why not take these guys up on their offer? I thought I might become a high school basketball coach eventually, which I knew I'd like better than teaching, but I figured I'd go down to Tennessee first and box this one time just for the experience. Most experiences in life you have to pay for. This one came with $500 in cash, so why not?

Once I went off to college, I pretty much stayed in Athens all the time, including in the summer. I went to summer school to earn extra credits, but the real reason was I wanted to get away from the small-town restrictions in Itmann and Mullens that had made my private life so difficult. I'm not suggesting Athens, West Virginia, was Athens, Greece, but it was far enough away that I felt free to live as a gay woman and go about my business. People there knew exactly who Christy Salters was. I don't know if they cared, but if they did, they never let on, which was a relief.

My problem now was a familiar one as your college years are coming to an end. I needed to start making enough money to become totally my own person. I felt if I was paying my own bills, I could live my life the way I wanted.

If my parents were still paying my bills, which they were, it was legitimately their business how I was living and with whom, which meant I was still hiding things from them.

I wanted to get on with my life, so I needed to become financially independent. Once I did that, I thought I could be totally who I wanted to be. If my parents didn't like that, it wouldn't matter. They would have lost the right to judge how I lived. That's the way I thought things would go. I found out later nothing is that simple. The baggage I was carrying was too heavy and not so easy to just drop and walk away from.

I never thought, when I put down that phone, that boxing would free me from any of the personal issues I was facing. At that point, I didn't even know women's boxing was a thing, probably because it really wasn't. It wasn't like you saw women boxing on television, like you do today. You didn't see them fighting anywhere except maybe in Toughman or a barroom. But what did I have to lose? My whole reasoning was do it one time so I could always say I'd been a professional boxer. Not twice, for sure. Just once.

The morning of the fight, "P" and I drove to Bristol, which I later learned wasn't the norm. Promoters don't want to spend a penny more than they have to on undercard fighters, and now that I'm a promoter I get it. But some promoters take it to the extreme. In this case, I drove down, weighed in, and then hung around all day in my room waiting for the bell to ring.

I didn't say much at the weigh-in. Later in my career, I could get pretty boisterous and intimidating at weigh-ins because I believed, like a lot of boxers do, that the fight begins long before you step into the ring. The mental side of the sport is so important. You have to get yourself past your own nature before you can fight effectively. Human nature is designed to protect you, so when you feel threatened your first reaction is to retreat, because all human nature cares about is survival.

The first caveman didn't run at the saber-toothed tiger, I'm sure. He ran away. But eventually he figured out that to eat, he had to catch something. So, you train yourself to come forward when most people are going backwards. That's the start of understanding how a boxer has to think. It's also why intimidation becomes a part of how you approach opponents. You want them to be asking themselves, "Is this really worth it?" But at that time, I didn't know enough to be intimidated or to try to intimidate. I just watched everyone else at the weigh-in and didn't ask any questions.

At that first fight, the roles were reversed from the way they would become later on. Angela knew everybody. I was the B side. I was shy and didn't know quite what to make of it all, but I knew I was the underdog in the opinion of the people there, because they didn't know a thing about me.

Being the underdog has always worked for me. It's how I saw myself most of my life. It brings out the fight in me, so it wasn't a disadvantage at all. The A side brings pressure with it. I was always aware that I didn't want to stink the place out when I was the A side. People were paying to watch me fight. Who cares about the B side? Nobody in that arena on September 9, 1989, I can assure you of that.

I can't say I felt confident, but I wasn't worried either, because I didn't know enough yet about the damage boxing can do to you. I had no reason to think it would be any different than another Toughman contest until I got to the arena, and someone told me I had to wear a chest protector.

I wasn't sure what they were talking about until they brought in this thing that looked like a catcher's chest protector, like I used to wear when I was playing Little League baseball. It was HUGE. It came all the way down to my waist. I'm so short-waisted it was really restrictive. It looked ridiculous, frankly.

I'd never worn anything like that in Toughman, but someone from the Tennessee Boxing Commission told me a woman fighter had to protect her breasts, which was the first I'd heard of that. When I saw it, I thought they were joking.

Later I'd learn some states required that kind of protection and others didn't. The funny thing is, my chest was an area I never did get hit in, but those were the regulations. In Las Vegas it was required, too, but a lot of times I'd just wear a sports bra and a shirt. If they made me, I'd stuff some towels inside my bra, but I usually got away without it because I was the A side then. The A side gets the breaks in boxing. The B side puts on a chest protector and doesn't ask questions.

The promoter owned what was then called Bristol International Speedway. It's the track now known as Bristol Motor Speedway, which is one of NASCAR's biggest venues. Larry Carrier helped build it in the early 1960s right off Highway 11-E on a piece of land that used to be the home of one of the largest dairy farms in the eastern half of the United States.

It had been sold a couple times by then and expanded quite a bit from when he first built it. It's a massive place on more than 100 acres with a half-mile oval track, miles of parking, a huge grandstand, and a small arena he built on it for boxing. Larry finally sold it all in 1996 for $26 million. By that time, the track had expanded to hold 71,000 spectators, and the new owners added another 15,000 seats after that. I'm pretty sure Larry did better on that deal than he did on my first boxing show.

That small arena around back is where the fight was going to be, and by the time I got there, I have to admit I was a little edgy. It wasn't that I was concerned about getting hurt or even getting hit. I just wanted to do well. Knowing you've never had any training doesn't boost your confidence. The truth was that the first time I fought professionally was the first time I'd ever been to a boxing match, which probably is not the ideal way to get your baptism in boxing. Neither was what happened next.

When I came out for the first ring walk of my career, it was pretty shocking. The crowd reacted like it was a cat fight. Like this was a circus sideshow. It was the opposite of coming out for a basketball game. That was an athletic event. You could tell the crowd looked at this differently. It was more like this was "send in the clowns," and I didn't like that. Not one bit.

I take things to heart, and I felt like the people in the crowd, which was almost all men, were laughing at me. That was a shot to my pride and my ego. I always thought of myself as an athlete, not a freak. I didn't feel like I deserved that kind of reaction, but I got it anyway.

You're standing there in shorts and a T-shirt. You have on big boxing gloves, no head gear, and the place seems as dark as a cave except far ahead of you, where the lights are shining on the ring. It looked miles away. Later I would at least have some familiar faces around me as I made that walk, but at this point, I didn't have anyone in my corner that I knew. The only guy with me that night was named Billy Mitchum. He worked the corner for a lot of the opponents Larry brought in. He was an ex-fighter who once fought Roy Jones Jr. early in Jones's career. He was a tough guy, and I came to like him, because the more I fought for Larry, the more I trusted having Billy in my corner.

Maybe I didn't know how to box yet, but I knew what I wanted to do. I wanted to beat the shit out of Angela Buchanan, which is exactly what I did. I knocked her down once, and she went down hard. It wasn't like she slipped or was off balance. She got knocked down, and those same fans who had been laughing at me seemed to be a little intrigued by that.

I learned a few things about boxing that night. The biggest lesson was that even though everyone knew I won, they called it a draw because Angela was what they call the "house fighter." What that means is she was the local promoter's fighter, and this was a local show. They couldn't protect her during the fight, but once the judges' scoring took over, they could. I didn't understand that when they call you to come fight their girl in a small-time venue, you're not supposed to win.

The other lesson I learned, and never did forget, was the less the officials have to do with the outcome, the more control you have over it. Pencils come with erasers, and in three judges' hands, they can erase whatever fighter they want to erase—or need to erase. But if you knock out the house fighter, there's no eraser for that. That's why I always came to a fight with bad intentions. Let your fists be the judges.

Despite the outcome, I wasn't really unhappy with how things had gone. It didn't matter much to me what those judges said, because it wasn't like I was going to make a living boxing. This was a one off, or so I thought, until Carrier came up after the fight and asked if I'd come back in three weeks for a rematch.

I agreed without really thinking about it. I hadn't won, but I also hadn't lost, so it was like nothing got settled, and I like to settle things. Plus, it was another $500 in the bank.

I still saw myself as a basketball player, not a boxer, so my focus was getting ready for my final season. My coach knew I was boxing, but it didn't bother him. Technically, I was now a professional athlete, but it wasn't like the NCAA was going to investigate the Concord College women's basketball program for professionalism.

When I came back for the rematch, it was still just for fun, but there was really more to it than that. The ring was becoming a safe place where I felt able to get out my frustrations and the anger that was locked up inside me. Even though women's boxing wasn't acceptable to probably 95 percent of the people in the world at that time, for the ones for whom it was acceptable, it was OK for me to go in there and be as aggressive as hell and as competitive as I wanted to be. No one would say anything about it. They might laugh at us on the way into the ring, but if we fought hard and did some damage, they'd cheer us on the way out. No one cared if you were angry, or what you were angry about. They didn't care if you were gay or straight. Whatever it was that drove you to fight was fine to the people watching . . . as long as you could fight.

So, three weeks later I was in Durham, North Carolina, for the rematch, and this time things changed. I knocked out Angela with one punch in the second round. That confirmed what I first felt in Toughman. What sold me on boxing was the crowd's reaction to a knockout and the adrenaline rush I got hearing that roar. When you knock someone out, fans go nuts. That fed my ego and propped up my sagging self-esteem. They liked me just the way I was.

That night, September 30, 1989, hooked me on boxing for the rest of my life. The approval of the crowd. My hand being raised. My opponent on her back. Having that mastery over another person, that control, really threw me. I loved it. Three weeks later I was back again, and it only took me one round to knock out a girl named Tammy Jones.

Carrier really liked those knockouts, because knockouts sell tickets, whether it's women getting knocked out or men. That's really what most boxing fans in the United States want to see. A few may want to see that smooth boxer, the Floyd Mayweather type who seldom gets hit and who makes his opponent miss. Smooth fighters embarrass their opponents more than hurt them. They make them pay a price, but not too high a price. They're like artists in the ring. They can turn a fight into a well-choreographed dance routine in which they are always leading, and their opponent is always following. Those fighters who are highly skilled boxers understand something about the sport that the rest of us don't. It's a style they appreciate more in Europe. In the United States, we like knockouts. That's what pays the bills.

After those two knockouts, Larry came to talk with me again. He wanted to be my promoter. Now I was his fighter, instead of Angela. He asked me if I'd come back in two weeks and fight a familiar name. He wanted me to fight Andrea DeShong, the girl who'd outboxed me at the Toughman world championships the year before. My answer came quickly. "Yes, sir!"

I understood I had a lot to learn, so I went out and found a heavy bag and hung it in my apartment back in Athens. I would watch fights on television and then go practice what I saw on the bag.

I really loved a guy named Hector "Macho" Camacho. Later he would become a dear friend of mine, but long before that I loved the way he moved in the ring and the flashy style he had. He was a showman as well as a boxer. He wore outrageous costumes into the ring and did things to sell himself to the crowd, but he also could fight. So, I studied him and other fighters and kept pounding that heavy bag. But I wasn't totally ready for the world to think of me as a fighter, so I hung a curtain around it. That way if anyone came over to visit who didn't know I was boxing, they wouldn't see it.

Never did I think my life would be defined for the next 20 years by that heavy bag and everything that came with it. One thing just led to another, like they often do in life, but at that time my real job was back in Athens, if you call working at Taco Bell a real job.

There was a guy who came in regularly who owned a private investigation agency, and he was always talking about his job. It sounded pretty interesting, and one day he told me he needed some help. It paid better than slinging tacos, so I started following people around for him. Mostly spouses who were cheating. That's how I became a private eye.

His company also repossessed cars, which I didn't like. You'd have kids crying and everything, and that really bothered me, but the rest of it was interesting work. The only time I was scared was when I went with another PI to repossess a car, and the owner got really mad. He came running out talking shit, which was expected, but when he reached behind his back for a gun, my partner took one look at him and said, "Get back in the car. This isn't worth getting shot over." I didn't argue with either one of them. I got in the car.

Some of the people I had to follow were smarter than others. Once I was following a woman whose husband was accusing her of cheating on him in a divorce case. I was tailing her, but I guess I wasn't exactly Magnum P.I., because she got onto me. I didn't know it, so I kept following her right into the police station parking lot. She jumped out and told the cops I was stalking her. They came out, and I told them, "Why would a college kid be following this woman?" They let me go, but they told me not to bother her again. Which I didn't.

My biggest case was a guy who was scamming an insurance company on a disability claim. He kept insisting he had a bad back, but the insurance company didn't believe him, so they had me trail him to find his house. That's not easy to do sometimes in rural West Virginia, but I finally found it off a main road up in what most people would call the mountains.

I let the air out of one of my tires, and limped into his yard and asked if he could help a girl out. I told him I was just a college kid who didn't know how to work a jack. I'd put my girlfriend back a ways behind a tree with a video camera to film what happened next.

That guy turned into Mr. Chivalry. He whipped those tires around, jacked up the car, and put on the spare like he worked for AAA. They were sure happy to see that film when I got back to the office.

So, I was working, playing basketball, living with my girlfriend, going to class, driving to Bristol every few weeks to fight, and spending as little time as possible talking with my family. My brother, Randy, who was four years younger than me, came down to visit once, but he didn't really know what was going on in my life. I'm sure he'd heard things back in Mullens, but he didn't ask any questions. All he wanted to know about was my boxing, so I had him make the drive with me to Bristol for the DeShong fight.

It was only two weeks since I'd knocked out Tammy Jones, and I was feeling pretty good about myself when I stepped into the ring with DeShong. It didn't take long for me to not feel quite so good. I realized in a hurry she was different than those other girls. She'd already won five straight fights, and it was obvious that she'd been doing more than watching boxers on TV and hitting a heavy bag in her apartment.

She knew how to throw straight punches and move in and out to change distances on me. I'd heard she'd been a kickboxer before Toughman, so she'd had some formal training in combat sports, and it showed. For some reason, kickboxing was always more receptive to women than boxing was at that time. Whatever she'd been doing, she was the first woman to hurt me. At least in a boxing ring she was.

She outboxed me for five rounds and landed cleaner punches. The fight was still close, but she won a majority decision, which means two judges had her winning and the third had it a draw. This time I knew they got it right, and I wasn't so sure it was worth it to keep going.

Right after the fight, Carrier asked me if I wanted a rematch, and this time I said no. She'd hit me so hard one time I didn't remember the rest of the fight. On the drive home, I asked my brother if she'd knocked me down, because I wasn't sure what had happened. He said, "Nope," which was a good thing, but at that moment basketball was looking pretty good to me. I was second-guessing myself and licking my wounds.

I'd never been hurt like that before. I was thinking this was not for me, but the truth is one of the reasons I survived all the things I've had to face in my life is I'm stubborn and I don't like losing. Not one bit, whether it's in life or in boxing. I may have my doubts, but I fight back. That was in me all my life. But box? That's a science, and I'd never spent a day in the science lab of boxing, which is the gym. That's where you learn the basics of what the famous *New Yorker* magazine writer A. J. Liebling called "the sweet science" and a lot of boxing guys call "the dark trade." Both names apply.

I didn't have the foundation I needed to excel. There's so much more to it than the average person thinks. People think boxing is just two fighters swinging as hard as they can at each other. It's a lot more strategic and scientific than that. It's counter and then counter the counter. It's movement and balance, and knowing when to come forward, and when to retreat. It's understanding the geometry of angles and how to navigate around the tight minefield of the ring. It's controlling your fear, too, by focusing your mind totally on your job.

Most of all its feinting and setting traps, getting your opponent to believe one thing when another thing is the truth. You're always trying to hide what you're planning to do next. In some ways, it was like being a closeted gay woman. You're always trying to hide who you are and what you're doing. You're trying to trick people into thinking you're about one thing when you're really about something else. You're hiding in plain sight what your intentions are.

In life I was doing that to survive in a world that wasn't ready to accept where my heart was. In the boxing ring, you're trying to trick your opponents into walking into a vulnerable position so you can take advantage of them, hurt them, or knock them out. In my life, I was trying to avoid the hurt, but in the ring, I was trying to bring the hurt. Maybe I was doing the one to avoid the other. People are interesting that way. We don't always understand why we're doing what we're doing when we do it. It has taken me years to sort it out, and I don't have it all worked out yet. I'm still healing, which was something I also had to do after losing to DeShong.

I didn't fight for five months, and that break was important. I was playing basketball again, and we had games every weekend, so that was one reason I wasn't available. But I also had to deal with doubt for the first time as an athlete. I was still working on the heavy bag at home, but I had no idea where I could find a boxing gym or a trainer. I didn't even think to go to the library and get a "how to box" instructional book. They didn't have *Boxing for Dummies* back then, but if they had, I would have qualified as a customer.

I was still watching fights on TV and mimicking what I saw in my living room, and my conditioning was good from playing basketball almost every day. I wasn't in boxing shape, which in my opinion is the best shape you'll ever get in, but I was in better shape for a rematch if I decided I wanted one.

The time away helped me forget what it felt like to get hurt and kind of black out. It gave me time to forget how I felt on that drive back to Athens with my brother. By the time Carrier called again, I'd changed my mind. DeShong had had two more fights by then, but what she'd been doing didn't concern me. I always believed when it came to a fight that it was about me more than who I was fighting.

About seven weeks after that fight, I had a Christmas to remember and an incident that took my mind completely away from boxing. "P" and I were living together in my apartment at school, and life was pretty good until her mother down in Johnson City found out and called my mother. I was home for the holidays, and the day after Christmas my parents sat me down and said they had something they needed to discuss.

As soon as they said that, I thought, *What did I do now?* My dad asked me in this sad voice, "You don't like men?" Then he started crying. He wasn't the kind of man who cried. He never showed weakness. I don't know that I'd ever seen him cry. It hurt me that something I was doing hurt my dad so bad. It made me feel guilty again. Not guilty for loving a woman, just guilty for hurting him. Only later did I understand my parents should have loved me enough to let me be me, because if not there would be consequences all my life that none of us could imagine. But at that moment I just felt sorry for him and how my lifestyle made him feel.

My mom said "P"'s mom had told her we were lesbians, and she was going to take her daughter to see a priest. I was completely blindsided. I didn't know if they were planning to pray on it or try an exorcism, but I thought it was crazy. Pray for what? To change her nature? I didn't know whether to laugh or cry.

My parents claimed they had no idea what had been going on and if it continued, they wouldn't pay for my apartment. I just said, "OK." But I didn't mean OK, I'd end the relationship with my girlfriend. I meant, OK, I'll get a job and pay for it myself. I told them I was in love, and we were staying together. That was probably the last time I stood up for myself in my personal life for more than 20 years. It was a long time before I could muster up that kind of courage again. I got up, packed, and went back to Athens that day.

My parents still insist they didn't know until then that I loved women. If that's true, which I don't believe, they weren't paying much attention. One time I told them about a party I was planning at my apartment for the girls' basketball team. There were only two or three gay girls on the team, but the party was girls only, because it was just for our team. When my mom heard about it, she asked me, "Aren't you going to have any boys there?" If she didn't have any suspicions about my sexuality, why would she ask that? Comments like that made me think they had more than an inkling of how I was living. But as long as they didn't have to confront it, they could stick their head in the sand and act like everything was how they thought it should be in a woman's life.

I left without telling them anything was going to change, because it wasn't. I made no excuses or explanations for us. I was 21 years old. When "P" got back, she said she'd told her parents she was going to continue living with me, and she did until I moved to Bristol a year later. I guess praying with her priest didn't take. If they tried the exorcism, her head may have spun around once or twice, but apparently that didn't take either.

We thought the whole thing was kind of funny, but those kinds of moments stay with you more than I thought at the time. They color how you feel about yourself and how you feel about your family. Those feelings are like a relentless opponent in the ring. You can fight them off, but you can't beat them. They just don't go away. But life has to go on.

It wasn't until spring that Larry called again, to ask if I was ready for a rematch. I don't know if I said yes because of the competitor in me or what.

I just thought I'd do better this time. I understood that if I didn't, my boxing days were over. It was either going to be closure on that chapter of my life, or I was going to keep fighting. I knew myself well enough to realize I had to find out if I could beat DeShong rather than wonder the rest of my life what might have happened if I'd tried one more time.

By the time we fought on April 21, 1990, I had my degree, which was a dream achievement for me. My college basketball career was over, and I was pretty sure I was about done with boxing, too. I didn't want things to end on a loss, but I understood that if I lost to her again, there was a message there that it was time to move on with my life.

The odd thing about it was even with all that, I didn't doubt myself. I still believed I'd find a way to win. I don't think I ever went into a fight thinking I wouldn't win. Even though she'd hurt me in our first fight, I believed I'd win the rematch. I didn't have any thoughts beyond that.

The rematch was another five-round fight, but this time it was different. It wasn't as exciting as our first fight. It was like the two of us were walking around and then throwing punches. She did bite me though, which really surprised me. I told the referee, "She bit me!" Maybe he didn't understand what I was saying, or maybe he did, but all he said was, "Shut up and fight." So, I did.

My skills still weren't as good as hers, but my toughness allowed me to keep it close. To be honest, I didn't know if I'd won or not. She hadn't hurt me like the last time, but she had a full team around her, including Jerry Thomas, the Toughman promoter, who was managing her. I had nobody in my corner, which makes it easier to get screwed. That's not just true in boxing. It's true in life. It's hard to accomplish much alone.

I came to really dislike that part of boxing, but I began to realize the reality of the business. As my career went along, I'd find myself on both sides of that. I didn't have the connections when I fought DeShong. Later I did when Don King was promoting me, and then after I left Don, I was alone again. I didn't have the edge anymore, and it cost me fights I believe I won. I tell the kids I promote today, that's the reality of the sport. Deal with it, overcome it, or find another job.

When they raised my hand, I was surprised, but this time it was a unanimous decision. My toughness had kept it close, and all three judges had me winning, so there was no doubt. I learned later that Jerry Thomas told Andrea sometime after that fight that she should retire and move back to her hometown, a place called Mingo Junction in Ohio. He told her it was just too hard to find fights for women, and we weren't earning any money when they did.

She took his advice and moved to Steubenville, Ohio, and became a massage therapist. She didn't fight again for six years, but she wasn't completely out of my life quite yet. She'd be back under some crazy circumstances a few years later.

I'm pretty sure if I hadn't won that night, I would have stopped boxing, and the only coal miner's daughter anyone would have heard of was Loretta Lynn, the country-western superstar. It wasn't like I was really improving a lot. Of that I was quite sure. And it wasn't like there were any female fighters I could look to as role models. There were some women trying, like Jackie Tonawanda, who sued the New York State Athletic Commission in 1975 for discriminating against women by refusing to license female boxers. She won, but she only had one professional fight, and that came six years later, so I'd never heard of her. I later learned she was legendary in gyms in New York for her toughness, but you can't make a living in the gym. All the women trying to find their place in boxing in those days were going in the same direction I seemed to be, which was essentially nowhere, but winning that rematch gave me a lift.

They told me in the ring I'd won some kind of title, which was news to me. They handed me a belt, but it wasn't like the real ones I would win later in my career. It was just a weight belt like weightlifters wear with a plaque attached. It turned out to be for the World Women's Boxing Association junior welterweight championship, so I was a champion, even if I didn't know of exactly what.

I was 3-1-1, and I'd settled my score with DeShong, but I didn't have a clue what was coming next. Maybe I'd keep working as a PI until I figured out what the future held, and if Carrier called in the meantime, I'd fight. I was having fun, but for the next eight months he never called, and I thought maybe that was it.

Larry was busy running the Motor Speedway that summer, but he finally brought me to Johnson City at the end of September to fight a girl named Jamie Whitcomb who DeShong had already beaten twice. I struggled to beat her, but a month later, just before Halloween, I had a one-round knockout win over a girl named Lisa Holpp back in Bristol. It was a spectacular knockout, and that gave Larry an idea to try to do something more with me.

The next time he called, he wasn't just calling about another $500 fight. He wanted me to move to Bristol and start training with a guy he'd hired to train his son Mark, who was a young heavyweight prospect. He said the guy really wanted to work with me, and Larry thought together they could promote me into something, because I'd developed a local following.

He was offering more than a trainer, too. He said he'd give me a job in a little Western store and tack shop he owned plus a place to live. It would be a chance for me to train like a professional.

I understood what life would be like outside of boxing. I had no idea what it would be like inside boxing, but I knew if I didn't try, I'd wonder for the rest of my life what might have happened if I'd given myself a chance. Otherwise, I'd be working the 9-to-5, getting up every day and going to work like all the people I'd seen trudge off before the sun came up and come home dog tired and not much farther ahead than they were the day before.

In West Virginia teachers weren't paid enough to even buy a house unless they were married or had two incomes. It wasn't the worst life, but I knew what that life would become, and I didn't think I wanted that. So I decided to give boxing six months, and then maybe I'd move to Florida to start being a grown up down by the beach.

I had a lot of different thoughts in my mind. What would happen to my girlfriend and me? Who was this trainer, and how could we make a profession out of making me a boxer? About the only thing I was sure of was I wouldn't stay in West Virginia for the rest of my life. I thought about all that over the Christmas holidays and decided to drive over to Bristol with my mom to take a look. I was 22 years old and heading off to meet a man who would lift me up and put me down for the next 19 years.

Down in Bristol, Jim Martin was waiting for me . . . and he wasn't happy about it.

Meeting My Mentor . . .
and My Menace

You don't have to be the most perceptive person on Earth to know when somebody doesn't want you around. In Jim Martin's case, it wasn't just that he didn't want *me* around. He didn't want *any* women around. At least not inside a boxing gym.

I could feel that the moment my mother and I walked into Carrier's gym in Bristol. I had my gym bag, my dreams, and a roadblock standing in front of me. Despite whatever Carrier may have thought, Jim Martin did not want to train a female boxer.

My mom and I drove down to Bristol a couple of days after Christmas to check things out. I was too shy to go alone, so we piled into my car along with my little dog, Casey, and headed off. It felt like an adventure until I walked through those gym doors.

There were some guys in there training but no women. Not many women were training in any boxing gyms back in 1990, so that didn't surprise me. What surprised me was the reaction my new trainer had when Carrier introduced us.

I could feel people in the gym watching us, which was to be expected, but it took a few minutes before Jim even came over, which was not. Let's just say he didn't greet me like a driver for Welcome Wagon.

Years later, after Jim and I began to have a lot of success together in boxing, he told *Sports Illustrated* how he felt the day I arrived. "I got a lady in my gym," he recalled to their writer, Richard Hoffer. "I got her mother in my gym. I got a little bitty Pomeranian dog in my gym. Women's boxing? This was not an acceptable idea unless you were promoting virtual emasculation. . . . I didn't think women belonged in the fight game. So there was no question (what he planned to do). I was going to have her ribs broke."

This was the attitude of the man Carrier said wanted to train me. I didn't realize all of that the first day I got there, of course, but I could feel he wasn't happy. We've all been in a situation like that in life where you know the person in charge doesn't want you around. That was me that first day. I could feel it.

What I didn't know until later was that Jim was a classic male chauvinist. Matter of fact, if you called him that and didn't add "pig" at the end, he took it personally. Women and boxing were never supposed to mix in his mind, and he never hid those feelings. I'll give him credit. On that score at least, he was an open book.

He didn't start telling that story about having someone break my ribs until we were away from Bristol, and my career had taken off. I'll never know if it was true, but the real story is it never happened, because he was smart enough to realize Carrier would not have been happy. This was all Carrier's idea, and he was the one paying Jim to train fighters. Later Jim would bite the hand that fed him when he shot me, because I was the one who'd been feeding us both for years. But he never executed his original plan to have me spar with an experienced guy named Richie Hess that first day.

Richie and I became close friends over time, and I really don't think he would have done what Jim wanted. But you never know. He only knew me then from my earlier fights in Bristol. We'd never sparred before, so I could have just been a girl someone put in front of him in the ring. He always told me he never would have, and I believe him, because we worked together a lot in sparring. and he never took advantage of me when I was learning, so I don't think that was in his makeup.

Maybe it would have been better for me if he had, but I probably still wouldn't have left. I'm a stubborn person, especially when people are trying to make me quit or telling me I can't do something. I'll fight you on that every time. and you better bring a lunch pail, because it will take a while to convince me otherwise.

All I ever want in anything is a fair shot. A chance to compete. That's all I was looking for that day. So, I did a workout with him despite my doubts, about his interest in me, hitting the bags and the mitts and doing footwork on the floor. It was decided I'd stay another day or two and do a couple more workouts, and then go home and make a decision about moving.

I didn't want to go back for that second workout, but my mom encouraged me to. I told her, "Mom, this guy hates this idea. He doesn't want to train a woman." When you work the mitts with someone, you're throwing punches at his hands, which are inside some flat, padded mitts. You're at very close quarters. If there's tension between you, you can feel it. It felt like he thought he was lowering his standards working with me.

I wanted to get in the car, drive back home, and get on with my life, but Mom kept insisting he wanted to train me. I thought she was being supportive, and I guess she was to some extent, but the truth is she wanted me away from "P" so badly, she saw what she wanted to see. She saw Jim and a gym in Bristol, Tennessee, as an antidote for the gay life I was living back in West Virginia.

So, I stayed for a couple of days, trained with him, and then my mom and I drove back home to celebrate New Year's. After a lot of thought, I decided I was coming back to make 1991 a truly new year, whether or not my first trainer liked it.

I still had my doubts, but in the end, what did I have to lose? I didn't have any idea Jim was thinking of having one of his fighters try to hurt me. I just knew he didn't particularly want to coach me, but I figured it was only going to be for six months, so I'd go off and learn a little something and live it up. Boxing wasn't the first thing on my mind at that point. It wasn't even the second. It was just something to do, sort of like junior year abroad with some fights thrown in.

When I got back to Bristol just after the first of the year, I already knew I had a fight scheduled in 12 days. Jim and I worked nearly every day in those two weeks to get ready. Whether or not he liked me, he liked losing less, so he did all he could to get me ready. But all he had time to teach me was how to throw a straight, hard jab and turn my opponent by using it effectively. So that's what I did.

I didn't feel like his opinion of women in boxing was changing, but I did feel like I was improving, and that's a strong motivator. You can learn the basics of boxing on your own, but you can't really teach yourself how to box. You need another set of eyes to see what you're doing wrong and correct you. You need sparring partners to remind you of the consequences of mistakes, which is getting hit in the face. Most of all, you need someone who knows more about what you're doing than you do, and Jim did. Of course, so did my Pomeranian.

I'd fought seven times over 18 months without a trainer and was 5-1-1, but I needed a teacher. Jim seemed like a professor compared to other people I'd run into. Later I'd figure out he was more like an adjunct professor than chairman of the department of boxing, but at this juncture it didn't matter. I was beginning to realize the difference between knowing a little bit about my trade and knowing nothing, but I was still nervous before the first fight with Jim in my corner.

My opponent was familiar to me. It was Jamie Whitcomb again. I'd fought her four months earlier and won a decision, but she hurt me a couple of times, so I knew what she was capable of, and now I had the added pressure of not wanting to let my coach down. I always felt responsible for making their efforts with me pay off.

When they rang the first bell, I walked out and did exactly what Jim had taught me. Jab, jab, turn her to avoid getting hit, and jab again. It only took about 30 seconds to see he'd made this fight easy for me, because she had no real skills. Jamie was tough, but now I'd been taught how to box well enough to keep her off-balance. She was never able to set her feet to punch, because I was either jabbing her or moving her. If you can learn how to throw an effective jab and turn your opponent, they end up following you around the ring and can seldom hit you. That amazed me.

She kept throwing this big right hand but would miss, and then I'd pepper her and slip away. She'd turn, and pop, pop, pop! Jim kept telling me, "Turn her like a top."

I was hitting her at will, and she couldn't hit me, which made her get desperate, and I tore her apart. I'd jab, step to the left, and she'd turn, and I'd hit her again. Every time she turned it took away her power. When you're turning, you can't use your power, because your power comes off your back foot. She ended up stuck between a rock and a hard place, and that hard place was me.

She was throwing big haymaker right hands that she'd hit me with in our first fight, but this time she kept missing. She finally missed with a wild right thrown so violently she fell into the ropes and threw her shoulder out. She nearly fell through the ropes. I ended up stopping her in the second round, and the next day in the local paper, the *Kingsport Times-News*, the writer covering the fight said I'd shown "vast improvement since the last time she fought Whitcomb." He rightly gave Jim credit for my displaying "fledgling boxing skills." I looked up fledgling in the dictionary and saw fledgling meant a young bird just learning to fly. I sure hoped Bill Lane, who wrote the story, was right, because I wanted to soar.

Jim was clearly proud, but it was more him saying look what he'd done with this girl in two weeks. There wasn't much acknowledgment of what I'd done. It was all about him. That would become a pattern in our lives whenever I accomplished anything in the sport, but at this stage I didn't care who got credit.

I'd won easily and that gave me confidence in Jim, so I did whatever he said when he was training me. Later on, I made the mistake of doing the same thing outside the ring. But at this juncture, I could see Jim was helping me improve, so I didn't ask any questions. He realized I listened and worked hard, and we were both enjoying working together. I thought he was a good teacher, and he began to realize I was a good student.

Sometimes "P" would come visit, and it was different there when we were together than it was back home. In West Virginia I knew my girlfriend wasn't welcome at my house. We couldn't go there and do family things, so there was always distance between me and my family. Either physical distance or just a spiritual absence. There was a hole in my life when I tried to go home. It was either the woman I loved or the family I loved. One of them was always missing. That's why I didn't try to hide our relationship when we were in Bristol.

She was a tiny thing and a beautiful girl. She got a lot of looks, but my life-style there wasn't much of a secret. It wasn't like I wore a sign saying "I'm gay," but in those days the stereotypical woman fighter was considered gay anyway, so in the fight world it was kind of expected. I didn't really care what the guys in the gym thought. They weren't family to me, so I felt free to be me a little bit.

The funny thing was, even though Larry knew I was gay, he was the one who first put me in pink. I used to wear red and black, so when he first suggested pink, I was like *really*? But he said we were going to do it, and I figured if he was going to pay for pink tank top and pink shoes and a robe, I'd wear it. I had no idea it would become my trademark over the years, but it sure did.

My life was a steady routine. I'd get up, run, go to work at Carrier's Western shop, walk to the gym to train after work, then drive out to the racetrack to a trailer Larry let me live in. It was free, so I couldn't complain, but imagine being a 22-year-old girl living alone in a trailer behind one of the biggest racing tracks in the country.

I had to unlock the entry gates to get inside, then lock them back up and drive to my trailer behind the stands. I was the only person living there, so it was pretty quiet and very scary. All I had was my little dog, Casey. He was my only companion and my only friend. I felt pretty vulnerable, more vulnerable in that trailer than I ever felt in a gym full of male boxers.

You can be lonely living anywhere if you don't know anyone, but at least in most situations you have people around you. Neighbors to say hello to or people you see in the hallway or the elevator in an apartment building. Living in that trailer was a different kind of lonely. You didn't see anybody. You didn't hear anybody. It was like being dropped off on Survivor Island. Once I got through the gate and went to my trailer, there was nothing but the sound of crickets. I never saw a soul. It wasn't like anybody came by to say hello and watch TV. I was totally alone for the first time in my life, and it was in a pretty odd circumstance. Being alone like that always freaked me out.

Once in college our team had finished its last practice before Christmas break. We all left to go home, but I went back to the gym to get a video of one of our games. I didn't see anybody around, but I went through a few doors to Coach Hill's office thinking he'd still be there. He wasn't, and when I turned to leave, I realized the doors had locked behind me. The place was dead silent, and I freaked out and started screaming. Maybe that fear of doors locking behind me and being all alone goes back to what happened to me when I was sexually abused as a kid. Maybe it doesn't. All I can tell you is I never liked that feeling of being alone in the dark.

Part of that loneliness made going out to dinner with Jim more attractive than it normally would have been. Just to spend some time with another person was a relief. From that, and the fact he was my trainer, I gave him an automatic trust that should not have been so automatic. I trusted him because I thought we were on the same team. I understood people could want totally different things from that, but I believed we were still in it together. The truth was I barely knew Jim Martin at that point. I was about to open up to a near total stranger, which is always unwise. It certainly was in this case.

I eventually told Jim that story about being locked in the gym at Concord, and when he realized I was still afraid of doors locking behind me, many times he used it against me by threatening to lock me inside. It was a way to keep me under control, because he knew how uncomfortable just the thought of that made me.

In that trailer I often felt locked in like that, but you figure out a way to get through it. It may not feel comfortable, but life isn't always comfortable. I suppose it says something about me that I felt more relaxed in a boxing ring with people trying to hit me than I felt when I was alone in a trailer, but comfortable or not, life moved on, sometimes weirdly.

With the distance between me and "P", faithfulness was becoming an issue for us. I didn't really have any opportunity to meet someone else, but she still had a lot of chasers, and once I was physically removed from the picture, some of those chasers became catchers.

Meanwhile, I didn't know anyone in Bristol, and neither did Jim, who had moved there from Indiana. So, we started having dinner together sometimes after training. It wasn't like a dinner date. It was more like, "I'm going to get something to eat, you want to come along?" Why wouldn't I go eat with my trainer if the only other option was eating alone with my dog?

Jim had a lot of boxing stories to tell, and he could be pretty charming. He told me about being at the pool at Caesars Palace before a big fight. He told me he'd taken guys to fight at Madison Square Garden in New York, which is the mecca of boxing. He always had a lot of details that made those stories pretty vivid. I found out later a lot of them weren't true, but I was a naive girl from a one stop-sign town. What did I know about the world? I believed him. That was me.

Why would I not believe him? I didn't tell him any lies. Why would I think he was telling me any? I wanted to believe what he was saying, because it was the only reason to think this whole, lonely life I was living wasn't a total waste of time. Listening to him at dinner was a way to pass the time before I had to go back to that empty trailer in the middle of the Bristol Motor Speedway. It was a way to dream of a new life with bright lights and big fights instead of dark coal mines and limited horizons. It was the only dream I had.

Six weeks after the Whitcomb fight, I was back in the ring against a tough girl from New England named Suzanne Riccio, and I won a five-round decision. She would have beaten me if Jim hadn't been training me. When the fight went to the judges, I was mad because I hadn't knocked her out, even though I was sure I'd won. I never went into a fight not thinking about getting a knockout. I was just wired that way.

But I was happier a few minutes later because they gave me my first real title belt, a leather one with the WWBA logo on it, not just some old weight-lifter's belt. I still have it, 30 years later.

It didn't take long after that for Jim to begin saying he was going to make me the best female fighter in the world and how I was going to make him a lot of money. Never us. Him. He accepted me in the gym by default, saying I worked harder than the men he was training, but he never gave me credit for winning fights. Those were always his accomplishments, not mine.

The more nights we trained together and the more times we went out to eat, the more I opened up to him. I told him I was gay, because I didn't want my trainer surprised to hear something like that from someone else, but there was more to the two of us getting together than that for me. I felt like there was so much pressure from my parents, the promoter, and the world not to be gay that I just slipped into spending more and more time with Jim, thinking it might take away some of the suspicions about me. My relationship with my girlfriend back in West Virginia was falling apart, and I just gave in to what it seemed people in my life wanted, which was a daughter and a fighter who was straight.

I began to spill my guts to him about everything that had happened in my life. I looked at him as my mentor. To me he was like Mr. Miyagi in the Karate Kid. He was 24 years older. He was devoting all this time to making me better, and I started thinking of him as a confidant, not just a coach. I'd come to regret that later, but at that moment it was a relief to unburden myself. I was telling him the secrets in my life, and eventually I told him all of them. I was trying to be true to me, and one way to do it was to open up to someone about who I really was.

He told me Larry had asked him if I was gay, and he claimed he'd told him no. Then he just asked me, so I told him the truth. The way he reacted should have warned me about him, but I was a kid who was pretty short on worldly ways. He asked why I'd want to be with girls instead of men. I'm trying to talk to him from my heart, and I realized later it was just sex talk to him.

When my dad had asked me if I didn't want to be with men, it was hurtful to me, because he couldn't find a way to understand I was different than what he thought I should be. As a parent of a gay child, you need to be accepting of who your child is, but some people can't do that. But Jim's attitude was more like a wise guy's response.

It was like he thought I was settling for women because I couldn't get a man, even though I told him I'd been with both and just felt more comfortable with women. Today if I got that response, I'd just laugh, because it wouldn't be worth explaining, but in my 20s I felt defensive about my sexuality. When you're young, you want to fight every battle, especially that one. So, I was a little angry about how he reacted at first, but I let it go. Later on, he would use everything I'd told him to threaten and control me. I paid for being honest with him those first few months we were together a thousand times over.

Once I started having real success in boxing, I became less interested in who I really was and more concerned about my career and my persona as Christy Martin. A few years later I would never have answered that question he asked about being gay. By then I'd decided I would do anything to keep my career growing. If that included convincing the world I was a happily married straight woman who knocked out girls and went home and cooked dinner for Jim, I'd do it.

I just didn't want my father to cry any more. I didn't want my mom or people who knew me upset any more. I tried to do all I could to make everyone happy. The problem was trying to do that ended up making me miserable.

In the gym, though, everything was good. I was like a sponge. I soaked up everything Jim was teaching me. When my next fight came three weeks later, I was well prepared to fight but not for what happened that night.

My parents came down to watch, and after my opponent, Pat Watts, got off the scale, my mom went nuts. Pat weighed 242 pounds! I was 140. My mom went to Jim and told him if I got hurt, she would kill him or find someone else to do it. Jim understood she meant exactly what she said. It was insane.

Carrier was so angry. He was yelling at Pat's manager about the weight and the guy said, "I thought you said you needed a girl who weighed 240." Carrier hollered back, "I told you 140, you idiot."

The girl was not only huge, but she had a gold tooth in the front of her mouth like Mike Tyson! Everyone was freaking out, but I knew enough to realize she wasn't going to beat me. She just didn't look like an athlete to me.

What never crossed my mind was how ridiculous it was for the Tennessee Boxing Commission to allow the fight to go on. They have weight divisions in boxing for a reason. Normally you can't have more than about a seven-pound differential between fighters, except for heavyweights. She was sure a heavy-weight, and I sure was not.

What the whole thing proved was that in women's boxing in those days, there were basically no rules. If there had been, nobody would have let us fight. Certainly, they never would have let two men fight with that wide a weight disparity, but nobody cared about women fighters. It showed women's boxing was not yet a truly legitimate sport. It was still a freak show, but at the time I didn't give it a thought. I just wanted to fight.

The night of the fight things got even weirder. I was in the back of the arena hitting the mitts with Jim to get warmed up. BAM! BAMBAM! BAMBAMBAM! All of a sudden, the door burst open, and it's Pat Watts. She walked in and hollered, "Don't you hit me like that!" My people pushed her out, and we went back to the pads. That was a little strange but not as strange as what happened next.

We get to the ring, and the referee was a guy named Deacon Bowers. Deacon is giving us our instructions, and Pat all of a sudden says, "Look, when I wave my hand like this, it means stop hitting me." Deacon was astonished. He finally told her, "You can't tell her that!"

All I could think of was wanting to knock her out before the fans realized she couldn't fight. I wasn't about to stop hitting her if she waved at me, that's for sure. It only took me about 30 seconds to get rid of her, but it wasn't fast enough to stop the crowd from laughing like they were watching a stand-up comedy routine. You want to go out there and be taken seriously, but how could they not laugh? I was laughing, too.

What was unfair about it was the truth: there are plenty of men who shouldn't be in the ring as professional boxers either, and nobody laughs at them. Maybe she didn't deserve to be in the ring, but she wasn't the lone stranger when it came to that. So why did they laugh at a woman who couldn't box but not a man? The answer was obvious.

Boxing was a pretty chauvinistic world at the time. That was a barrier that had to be broken before women would be accepted in the sport, but I wasn't looking to legitimize women's boxing. I wasn't trying to break any barriers. That wasn't why I was fighting. I just wanted to be great, and I didn't want to be laughed at for trying.

Two months later I had another first round knockout to get my record to 10-1-1. I'd won four of my last five fights by KO. Everything was going well, I thought. But I was soon to find out otherwise, because by that time my relationship with Jim had changed. He had become more than a confidant. I hesitate to say we became lovers, because that would mean at some point I loved him and I didn't. I just wasn't strong enough yet to be who I knew I really was.

Jim was a smooth talker, like most con men, and I guess I wanted to be conned. It became kind of easy to get into at first. I knew it didn't feel right, but once again, I took what I thought would be the easy road.

I'd begun getting phone calls from a man who used to call me back in West Virginia claiming he was a big women's boxing fan. He used to ask me who I wanted to fight, and was I willing to fight this girl or that one. Somehow, he got my number in Bristol and started calling again, and I told Jim about it.

Jim suggested the next time he called, I get his number, then come over to Jim's place, and we'd call him together and see what he was about. So, I did and somehow, some way I didn't leave that night. I wish I could say I was drinking, but I wasn't. That's how it all started between us. On a lonely whim.

The next day I was thinking that hadn't been the greatest idea. Jim had an ex-wife and a couple kids back in Indiana, and he'd told me when he went home to visit, he stayed with them. So I didn't know what was going on there, but when I got to the gym nothing was said, so I trained and went home. The last thing I was looking for was a relationship with a man, so the silence was a relief.

I have to admit I was intrigued by him and his boxing stories, but I wasn't attracted to him. I was never passionate about him. Yet a couple nights later, I was at his house again, and pretty soon I was staying there more than I was in my trailer, because it was easier than being a lonely lesbian in 1990.

At some point, Larry found out about it, and Jim told me Larry was not happy. Carrier never said anything to me, but Jim claimed he told him his being in a relationship with me would take time away from training his son. The truth was Larry's son didn't really like to train. There were days he didn't show up and days he didn't put much into it when he was there, but Larry couldn't see that, I guess.

I was on the fence about the whole thing. I wasn't really in and I wasn't really out. I didn't know what I wanted to happen, but about a month or so later, his ex-wife showed up in Bristol while Jim and I were at dinner, and that opened my eyes. She was not happy.

She started making a scene in the restaurant, and my first thought was to leave, but I stayed a little longer, which was a mistake. As I was walking out, she tried to run me over with her car; and after I left, I was afraid she was going to run me off the road. It was crazy. Right there and then I decided I was moving back to West Virginia. My promoter was through with me, and there was too much drama at a time when I was trying to figure out who I was as a woman. I actually felt relieved.

There was no more reason to stay in Bristol, so I packed up and moved back home. I didn't have a job or any money. I felt like a failure. Here I was the first in my family with a college degree, back living with my parents.

Jim kept calling at all hours. He told my mom he was in love with her daughter and that's all she needed to hear. If Count Dracula had told her he was in love with her daughter, she would have told me, "Good deal. Sign up." She began encouraging me to let Jim back in my life. She bought into what he was saying completely, because it fit the narrative she was hoping for me.

I wasn't in love with him, but when you get in a jam, you're just trying to figure a way out. My dad hated the idea of me being with a man older than he was, but he didn't get involved or say anything. My mom kept pushing. Jim kept calling. Finally, I gave in again.

A couple weeks later I drove to Bristol and brought him back to my parents' place. I had decided if this is what the world wanted, I'd show them I wasn't gay. I knew I was attracted to women, but I was going to make this thing work. Everybody would be happy, and I'd have my trainer and boxing back in my life. I thought that would be good enough, because nothing had felt totally right outside of boxing for a long time. It was the only true love I had.

We put a heavy bag, a speed bag, and a double end bag in my parents' basement, and I started training again. Jim never even tried to get a job; and whenever I talked about getting one, he'd tell me I had to concentrate on my career. What career? Fighting women who outweighed me by 100 pounds?

So, there I was. A closeted gay woman athlete in a sport that barely existed with a boyfriend older than my dad who spent most of his day on the sofa while my father supported us by working in a coal mine. I felt guilty, so I kept a ledger of everything my father paid for, and when I started to earn big purses, I paid it all back with a little more. For a while I gave my dad 10 percent of my purses to repay him, but at this point I had no purses. So he was getting 10 percent of nothing.

My dad used to bring us pieces of metal he picked up at work, and we'd strip them for the copper inside and sell it. I also started doing some part-time work with the private investigation firm again, but Jim kept saying boxing would work out. He insisted we just needed to be seen by the right people. Who the hell were they, and without a promoter, where would they see me?

I hadn't fought since May when Jim came up with the bright idea of suggesting my mom get a promoter's license in West Virginia and finance a card with me as the main event. That's how, on September 10, 1991, Joyce Salters made her promoting debut in a bar owned by the brother of my old boss in the private investigation firm. After a four-month layoff, I knocked out my opponent in two rounds. I'm sure Mom lost a little money, but she gave me a couple hundred dollars, and I helped out by selling some tickets up at Concord College. What neither Jim nor my mom realized was I did that to stay in touch with my gay life. That's who my friends mostly were at college, and it was good to see them again.

By this time, I'd committed to a relationship with Jim to some extent. My family's happiness was tied up in the presence of Jim, and mine was tied up in the presence of boxing in my life. One of my ex-girlfriends from college was the only one who kept asking me about the situation. She told me once, "If you're happy, fine, but what are you doing?"

What I was doing was hiding in plain sight again. I told her I was happy with my choice, and I wasn't lying, so it was easy to say. What she didn't understand was I had chosen boxing, not Jim. Whatever I had to do to keep that part of my life pure, I would do. As for the rest of my life, I was used to being unhappy.

What became more and more obvious was I was really improving as a boxer. We were doing a lot of technical, one-on-one work on the pads and with my footwork, but learning the science of boxing and translating that to a fight are two different things. There are a lot of fighters who look like a million bucks hitting the pads or the bags, because they aren't facing two things. They aren't facing any resistance, and they aren't facing the reality of the arena. A lot of boxers look good sparring in the gym, because it's a controlled environment, but they panic or freeze when the lights come on and an opponent is throwing back at them. Fight night is the final exam in boxing. It's that way in life, too. The fight is what tests your mettle. You need to feel resistance and answer it. Like it says in the Bible, steel sharpens steel.

But in Itmann, West Virginia, it's not too easy to find the kind of steel I needed to face. Coal we could find, but steel? We needed some help with that, and my brother came up with a potential solution.

He was spending time with kind of a rough crowd in those days, and he knew a girl who was a legend all over the area as a real badass. Everyone, male and female, was afraid of Ramona Brown, and with good reason.

So, we arranged for her to spar with me. She was tough in the street, but she didn't have a clue how to box, so she wasn't that helpful. After my career took off, she used to joke about how Christy Martin whipped her ass. We both used to laugh about it before she passed away a few years ago. I know this: in the street I would not have wanted to mess with Ramona Brown.

That summer I went down to Daytona Beach with Jim and my family and met a local promoter, Lenny Del Percio, who said he could get me a fight in October. He offered us a cheap apartment if Jim agreed to do some maintenance, so we picked up and moved. My career was stalled, and my personal life was a mirage, but at least I'd finally gotten to the beach.

Lenny owned some strip clubs and a few apartments, and he put us up in one in a pretty rough part of town. Most of the tenants seemed to be strippers or small-time drug dealers. Maybe they weren't, but it looked that way to me.

The October fight never came off, so I ended up fighting in Grundy, Virginia, in early January. It wasn't exactly Vegas, but I got another first-round knockout, and two weeks later Del Percio finally put me on a card in Daytona. My opponent was long and lean and looked like a female Thomas Hearns, the great five-time world champion who had those great fights with Sugar Ray Leonard, Marvin Hagler, and Roberto Duran on his way to the Hall of Fame.

Jackie Thomas had power and a lot of skill, but I caught her with a perfect overhand right in the third round, and her head spun around like she was an owl who'd heard a noise behind her.

She went down hard, struggled up at the count of eight, and was out on her feet, so they stopped the fight. It was a classic turning point in two boxers' careers. I was on the rise, and she never fought again. Someone's success always comes at someone else's expense.

About 20 years later I'd be on the other end of that story, but at 22 I had no idea of the arc of a boxer's career. I was 12-1 with nine knockouts and had stopped six of the seven fighters I'd faced since Jim took over. I still didn't see how boxing was going to pay the bills, but I was rocking and rolling.

Unbeknownst to me, I was soon going to be rocked in a different way and, like the punch Jackie never saw coming that night, I would be emotionally blindsided and utterly unprepared for what was going to hit me or the mistake I'd make to cope with it.

What Kind of Proposal Was That?

Regardless of whether you're gay or straight, we all have a vision, or maybe just a hope, of what our marriage proposal will be like. Maybe that's truer for women than men, but I kind of think we all have an image in our mind of what we think it should be.

I had one, too, but my reality turned out to be, as Don King would say, SKD! It was "somethin' kinda different" . . . to be kind about it.

The night Jim Martin proposed to me should have been a warning not to go down that path, but once again I erred on the side of everyone in my life but me, and accepted. A gay person marrying a straight person is hardly new. It's been happening for years and years and still does, usually for the same reasons I did it. It's another way to lie to the world about who you really are, because you think a lie will protect you better than the truth will, which it won't.

At the time I was not thinking about marrying Jim, even though we were living together in Flagler Beach. I didn't know where I was going in life, but it wasn't going to be there. Or so I thought. My focus was elsewhere.

Despite only being paid a few hundred dollars a fight, I loved going to the gym every day to train, and I loved the bright lights in the arena on fight night. I wasn't happy about our financial situation, but I loved my job, which was training to become a solid professional boxer.

My dad was helping us out financially, and Jim finally did break down and take a job for a while working for a pest control company, which he hated. But here I was with a college degree and not using it, because Jim wouldn't let me work. I wanted to get a job, but every time I mentioned it, Jim would say, "OK, then, we'll have to quit boxing."

I can see now that was another way of controlling me, because he knew the one thing I loved was boxing. I loved it more than anything in my life. It was the only part of me that felt truly me at the time.

Jim kept insisting that if I went to work, he wouldn't train me anymore, and I'd be out of boxing. The truth is a lot of fighters work day jobs and train at night or vice versa. I was willing to do that, but Jim said no, and I went along with him, thinking he knew more than I did about the world of boxing.

He kept telling me I just needed to be seen by the right person, so I should concentrate on training and being ready when our chance came. He was very convincing, and I guess I wanted to be convinced. I didn't really believe him, but what else did I have to believe in at the time? I had no idea how to get anywhere in boxing. Nor did I have any notion of where I was going, so "we'll see what happens" became my approach to life.

Maybe Jim was sincere about what he was saying to a degree, but I understand now that it was also another way he found to control me and keep me away from other people who might have an influence on me, which is how most abusers operate. Slowly they cut you off from friends, family, and everyone else. Your circle becomes smaller and smaller until your abuser is really the only person you have a lot of contact with.

I didn't understand this was beginning to happen to me, but I must have sensed that I was losing control of my life, because every year on my birthday and Christmas I'd give myself a present. I'd tell myself, "You're getting out of this relationship." But for years I didn't. I just got in deeper, which is what happened on March 19, 1992.

Not long before that day, Jim and I got into a nasty argument, and he dropped me to my knees with a body shot. It didn't happen in the gym during a sparring session. It happened at home. I never told a soul about it.

Why I didn't I don't know, but victims of domestic violence don't talk about what's being done to them. If we do, we make excuses for our abuser, or we blame ourselves. Or we keep silent and start to think we deserved it.

To go to my parents with something like that, I needed to be sure I was done with the relationship, because they weren't about to forget it. So, I stayed quiet. I wish I could say I stayed quiet because I knew where we were headed professionally and decided not to risk things, but that would be a lie. Why would I think at that stage of my career that Don King one day would give me a chance to fight on the biggest shows in boxing? There was no reason to think such a thing, but not long after that happened, I decided to visit with an old friend, someone Jim knew all about.

She was the last woman I had a relationship with from college before Jim and I met. She was in Florida at the time visiting her grandmother, who had a condo on Flagler Beach, not far from where Jim and I were living. I was still in love with her, but we'd only had sporadic contact since I left West Virginia for Bristol to begin my boxing career. She knew I'd moved to Daytona Beach. One day she contacted me and I drove over to see her.

We went for a walk along the beach and then went out to a gay bar. I'd never been a person who wanted to go to gay bars, but it was the middle of the day, so it's where we ended up.

It was pretty quiet, and at some point, I suggested we head over to a place called Punchy Callahan's on Sea Breeze Boulevard in Daytona Beach, which was not far from where Jim and I were living. It was kind of a biker bar with a lot of outlaw types who hung out there, but I liked it.

It was actually a pretty stupid decision, because it was a place Jim and I used to go to a lot. We had been in there drinking for a while when Jim walked in. I think that was just an accident, because I know he wasn't following us as I had the only car we owned at the time.

Regardless, he came over and asked me to come outside. He said he needed to talk to me, so I agreed to go with him. The woman I was with was kind of pissed about it, but I went. Once we got onto the street, Jim said he'd talked to my dad and told him I might be a lesbian. Might be? Jim already knew I was, but he said he told my dad that, and he claimed my dad told him my family didn't want me if I wanted to be with a woman. He said they would throw me away and claimed my dad told him, "If that's true, throw her stuff in the ocean."

I was half drunk, but that shocked me. It hurt me worse than any punch ever did. My dad said that? I didn't even know what to say. Not once did I think to call my dad and ask him. I was too afraid to hear the answer, I guess.

Jim had already told me a number of times by then that he'd kill me if I ever left him, but who believes that? I was 23 years old and just thought that was ridiculous, so I ignored it. I've learned over the years from working with domestic violence experts that it happens all the time, and very few women believe it until they're in that life-threatening moment I would eventually find myself in. Then it is usually too late.

Jim didn't say that to me that night though. Instead, he shocked me again. He got down on one knee right on Sea Breeze Boulevard and asked me to marry him. That certainly wasn't what I pictured a proposal would be. A man telling me that my family would disown me if I was with a woman, and then asking me to marry him instead. Let's just say it was not a particularly romantic moment.

It was a proposal, but it came with a not-so-veiled threat. I was a young woman who didn't know a damn thing about life. I grew up in a town without a traffic light. I certainly didn't have the life experience to cope with any of this. So instead of finding a phone and calling my dad, I kept thinking they were already unhappy with who I was. Why would they accept me now?

The real reason I had started in a relationship with Jim, beyond my loneliness, was to be straight. Or at least look like I was. I thought I could be content with that, because if everyone around me was satisfied, maybe I would be, too.

When he finally proposed out in the street like that, it just seemed like if I didn't say yes, I would lose my family, my trainer, and my boxing career in one night, half drunk in the street. I'd be lying if I said I stayed with him because I thought he was going to kill me. I didn't think that for a minute then. It just seemed like marrying him was my only choice.

My family now says they never had that conversation with Jim. They insist what he told me that night wasn't true. To this day I'm not sure what the truth is, and that's the hardest thing to cope with. I don't know who was telling me the truth about a night that nearly ruined my life. If you like baggage, I've got a trainload.

After he proposed, I just felt like what other choice did I have? I was really choosing my family and my boxing career, not Jim Martin. So, I made up my mind right there in the middle of the street. I chose boxing. That's who I agreed to marry that night.

When we went back inside, my friend got a little angry because Jim was still there. She didn't really know yet what had happened. A friend of Jim's drove her back to her grandmother's place while I kept drinking until Jim and I went home, and I passed out. The next day we got married. It was March 20, 1992. The first day of spring.

Now that I'm sober and free and looking back 30 years, it makes no sense that I ever agreed to marry Jim. But when I remember the girl I was then, a naive kid from Nowhere, West Virginia, I can understand what I did. Was I going to leave the trainer who was making me a good fighter in the middle of my boxing career when he's saying he'll out me and nobody else will be willing to train a gay female fighter? No, I was not.

In my mind, Jim was my one link to where I wanted to go in the sport. He told me he could pick up the phone any time and talk with Don King, who was the biggest promoter in boxing at the time. I knew people lied in boxing, but saying he could call Don was a pretty big lie, so I believed him.

It's crazy to think about it now, and it was crazy to do it then, but I know why that girl did what she did. She couldn't see another option, because she had no reason to believe she had one. So, she put her head in the sand and went to the justice of the peace and got on with life.

The next day we went to the courthouse. No one else was there. Just Jim, me, and that justice of the peace. Well, one other thing was there. A pounding headache. I was completely hung over.

I felt like I was surrendering. Like I was giving up my life. What kept me going was the thought that maybe something would happen with boxing. From that day forward, for better or for worse, for richer or for poorer, in sickness and in health, I was married to my sport. That's where my passion was.

It is crazy: the crossroads in my life. That night, when Jim came and proposed to me in the middle of the street, I had a chance. I could have gone back in the bar to a woman I truly loved at the time. I might have lost my family and my career, but I would not have married a man who would try to murder me. I loved that woman at that time. I never loved Jim. How different life might have been if I'd made that choice. But I didn't.

Some people will say I would not have been the boxer I became without Jim. They say I would never have earned millions of dollars, or had incredible moments and memories, and certainly no International Boxing Hall of Fame induction. Maybe they're right, but maybe I would have been good enough to make it anyway. Maybe it didn't have to happen the way it did, but I didn't have the courage to take that chance. I wasn't strong enough to bet on myself yet, because I wasn't sure who I really was.

I didn't really believe then that I would ever achieve the things I did. There was no woman fighter out there doing anything but barely surviving. In the end, people say I was a pioneer for women athletes, but at 23 you're not thinking about blazing a trail for yourself or anyone else. You can't even see the trail, because there isn't one. So, I did what I'd always done. I put my head down and kept punching.

Two months later I won an eight-round decision from a girl named Stacey Prestage. It was my worst performance in some time, and Jim claimed it was because I wasn't listening to him anymore. He said I was trying to train myself and run my own camp. I didn't think so, but clearly something wasn't right.

I did knock her down about 30 seconds into the fight, but she got up, and it was a war from that point on. After it was over, my face was swollen, and I was pretty bruised up. The fight had been a lot harder than it should have been, and Jim snapped at me, "You want to run your own camp, this is what you get!"

How could I be trying to train myself? I didn't know what I was doing yet. All I knew was that night I wasn't in great shape. I think that was the first time I stopped totally trusting in Jim to look out for me in boxing. I began to think maybe I better look out for myself a little bit.

When I got back in the gym, I started working harder. Because I was around better-quality male fighters, I began to see the intensity level they worked at. I reacted to that. I worked even harder than I had before, and I listened to Jim and tried to do whatever he told me to do.

All my passion came out in the gym, because there was none at home. We got along all right in those days, because we had boxing in common, and that was our main focus. But I never had a passionate moment with him. I'd say in those years we were married, I was really asexual. It got to the point where I didn't care about sex at all. I wanted to be in love with someone, but I replaced that desire with a love for boxing. For a long time that was enough for me—until it wasn't, and everything went sour. But that was a long time coming, because after the Prestage fight I went on a tear. I knocked out six straight women in 13 months and began to create a little buzz around me in local boxing circles. Some fight people in Florida were starting to notice the little girl who kept knocking people out.

If I had been a male fighter with a 19-1-1 record and 15 knockouts, I would have been viewed as a hot prospect who bore watching. People would have started talking about putting me in against more skilled opponents to see if I was ready to become a contender. But how could you be a contender when there weren't any recognized women world champions at the time? Contending for what?

That winning streak and those knockouts got me more low-paying fights, but that didn't put an end to the indignities women fighters had to face in those days. Even with all those knockouts, money was always really tight. The paydays were small, and with Jim only working sporadically, we were always broke. Lenny Del Percio, the local promoter who first asked me to come to Florida to fight for him, was promoting some of the shows we were on. He had originally put us up in one of his apartments, but we moved into a house he owned in a pretty tough section of Daytona. It was in the 'hood, to be frank about it.

We shared it with two of the guys who trained in the same gym with me, but they didn't have any money either. There were times we literally lived on corn flakes and popcorn, which you best believe is not the breakfast of champions. Or the lunch and dinner, either. There were enough roaches in the place that we kept the cereal in the refrigerator to make sure we weren't sharing it with them.

We had no furniture, so at first, we slept on the floor. My mother and my brother, Randy, came down to visit, and they went to a Goodwill and bought us a pullout sofa so we had a bed to sleep on, but the rest of our stuff was in cardboard boxes.

Jim was working sometimes for the pest control company, but people used to call about jobs, and I'd page him, and he wouldn't answer. I don't think he controlled too many pests at that time. I know he didn't bring home much money.

Jim was a hustler all his life. He loved the hustle over the 9-to-5 life, and maybe that's how he saw boxing. Boxing is a hustle for sure, especially when you're on the bottom rung of the sport like we were, but it's a tough hustle even at the top.

He kept telling me I'd become a star and make him a lot of money, but until that happened, we needed another way to supplement what the fights brought in. Jim came up with quite a solution. He wanted me to fight men in their hotel rooms. He said he'd heard there were guys who got off on it, and they'd pay me to beat them up. When he first suggested, it I just hollered at him, "Bitch! Get a job!"

How you can be a man and not want to get a job and support your family is beyond me, but it didn't take him long to convince me to do it, like he did with so many things I wish had never happened.

Men can be odd, which will not come as a surprise to most women. Apparently, some guys get off on women hitting each other, and a few get off on women hitting them. That's the reason I never wanted to fight on all-girl boxing cards. To me that was more of a circus act than an athletic contest. Its different today, with so many women fighters around, but back in the early 1990s, all-girl cards would have been looked at like mud wrestling. More of a sex show than a boxing show, and I never wanted to be a part of something like that.

Call me naive, but I never looked at women fighting as women fighting. I saw it as two boxers fighting. Two boxers trying to put on an entertaining athletic contest that people wanted to watch, because they wanted to see good boxing.

Jim told me some men had contacted him to ask if they could box me for money. He said they'd pay me to spar with them, and we needed the money, so I finally said I'd do it. But I thought it was going to be in a gym, like regular sparring. It wasn't.

The first time was in a hotel room in Fort Lauderdale. I'm in this guy's room ready to fight, and all he kept trying to do was grab me and hold while I beat the bejesus out of him. The guy seemed to like it. Go figure. As I said, men can be weird.

When it was over, we took his money and left. I felt like a prostitute must feel the first time. I felt dirty. I knew that hadn't been about boxing. It was a sex thing from the start for the guy. I said I'd never do it again . . . but, of course, I did.

When you need money, and all you have to do is punch some guy around in his hotel room, it's easy to find an excuse to do it again. The second time it was easier to accept. I still didn't feel right about it, but you find ways to justify it. I told myself whatever it is for the guy, it's just boxing to me. It wasn't sex for me, but I knew it wasn't boxing for those men either.

Even though I tried to justify it, every time I did something like that, something that diminishes you on the inside, I left a little piece of myself back in that room. A piece of my dignity had disappeared.

Why did I do it? I told myself we needed the money. I wanted to buy Christmas presents for my parents. I wanted to stop eating corn flakes and popcorn. I mean, I did need the money, but did I need to do that? Apparently, because I did it five times, and only one guy came to our gym to box. We closed it down, so it was just me, Jim, and the man I was fighting. I didn't want anyone else to know. I beat his ass, but at least that guy tried to fight a little bit.

He tried to hit me. The others were just interested in grabbing at me and getting punched in the face for trying. None of them called for a rematch. In a way, that was a victory for me. Just like a lot of women fighters back then, they didn't want to fight Christy Martin twice.

A couple of fights before my big break finally came, I was set to box at a small arena in Punta Gorda, Florida, against a girl named Deborah Cruickshank. The day before the fight, I went over for the weigh-in and to get my physical. I walked up to the commission doctor, and he looked confused.

"Why are you here?" he asked me.

I told him, "For my physical."

"The ring card girls don't need to have a physical," he said.

I told him I wasn't a ring card girl, who are usually models or strippers who earn a few extra bucks carrying a card in the ring between rounds with the number of the next round on it. I was more shocked than insulted, so I just said, "I'm a fighter."

"No, you're not," he told me. What do you say to that?

Later, we got that straightened out, and the next night I went to the arena to fight. Jim and I kept looking around for our dressing room until somebody finally asked, "Are you the girl fighter?"

I told him I was, and he took us down a corridor and pointed to a door. My "dressing room" was a janitor's closet. When he opened the door, there was a mop and a bucket against the wall and water on the floor. I really felt degraded as an athlete and as a person. It made me feel like I wasn't being taken seriously, but fights were hard to find for a woman then, so you took whatever you could get and tried to do your best and ignore the rest. Being treated that way pissed me off, and I took it out on Deborah. I stepped inside that closet, changed into my boxing clothes, and when I came out, I knocked her out in one round.

That wasn't the only reason I was angry though. That week is when I first met a woman named Jackie Kallen, who was a fight manager from Detroit who had once worked for Emanuel Steward's famous Kronk Boxing Team. Kronk was a legendary gym in boxing circles, a stuffy basement fight club where Manny kept the heat up to more than 100 degrees. That place produced a long line of world champions including Thomas Hearns, who was one of the greatest fighters of the 1970s and 1980s.

Jackie started out in public relations for the Kronk team, but eventually she wanted to manage her own fighters and signed a middleweight named James Toney. James would go on to win world titles in five different weight classes and twice be named Fighter of the Year by the Boxing Writers Association of America. The year before I met Jackie, he had won his first world title, so Jackie was the manager of the middleweight champion of the world, which meant her reputation in boxing was growing.

She had arranged for Cruickshank to fight me, but she'd also told my friend Jessie Robinson that she wouldn't cross the street to watch two women fight. Jessie told me that, so I concluded she'd brought this girl in to beat me. As soon as I got wind of that, I got pretty surly, which in those days didn't take much doing. I was going to show her I could fight.

I dropped Cruickshank once and then knocked her out with a body shot to the liver. Then, I'm ashamed to say, I spit on her while she was down. That's terrible to admit, but that's who I was at that time.

It was really aimed more at Jackie than Cruickshank, but nobody knew that but me. It was pretty messed up. I should never have done it. It just happened because I was so offended, but the funny thing is the crowd went NUTS!

When Jackie saw that crowd reaction, she was on me hard. All of a sudden, she was more than happy to walk across the street to watch me fight. I guess she realized the way that crowd reacted showed there was a chance to make some money with me.

In boxing, it's not just how you fight or that you keep winning that sells. It's are you pleasing the crowd? It doesn't matter if they love you or hate you as long as they're willing to pay to see you again.

You have to do something to separate yourself from other fighters and make yourself stand out in the minds of the fans. Spitting on your opponent generally is not one of those things, but it was that night.

After we got back to the janitor's closet, Jim didn't sit me down and scold me or give me a lecture about being more professional. He just said he couldn't believe I'd done that. Frankly, neither could I.

Now Jackie was all about getting on board with Christy Martin. She kept trying to make sure she was in the pictures after the fight, trying to separate me a little bit from Jim.

My next fight was back in Punta Gorda three months later. Same arena. Same janitor's closet. Jackie was back, and this time she brought me some red roses to throw to the crowd on the way into the ring. After I knocked that girl out in the first round, the crowd started throwing the roses back into the ring at me. I never found out whether Jackie set that all up, or it just happened, but I wouldn't have put it past her, because she understood how to get publicity.

She had first gotten wind of me through Jessie, who had seen me working in the gym in Florida while he was training one of King's heavyweights. He kept telling me he'd get me signed with Don, but King wasn't interested initially, so he spoke with Jackie. After those two knockouts, she wanted me to fly to Detroit to fight at The Palace of Auburn Hills, where the Detroit Pistons played their NBA games, and she wanted me to come without Jim.

I was already overwhelmed by how fast things were suddenly moving, and I thought Jim knew more about this world than I did, so I wasn't going to do that. The problem was Jim didn't like her at all.

Jackie was flashy, brash, and opinionated. Jim didn't like women in general. Other than me, he didn't like women in boxing, so he sure didn't like a powerful woman in boxing. He got offended right off the bat when she tried to stand right beside me in photos after those fights. He didn't like her, and he didn't want me to like her either.

We went to Detroit together, and Jackie had some promotional pictures taken of me and had me doing media around the city before the fight, which was on October 3, 1993, against a girl named Beverly Szymanski. Jackie was trying to make me feel like we were a team even though we hadn't signed a contract.

I'd never been in a venue that massive. It had 23,000 seats and was only a few years old at the time. It was a big jump from a janitor's closet to The Palace of Auburn Hills.

A few days before the fight, I was training at a gym in Detroit, and Toney was there sparring a local fighter named Booker Ward. After the bell rang and Booker turned to walk back to his corner, Toney punched him right behind the head. I could not believe it. This was not some playful tap. I'd never seen anything like that. Ward turned around and just stared at James. The next round was a war.

After they were done, someone said for me to get in and spar with James. I thought, "Forget that!" First off, he's a man. Second, he's the middleweight champion of the world. Third, and most important, he just hit his sparring partner in the back of the head after the round was over as hard as I'd ever seen anybody hit anybody.

I didn't want to do it, but in that kind of situation, you really have no choice. I got in with him, and he worked with me fine, but when the bell rang to end a round, I sprinted back to my corner.

I knocked Syzmanski out inside three rounds, and it was a good knockout. I was really on my game that night. After she was counted out, I was so excited I started running around the ring and almost tripped over her. I had to step over her to continue my celebration, so that's what I did. I should have just gone to my corner until she was on her feet. I should have acted like I'd been there before, but the truth was I hadn't. Not in a place like that.

I think Jackie wanted to bring me there to test me a little bit. See how I'd react to a bigger venue and more publicity. Frankly, if she'd put a managerial or promotional contract in front of me that night, I would have signed it even though I heard her matchmaker say something after the fight that really bothered me.

I overheard him tell someone, "We can put her in with a man and make a lot of money." That really shocked me.

That was not what I wanted. I never wanted to fight a man. I wanted to be taken seriously as a boxer, but not by fighting men. I understood that was a losing proposition for me.

I'm sure they could have found a male boxer I could have beaten. Maybe a few of them. But if I kept winning, I would have to fight better and better men, and eventually I'd get hurt. There's just no way around it. So, no thanks.

Still, considering my financial situation at the time, if Jackie had written me a check and offered to manage me, we would have had to take it and sign. But that didn't happen. She let me get out of Detroit without signing anything, probably figuring nobody else out there had heard of me or would be interested. She wasn't far off, but she forgot one thing. She forgot the guy who had brought me to her, Jessie Robinson, also trained fighters for Don King, and within a couple days after we got back to Florida, Jessie called with some interesting news.

Don King wanted to see me.

CHAPTER EIGHT

Enter Don King

To be a boxer told in the 1990s that Don King wanted to meet with you was like a young actress being informed that Steven Spielberg or Martin Scorsese was calling. This was the moment you hoped for but also dreaded. This was the man who could change your life . . . if you were good enough to make it happen.

The aura King carried with him at that time, not only in the world of boxing but also in the larger universe where he had become a celebrity far beyond his sport, is difficult to fathom today. He turned 90 in 2021 and hasn't been involved in a major boxing promotion in half a decade, but in those days there was no bigger name in the world of sports than Don King.

So, when Jessie told me a couple of days after Jim and I got back from Detroit that King wanted to see me in his Deerfield Beach office, it was unfathomable. Jessie had some of his fighters working at King's training camp in Ohio, and King had recently signed one to a promotional deal. So, Jessie had an established relationship with him and had told me several times he was going to convince King to promote me. I liked Jessie a lot. I still do. But I didn't believe him for a second.

Why would King sign me when he'd never promoted a woman fighter, nor shown the slightest interest in our side of the sport? He promoted the biggest names in boxing. None of those names belonged to a woman.

Jessie had first become interested in my career when he saw me working in the gym, but what convinced him King should take a look at me was the Prestage fight 18 months earlier in Daytona Beach. Jessie always says "when you fought that truck driver, I knew you had something special." I don't know if Stacey was a truck driver, but I know she was a warrior and that night so was I, which impressed Jessie.

He went to Jim and told him, "This girl needs to be on TV. She needs to make some money." He kept saying I was the Mike Tyson of female fighters, because I was pretty much all action. He loved the fact that when I got in the ring, punches would be thrown in every direction.

Jim didn't believe Jessie at first, but Jessie had brought Don a number of fighters that he'd made money with, so he was willing to listen, even though he had never heard of me. Frankly, neither had any of the other major promoters, so it wasn't like he was a holdout. We got our fights in those days mostly from small-time promoters on local shows, which meant we weren't likely to go very far or make any real money. In the public's eyes, we were just girls who liked to fight, not fighters on our way to something big.

As with most things, to advance in your career at some point you need a boost from someone with juice. And in those days, nobody had more juice in boxing than Don King—which is why the idea of going to meet him was so intimidating.

I knew this was the opportunity of a lifetime, but it was also scary to me. It's scary to take the step from the small time to the big time, because even though that's your dream, you never truly know if it will become a dream or a nightmare. In my case, it turned out to be both.

Jim was a little scared, too, because despite all his talk and bluster, this was way out of his league. He understood I was about to see the truth: he didn't know Don King or any of his people. He was as small-time as I was, but Jim Martin was a chameleon. He could blend into the woodwork. Fake it until you make it. That was Jim.

So, we got in my broken-down Plymouth Laser and drove to Deerfield Beach, where Don was just opening a big new office after moving to Florida from New York to beat state income taxes. I was pretty nervous, and it didn't help that as we got close, my car started smoking. I had no idea it needed an oil change, and Jim hadn't bothered with it, so we rolled up to the office of the biggest promoter in boxing with a car that's smoking like a three-alarm fire. Great first impression.

When we walked into his office, I was totally in awe of King. Talk about feeling way, way out of your league. That was Christy Martin when we walked in, and I saw this larger-than-life character whose hair was shooting up toward the sky like a volcano erupting. King all but ran the sport of boxing in those days. I would have signed whatever he put in front of me just to be able to say I was promoted by him.

I'd brought along a VCR tape, sort of a highlight film, but no one could find a machine to play it because the office wasn't totally set up yet, so Jim told me to shadowbox for King. Fortunately, Jessie was there, too, so I didn't feel totally uncomfortable until Jim told me to show Don how well I threw a left hook to the body.

I did it, but then I realized Julio Cesar Chavez, who is considered the greatest Mexican fighter in history, was in the building because King also promoted him. Chavez threw the most devastating body shots in boxing, and here I am showing King mine?

King watched for a couple minutes and then he just hollered out, "Write her up a contract!" That was it. There was no negotiating. No lawyers or accountants. Nobody. Just sign the deal.

The deal was for five six-round fights a year at $5,000 a fight. Considering that I had been making around $500, $600 a fight, about $100 a round, I felt like I had made it. A starting teacher's salary back then was maybe $25,000, $30,000 a year, and I knew there was no woman fighting anywhere in the world at that time making anywhere near $5,000 a fight. Up to then my best payday had been in Detroit, when Jackie paid me $1,200 plus expenses, so all I could think was, "Man, I am making it now."

The whole meeting lasted maybe 40 minutes, and after I signed, someone said there'd be a $1,000 payment up front. I was so naive I thought that meant I had to pay King $1,000, which I didn't have. Finally, someone in his office said, "Christy, you get the $1,000." That was an amazing feeling.

After I signed, we left for the weigh-in for a big card King was running that weekend at the Broward County Convention Center in Ft. Lauderdale. Felix Trinidad was the IBF welterweight champion, and he was defending his title against a guy named Anthony Jones. King promoted both guys, which I would later learn was standard operating procedure for King whenever possible. That way he couldn't lose. No matter who ended up as the champion, King already had him under contract.

A contract with Don was like an octopus. It had many ways to tie you up, but one good thing for me was that at the time, there were no organizations with recognized women's world champions. So he couldn't sign me to one of his roll-over deals where every time you successfully defended your title, it extended his contract with you. I was barely 24 years old and someone who had never really been anywhere, so I had no understanding of that type of thing at the time, of course.

When we left his office, you'd think I would have been elated, but I wasn't. I was happy I'd finally cracked into the world of big-time boxing, but I was more scared to death than elated. This was what I had dreamed of—but whose big dreams really come true if you come from a coal camp in the West Virginia mountains?

That day I met Chavez in Don's office before we left to see Trinidad. To be around fighters like that made me feel so inferior. It was exciting, because for the first time I felt like I was close to achieving something in boxing. But I didn't feel like I'd made it, because I knew I still had to prove I could do it. Prove I could fight at that level. I suppose it's what a young baseball player feels like when he's called up from the minor leagues to the Yankees.

The next night, October 23, 1993, I was sitting at ringside watching Trinidad. Sitting right near me was Chavez. This was the biggest fight I'd ever been to in my life, and all the time I kept wondering how I was ever going to fit in with these kind of people.

The answer, of course, was obvious. Keep winning and keep knocking women out. That's what Don King was paying me for, and it didn't take long for me to earn my keep, because three months later I was standing in the ring at the MGM Grand in Las Vegas, but I wasn't standing there for long.

About a month earlier Don had brought Jim and me to New York to promote my first fight with him. I'd never been to New York, and they put us in a hotel overlooking Central Park. I couldn't believe how small the room was or how big the price was. The room was barely the size of my bed, which I would later learn wasn't that unusual even in swanky New York hotels.

They asked me to put up a credit card for incidentals. I'd never heard of such a thing, and I didn't know enough to say I wouldn't have any incidentals. They put like $300 on my card, and I was petrified it was going to stay on there, because that was about my credit limit. At that time $300 was important to me. It still is, frankly, but not like it was in those days. I was relieved when we checked out and they told me no charges were on my card. It's kind of funny to think of me as that girl now, but at that time I didn't know anything about how a lot of the world worked.

What I did know was how things worked in the ring, a point I made clear to King on January 29, 1994. That was my first fight for Don, and the fact it only lasted 40 seconds was a pretty auspicious beginning, I have to say. I'd never been to Las Vegas, so I was just as stunned as most people are the first time they see all that neon reflecting up and down the street and all those casinos along The Strip.

I also had no understanding of what January in Vegas could be like. I figured we were going to the desert, so why bring a coat? Turned out it was freezing. Maybe that was my first lesson that in boxing, like in life, things are not always as they appear.

My mom and dad made the trip out, and they had to buy me a coat because Jim and I still didn't have any money. Until you become a star, a boxer doesn't get paid until after the fight. Maybe you get some training expenses, but I couldn't go to Don like Chavez used to do all the time and demand an advance. There's no advance on a $5,000 purse. Show up and fight, then you get paid.

That first fight was at the newly opened MGM Grand Garden Arena, a venue that sat more than 17,000 for boxing. The man running it was Dennis Finfrock, a former high-school wrestling coach. He got into business in Las Vegas running first the Thomas and Mack Center on the University of Nevada Las Vegas campus, and then he moved to the MGM to open the Grand Garden Arena. For whatever reason, he took a liking to me, maybe because he could sense I was in awe of the whole scene. He was so nice to me that it relaxed me a bit, but the one thing he could not do was prepare me for what would later become a staple of fighting for Don. Nothing could prepare you for a Don King prefight press conference.

What a production. It went on forever, because Don would drone on and on in, as he would say, his "inimitable style." Later I became like Tyson and Chavez and the rest of his headliners and would just sit there clearly bored, but not the first time. His material was all new to me then, and I was all ears and wide eyed. It was really something to be part of when you were used to being promoted by small-time operators and once even my mom.

My opponent was a girl named Susie Melton. She was from South Carolina, and boxing people had always told us to stay away from her. She was 2-1 at the time and had lost a decision to my old nemesis DeShong, so I was a little nervous. But I figured out in a hurry she couldn't really fight, so I went for the kill. Whenever I found myself in that kind of fight, I wanted to get rid of the girl before the crowd figured out she couldn't really fight, and in her case, I did. She'd never been stopped before, but I knocked her out in 40 seconds, and she never fought again.

After it was over, I could tell the way I threw punches had surprised a lot of boxing people in the crowd. They didn't expect to see a woman who threw a straight, hard jab and a solid hook. I have to thank Jim for that, because just being able to move and punch like a professional distinguished me from a lot of the competition.

I fought four times for King that first year and three the next, meaning we were three fights short of my guarantee, but we weren't in a position to say anything about it. After all, I'd just made $35,000 in purses in two years with King, which probably sextupled what I'd earned before.

My only slipup came May 7, 1994. King put me in against a Mexican girl named Laura Serrano. They told us she had no professional fights, but the minute they rang the bell, I knew that was a lie. At least a boxing lie. Laura could fight.

We learned later she'd had a lot of off-the-books fights in Mexico, which wasn't that unusual then and probably still isn't today. Whatever she'd been doing, I didn't have to be in with her for very long to realize she knew how to fight.

She also had a second edge we knew nothing about. She was left-handed. I'd never fought a southpaw before, so that made the fight more complicated. You may wonder why that's a big deal for someone who is right-handed, and if you've never boxed, I understand why you might figure boxing is boxing. It is, but like with most things, there is technique involved, and when you face someone who is left-handed, everything is backwards.

I'd sparred with a left-handed girl once, and she popped me in the face the whole sparring session. I couldn't get adjusted to punches coming from different angles than they would from a right-handed fighter. That girl beat the hell out of me that day, and after we were done, she told me I should stay away from southpaws, which we'd done until Laura showed up.

We were totally unprepared for the complications, and I paid for it, but at the time you didn't know anything about your opponents if you were a woman fighter. That's how it was for all of us at that time. The matchmakers had trouble just finding us opponents in the first place; and when they did, they usually didn't know anything about them except they were alive and had a boxing license. So I really can't complain about what happened that night.

Laura being left-handed wasn't the only problem for me, though. I'd also made the mistake of walking all up and down The Strip with my mom looking at the sights. I walked my legs off that week, which was pretty stupid but my own fault. I just didn't know any better. What's the problem with long walks in the desert in May? I was about to find out.

Three rounds into the fight my legs went dead. I was having trouble finding safe places to throw punches and safe harbors to avoid hers, because everything was coming at me backwards, and now I could barely move. Jim had taught me a shifty little move when I was backed into a corner, where I would bounce off one rope and slip to the other side and then come back with a right hand. It was a good little move, but when I tried it against Laura, I kept bouncing right into her left hand. Before I could throw, I was exposed and—bang!

You train to slip punches a certain way, but you're doing it against right-handed fighters, so you slip to avoid a punch the same way against a left-hander, and you're moving right into their left hand. You might think, well, alter your approach, but you train and train offensive and defensive moves for hundreds and hundreds of hours, and it becomes muscle memory. Training becomes habit, and then habit becomes second nature to you. It becomes instinctual. Then, after facing 30 or 40 right-handed opponents, you find yourself in with a lefty, and everything is coming at you from the opposite direction. You haven't trained for that and didn't have the time to break those habits.

You might ask, "Isn't it the same for the left-handed fighter?" It's a logical question, but it isn't because the left-hander sees a lot more right-handed fighters. They see them all the time in training and in competition, but the right-handed fighter doesn't see many lefties at all. In fact, most of us avoid them as much as possible. In our eyes, everything they do is backwards.

It's the same thing with your footwork. Against a right-handed opponent, you lead with your left leg, sort of splitting them in two. They're doing the same. No problem. But the lefty is leading with her right leg, so you're both fighting for the same spot. You're trying to keep your leg outside theirs, which is in the way and can cause you a balance problem.

You're going after the same area, and you tend to step on their foot and slip. If you get hit at the same moment, you can go down without really being hurt, which hurts you with the judges.

If you haven't trained for it, you can spend much of the fight off balance, which is what happened to me that night. You start to spread your legs too wide to find a comfortable spot, and that affects your balance, too, and you lose punching power because you aren't properly set to punch. What made it worse for me was I usually fought flat-footed. I was kind of a plodder in that way, always looking to throw power shots. When your balance is off, it's hard to do that effectively, which I didn't in that fight. Maybe the best way to explain it is it's like a right-handed person trying to paint left-handed or write left-handed. It's difficult to be smooth in your movements, and that really affects a boxer. Had we known she was left-handed, we would have at least tried to find sparring that was similar, but we had no idea. If we had, I would have worked on throwing a right-hand lead, which is effective against lefties but not something you'd do against a conventional fighter.

So, I struggled all night and felt I had to win the final round to get the decision. I kept trying to land a big shot, but I couldn't do it. In the end they called it a draw, and the crowd booed the decision. That didn't surprise me. The crowd was heavily Hispanic because Chavez was the main event in a title defense. What were those people going to do? Cheer for the girl from West Virginia? They would have booed if I had knocked her out, too.

I was afraid after the fight that King was going to say, "Get her out of here." It was the only time I had doubts about boxing while I was a professional. After the fight I questioned myself. Was this really for me? I decided it was, but what about King?

Don didn't say much of anything after the fight. I was afraid we'd never hear from him again, contract or no contract, but in September I was back in Vegas to face a tough girl named Chris Kreuz, whom I stopped in four rounds. It was a good night because it was when one of King's top employees, Dana Jamison, told me she noticed how excited the crowd got when I fought. She was sitting at the scorer's table, but instead of watching the fight, she started watching the crowd respond. We rocked the house that night.

Kreuz had an outlaw motorcycle gang from Chicago behind her, so the crowd got pretty wild. I did notice one thing though. This time I wasn't at the MGM. The fight was at the Silver Nugget, which was an older casino over in North Las Vegas, not on The Strip. If I'd thought about that I might have thought it was a demotion, because the draw with Serrano had set me back with King, but the purse was the same, so that thought never crossed my mind.

The next fight was at another smaller venue, an odd place called Buffalo Bill's Casino in Primm, Nevada, out near the California state line. I'd never seen anything like it. It had a Western motif with a pool shaped like a buffalo and a huge roller coaster called The Desperado. I kid you not. The Desperado was 225 feet high, and they claimed the cars hit up to 80 mph at some points on the way down. This place wasn't the janitor's closet in Punta Gorda, but it wasn't the MGM Grand either.

Actually, the card at Buffalo Bill's was a week before a King fighter named Oliver McCall was defending the heavyweight championship against one of the great heavyweights ever, Larry Holmes, at Caesars Palace. I tried to get King to put me on that show instead, but Don said no.

Maybe because I didn't want to stay too many more times in the Annie Oakley Tower at Buffalo Bill's, or maybe because I'd had a six-month layoff and felt I'd better do something big, I came in feeling fresh and aggressive for my rematch with Beverly Szymanski. I knocked her out in the fourth round, which was not much different than what had happened when we fought in Michigan, but it was a spectacular knockout.

I nailed her perfectly with an overhand right, and she went tumbling down. She almost went through the ropes and landed in the lap of World Boxing Council president Jose Sulaiman, who was another powerful force in the sport and an ally of King's. The look on his face was utter shock. I don't think he'd ever seen a woman knocked out like that. I mean she wasn't just out. She was *out*.

King went crazy after the fight because he loved knockouts. They were good for the business we were in, which is, after all, the hurt business. Don ended up pulling out a wad of bills and paid me a $5,000 bonus. That doubled my purse and made it probably the biggest purse in the history of women's boxing at that point. My next fight I was back at the MGM Grand and looking at another familiar face.

King put me in with Angela Buchanan for the fourth time, and I knocked her out in two rounds. It's pretty unusual to fight the same person that many times, especially when you're not talking about championship rematches, but it was hard to find opponents in those days. It still is, frankly. The talent pool was very shallow in the early 1990s. You have to remember at that time we were creating a new sport for women. There was no amateur boxing for women when I started, and fewer girls around who were well trained and could fight.

Regardless, that win lifted my record to 24-1-2 with 20 knockouts, including two straight for Don since the draw with Serrano. Everything was on the upswing, and it got even better when Don called and told us he was putting me on a show in Philadelphia two weeks before Christmas 1995. I was astonished to hear him say I was going to fight on a card with Mike Tyson, who was the biggest name in boxing then and still is, well into his fifties. There's no bigger buzz at ringside than the one Mike Tyson causes.

By then Tyson was already much more than a fighter or even a champion. He was a phenomenon like few in the history of sports. Every time he fought was an event, regardless of the opponent. He shattered pay-per-view records, terrorized opponents with his power and speed, and made headlines as much for the wildness of his lifestyle as for his success in the ring. He was a wrecking machine, whether he was wrecking an opponent or his own life. No one made headlines like Mike Tyson.

I loved to watch him fight, and so did the rest of the world. He was so explosive. It wasn't just that he hit hard. It was that he could hit you so fast. Opponents would think they were at a safe distance; suddenly, he was on them and hitting them with three or four punches in combination before they had time to blink. It was incredible to watch because of the combination of the speed with which he could move his hands and the power he carried in both of them.

By then things had gone south to a degree for Tyson. He'd lost the heavyweight title, been convicted of raping an 18-year-old beauty queen at a pageant in Indianapolis in 1991, and served roughly half of a six-year sentence at a prison called the Indiana Youth Center, which today is known as the Plainfield Correctional Facility.

He'd been offered an early release if he agreed to admit his guilt, but he refused, choosing to remain incarcerated rather than admit to a crime he did not believe he had committed. Even in jail he cast a long shadow over the sport, because in the fans' eyes no one could really claim to be heavyweight champion until they beat him.

His comeback fight had grossed more than $96 million, including a record $63 million from U.S. pay-per-view sales, and it only lasted 89 seconds. No one wanted their money back. It was what the public had come to expect from Tyson. Rapid destruction, in this case of an overmatched journeyman named Peter McNeeley. Now he was preparing for his second comeback fight against Buster Mathis Jr., the son of a former Olympic boxer and heavyweight contender, and here was Christy Martin on the same card as the biggest name in boxing. I had my dreams, but I had never dreamed this big.

Even though he wasn't the main event that night, to me, when Tyson fought, it was always about him. The buzz was louder and tinged with a sense that mayhem wasn't far away. He had also become a lightning rod for things way beyond boxing, including advocates who opposed sexual assault and domestic violence. Tyson had been accused of both, so that week there was a lot of negative stuff swirling around.

Women activists felt like he shouldn't be allowed to fight, even though that was his job, and he'd served his time after the rape conviction. He continued to claim he was innocent, and that irked a lot of people, so the word was there would be protestors at the fight out in front of the Spectrum, the arena where the Philadelphia 76ers and Philadelphia Flyers played pro basketball and hockey.

Even though I didn't know Tyson at the time I didn't think that was right. Even if I'd thought he was guilty, which to be honest I didn't, he still had the right to go to work and make a living, didn't he?

After I first learned I would be on a Tyson card, I asked a friend named Tom Casino, a photographer who always seemed to be ringside for every big fight, if he could get a highlight video of my fights to Tyson. Tom was friends with a guy named Jay Bright, who had grown up around Tyson up in the Catskills after Cus D'Amato discovered Tyson in a reform school and began to train him.

It was an old VHS tape, kind of grainy because the lighting in most of the venues I'd fought in wasn't great, but Tyson watched it with Jay. Later they told me he saw a little sidestep move I made to set up a big punch, and he liked it. A little later he was only half watching and—BOOM! I knocked some girl out cold, and he told someone to rewind the tape because he wanted to see it again. I guess after that he thought I could fight, because he was always respectful to me.

When I got to the hotel a few days before the fight, I was sitting in the lobby where all the fighters were staying, and in walked Tyson surrounded with what seemed like a 50-man entourage. As soon as I saw him, my heart started racing. This wasn't just another fighter. It was like meeting Michael Jordan. This was Mike Tyson.

All of a sudden, he turned and walked right over to me and shook my hand. He said he'd watched my tape and was glad I was on the show. He told me he liked that I came to fight. Then he and his crew just walked away. I was dumbfounded, but it made me feel like maybe I belonged in this world I was crashing.

Later I realized we were staying on the same floor, but he had guards in front of his room, so I never saw him again until the weigh-in. No one bothered to post any guards in front of my door.

The way things worked out, it was so cold that night he really didn't need protection from anyone, his opponent or the protestors. It was cold as a meat locker outside, so the protestors decided to wait for another day, and Mike knocked Mathis cold in the third round with his signature right uppercut. That night it didn't look like anyone was ever going to beat him.

As for me, the way the card worked out, I ended up fighting after his fight instead of before. My fight was what's called a swing bout, meaning they insert it when needed if some fights end early. The hardest thing about a swing bout is having to wait to go on with no idea when that might be. It's hard to warm up, then not go on, and then get ready again. You get tired both physically and mentally, but the mental part is the hardest, because it's the most important part of being a fighter, assuming you can fight, of course.

None of the fights were short enough to squeeze me in until Tyson, and by then it was time for the main event, which was a junior middleweight unification title fight, so I didn't come on until after that, making it the "walkout bout." The name implies exactly what you probably think it means. A lot of people were walking out when I walked in.

I really wanted the opportunity to fight in front of a lot of people and on TV, and the walkout bout doesn't get any of that, so I was a little mad about it. Sometimes they even cancel that bout and just pay you without fighting. There are some fighters who would be OK with that, but not me. I trained to fight because I wanted to fight. I loved it and, frankly, because of the mess my private life had become, I needed the release. In the ring I was free. I was totally in control of what would happen to me. For however long I was inside those ropes, I was free to fight back.

Every day I was either fighting in the ring or fighting myself and the world around me over the way my non-boxing life was going. Jim wasn't hurting me physically at that point—that wouldn't start until later—but it was a constant mental beatdown, and I was losing that fight, so I wasn't going to lose this one.

As I climbed into the ring, I could see people leaving. I tried to ignore it, but it made me angry, and I made my opponent pay for it. When the first bell rang, I tore out after her and knocked her mouthpiece flying. The fans who were leaving heard the crowd react. They didn't expect that level of aggression and violence from a girl, I guess, and some of them started trying to get back in, but it was over before they could get by the ushers. Poor Erica Schmidlin didn't get out of the first round before they stopped the fight.

Later I would learn Tyson loved the way I closed his show and how I fought. I fought like I had demons, and so did he. We both had plenty of them buried inside us. Eventually he liked me for who I was, too, but he's said many times his first attraction was the way I fought. Birds of a feather. Troubled birds who had both found a place where we could express ourselves without condemnation.

That evening turned out to be the first of six times I'd fight on Tyson cards, including two of the biggest ones in history—his two fights with Evander Holyfield. They were my stepping-stones to a world I never knew existed—the big-time side of boxing.

I'd ended 1995 with another first-round knockout. I was 25-1-2, had knocked out 12 of my last 13 opponents and had 21 knockouts on my résumé. I was 27 years old and being promoted by the kingmaker of boxing. My personal life may have been as cold and dark as that winter night in Philadelphia with me burrowed deep inside the closet, but in 28 days Don King was going to fall in love with me for the same reason Mike Tyson did.

He was going to realize a lot of people were ready to pay to watch me put people to sleep.

The Fight That Legitimized Me and Women's Boxing

You never know when your moment will come. Often, it's when you least expect it, and if you're not ready—or if it comes before you've had time to prepare yourself for it—that moment can slip away and change your life without you realizing it. That certainly happened to me several times in life but never in boxing.

The night Jim Martin proposed to me I was ill-prepared to do what would have been best. I wasn't strong enough to declare to the world who I really was when I was a young woman. Those moments slipped away. The same was true when I was that 6-year-old child trapped in my parent's basement with a 15-year-old predator next to me. I couldn't say the words that needed to be said, so I suffered for it, and so did a lot of my family for a long time.

Yet when it came to sports, I always knew who I was. I knew it as a kid playing baseball and basketball with the boys. I knew it in college when I had to figure out a way to change my game to make a spot for myself on the floor at Concord. Most of all, I knew it inside a boxing ring. For a while I didn't know what the hell I was doing, but I knew one thing for sure: Christy Martin was a fighter, so let's get it on.

As my skills improved, I learned that forward motion wasn't always the wisest choice, but it was always the ultimate goal. You had to set things up, lay the groundwork to get things done, move backwards sometimes to get in position to attack later. That is not only true in a boxing ring, but also in your own life. Have a plan so when your moment comes, you're able to fight for yourself using whatever means necessary. There were moments I didn't do that when I was a young woman and learned later that the cost of not fighting for who you are is higher than whatever I thought the consequences might have been had I done so at the time.

The more I learned about boxing, the easier that became to do in the ring, but one thing never changed: I was always coming to win as fast as I could. My opponents knew that and understood it put them at risk. Often it unnerved them. It also began putting fans in seats, because they understood what was coming, too, and they liked it.

King called me on Christmas Day in West Virginia, where Jim and I were visiting my family. He said he had a fight for me in three weeks. That was less than a month after I'd won in front of Tyson in Philadelphia. It wasn't much time to prepare, but King would often call me on short notice with a fight, so I basically just stayed in shape the entire time. I was never out of the gym for very long, because I never knew when he'd call, and I wasn't about to ever turn down a fight Don King was promoting. If King was involved it was an event, and that's where I wanted to be.

So, on January 13, 1996, Don put me back in the ring at the Miami Jai Alai Fronton, a place that sat around 6,500 people. That was fine with me. He wasn't paying me much yet, but I wasn't fighting to pile up money. It was to be part of the big shows put on by the greatest promoter ever. Not just the greatest boxing promoter. The greatest promoter of anything. Every time I was on a King show, it made me feel like I'd begun to make it in boxing; and on this night, King made it clear that I had.

The main event was a welterweight championship fight between Frankie Randall, who had just upset Chavez, and Juan Manuel Coggi. I was set to fight a woman named Melinda Robinson on the undercard. I knew she was tough, but I also knew I was 26-1-2 and feeling bulletproof; so I went out and took it to her in the first round. At the end of the round, I came back to the corner and told Jim, "She can't keep taking this!" Turned out I was wrong about that. She could, and she did.

I was beating her up and down, but Melinda would not back down. In the fifth round, I leaned back into the ropes and waved her to come in and try to hit me, which is a pretty bold move. When she did, I feinted and nailed her with a hard shot coming off the ropes, and I could see King in the crowd waving his hands and hollering.

I ended up winning a lopsided decision, and when I came out of the ring, King was right there beside me. He kept hollering, "My champion! My champion!" He walked back to the dressing room with me, too, which he'd never done before. That was the first time I felt like I'd made him take notice of me.

I was happy with King's reaction and with my $15,000 payday. I'd now made $30,000 in 28 days, which was a fortune to me. Most girls fighting then weren't making that much in their careers.

Although my private life was like living in Seattle in February, dull gray with occasional sunshine, I was so happy with my boxing career it didn't really matter to me. I loved to fight, and King was giving me that chance and paying me better than any other girl in boxing to do what I would have done for Toughman wages. How could it get any better than that?

Don had boosted me from $5,000 a fight to $15,000 for the second time. It was really Dana Jamison in his office who upped my pay, not Don, but he OK'd it. That was a great payday for a female fighter then, and it still is to this day, which is kind of sad, but it's the truth. I don't believe there were any female fighters making $15,000 a fight at that time but me. Fifteen thousand a fight is nothing . . . except when everyone else is lucky to make $1,500. Then it's a lot, and I understood that.

In the end I would fight six times in 1996; and as my success and reputation grew, Jim became increasingly more controlling. In addition to demanding more and more that I limit my interactions with other friends, he would often intercept calls from my family, telling my mother I was training, sleeping, in the shower, or out. He'd assure her I'd call back but seldom informed me that my family had called. This led to fewer and fewer conversations with my family and more and more focus on life with Jim. I began to think they weren't interested in me, and they started to believe I didn't care about them. The walls were going up and closing in.

Jim became obsessive about my weight to the point he would weigh me as soon as I woke up in the morning, before and after training at the gym, and again before I went to bed. I understood he was my trainer, but he was also my husband, and I started to wonder, "How many husbands weigh their wife when she gets up in the morning?"

Normally you would see your trainer in the gym, and maybe he weighs you there, although not every day unless you have a fight coming up. He surely doesn't go home with you and weigh you morning and night. I realize now Jim's obsession wasn't solely about concern over my weight. It was because he knew I had always been very conscious about my body. My weight was always an issue for me, and this was his way of both controlling me and insulting me, implying I might have trouble making weight for my fights, which I didn't.

In my view, I had a soft body. I never had that cut look like some women, and a lot of professional athletes of both genders, have. That just wasn't in my genes. Evander Holyfield can wake up any day of the week and look like the statue of David. Me? The only way I would ever have a six-pack is if I bought one in a liquor store.

Jim knew that bothered me, so as my profile started to rise, he began to erode my self-esteem with things like that. The larger my profile became, the stronger the criticism, and that just tightened his hold on me.

The funny thing was he'd criticize me in private, but he didn't want anyone else doing it. As the boxing magazines started to write stories about me, he'd have the other boxers read them first, and if there was anything critical, he'd try to keep it from me.

Once he even told me King had said he wouldn't put me on television any more if I didn't lose weight. I never asked King about it because I didn't believe that came from King. It was just Jim's way of keeping me constantly on edge and uneasy about myself. He was an insecure guy always criticizing other people. Fat people. Gay people. Black people. His wife. It didn't matter to him. I used to tell him anyone who was as big a homophobe as he was must have doubts about themselves. That would piss him off, but I came to believe there might be some truth to it, not that I cared.

Despite my professional success, it was a hard time personally. I could feel my boxing career expanding, but personally my world was shrinking, and I was growing unhappier the longer we were together. By this time, I had been with Jim for more than five years and had really become asexual. I used to say I was no-sexual, because months would go by, and we wouldn't have sex. Every now and then I'd think maybe it was time, so I did my duty, but I had no interest.

The absence of sex in our marriage or with another woman wasn't the real problem. It was a symptom of something much bigger that was missing in my life. I was a married woman who always felt lonely. Certainly, we had some fun times together, but on a day-to-day basis I felt alone in the middle of an expanding crowd.

I always had people around me in those days, whether at the gym or when we were traveling, but I always felt detached. There was distance between us because they had no idea who I really was. I had my regular sparring partner, Jimmy Maloney, and Jeff Bailey, who we called Elvis because he dressed and wore his hair like Elvis, usually with me. That was awesome, but at the end of the day they went home, and I felt alone, even though Jim was right at my side all of the time.

There was just this underlying sense of sadness I felt about being with someone I didn't love and didn't totally trust. While I was on the ascent in boxing, that was enough for me to cope with what was missing in my life, but it was just a Band-Aid. When I saw the end coming, I lost my edge and, eventually, my mind.

I can blame a lot of people for the situation I was in, but the truth is I put myself there. Nobody else did. I made the decision to make myself secondary, so the responsibility for the consequences is on me. You can only live like that for so long, especially when at the very foundation, I was a gay woman living a life of lies. The only real truth came inside the ropes of a boxing ring.

On top of that was this constant pressure I felt to perform. Every time I fought for Don King I didn't want to let him down, because he had taken a chance on me. He could have signed any woman he wanted, but he chose me, and I understood being promoted by King gave me that extra push the other girls didn't have.

I was reminded of that about a month later when King matched me against a girl named Sue Chase, whom I knocked out 27 seconds into the third round. It was February 10, 1996, at the MGM Grand Garden Arena. We made history that night because King managed to get me on Showtime for the first time. It was the first televised bout in U.S. history between two professional female boxers. Maybe I hadn't broken through the glass ceiling of sports yet, but at least I'd gotten through a previously locked door.

The fact that the fight was on premium cable, which really was where all the big fights were being televised then, made it an even bigger breakthrough for women athletes. That night was also memorable for another reason though, and it had nothing to do with me.

That week a former heavyweight champion named Tommy Morrison was supposed to fight a journeyman named Arthur Weathers with the idea being to build him up for a big fight with Tyson. Morrison was being sold as the "Great White Hope." He was the guy who would derail Tyson's comeback and begin his own star turn. Like Tyson, Morrison was a powerful puncher who had captured the public's imagination through skillful public relations. But the night before the fight, the Nevada State Athletic Commission learned Morrison had tested positive for HIV, the virus that causes AIDS.

In those days that was considered a death sentence, and it came as a shock, because at the time it was believed to be a disease that affected only gay men and intravenous drug users. Morrison was neither. What he was, it turned out, was incredibly promiscuous, and apparently, he somehow had gotten the virus through unprotected sex.

Whatever the cause, it was a bombshell the commission tried to hide, but when they announced he would not fight the next day, it wasn't long before the reason why got out. That only served to bring even more attention to the card.

Tyson was at ringside for my fight, and he was going crazy in his seat because Sue took a beating that night. At one point I did a little pivot move to change angles like Tyson often did and landed a body shot followed by an uppercut. It was the signature Tyson combination, and when I landed it, Mike was rocking back and forth and throwing punches in the air. The whole crowd noticed that the most famous fighter in the world was into women's boxing.

Sue had a sense of humor about how things had gone for her. At the time, there was a rumor I might be in line for a Revlon makeup commercial. At the post-fight press conference, she came in kind of bruised and said, "If anyone needs a makeup endorsement it's me." Everyone in the room laughed. It was another little step toward separating myself from other women fighters, although what would really separate me was about to happen in six weeks.

King had put me in an easy fight in Richmond, Virginia, two weeks after I knocked out Chase, figuring Richmond was close enough to coal country that he could capitalize on the fact I was now known as "the coal miner's daughter." That nickname came out of nowhere one night when King's usual ring announcer, a high-school principal from Los Angeles named Jimmy Lennon Jr., introduced me that way.

I'm standing in my corner waiting to fight and Jimmy says, "Fighting out of Mullens, West Virginia, the coal miner's daughter, Christy Martin!" It took a second to register, but that's who I was from then on in the minds of the public. It was a good way to be noticed because Loretta Lynn, who wrote that song, was also a coal miner's daughter, and she took an interest in me, and that meant a lot.

A few days after that fight, King said he wanted to put me on a monster promotion in three weeks. Three fights into his comeback, Tyson was going to challenge WBC heavyweight champion Frank Bruno, and King was adding three other world title fights to the card along with me against an unknown Irish girl, Deirdre Gogarty. This would be my fifth fight in 3½ months, but there was no way I was going to turn down a chance to be on my first Showtime pay-per-view card, especially one that was so loaded with title fights.

I knew this was a special opportunity. No woman had ever fought on a Tyson pay-per-view card before. That meant I was going to be seen by millions of people around the world. That was important for me and for women's boxing.

I was still in the gym, so I was in good shape, but Gogarty was only given about 10 days' notice. Originally King was looking for someone else but then decided with Bruno being from England that adding another fighter from the United Kingdom might attract more British fans to come to Las Vegas.

More than 5,000 of them showed up that week, and they were loud and often drunk. That seemed to bolster Bruno, who had wobbled Mike in the first round of a fight seven years earlier before being stopped in the fifth round. He talked confidently all week and looked to be in great shape at the weigh-in, but I was more focused on Gogarty, who I would learn later had some real issues that day.

I didn't know one thing about Deirdre, but I did notice something that made me nervous. Her trainer was a guy from Louisiana named Beau Williford, and he seemed to know everybody in boxing in Vegas. That made me think they'd brought in someone with the intention of beating me.

I'm not sure why I thought that, but it speaks to how little trust I had in people. Why would King want to get me beaten with my career on the rise? That made no sense, but there's so much gamesmanship in boxing, I began to wonder. Boxing is psychological warfare as much as physical, and I kept thinking, *"Who is this dude?"*

A couple of days before the weigh-in, WBC president Jose Sulaiman named me the women's lightweight champion of the world. It was kind of a ceremonial thing, because I hadn't had to fight anyone to win it, but it was still a big deal to me. The WBC belt has always been considered as big as it gets in boxing. Every fighter wants to win one of their green title belts, so having Sulaiman recognize me and support what I was doing meant a lot. I also thought with a WBC title belt around my waist it might help keep King on my bandwagon.

At the time, there weren't even any women's ratings, but I began to realize it was another bit of recognition for women's boxing. It was another step along the way to being legitimized in the sport, and it was another first for me.

Even though I say that belt didn't mean anything to me, it must have meant something, because I kept it on the dresser in my hotel room at the MGM all week. It was the first thing I saw in the morning and the last thing I saw before I fell asleep at night. It was a little more motivation for me, not that I really needed it. My ego and my desire to win were enough, but if they were going to hand out belts, I wanted the first one. And I got it.

At the midweek press conference, I said, "I just didn't get my foot in the door first, I got my foot in the door because of my fists! I'm going to show that Saturday night when I stop Deirdre Gogarty in such spectacular fashion that everybody's going to leave talking about it." Deidre recalled later that when I said that, Tyson gave her a grin, and she took it to mean, "Girl, you're fucked!" Considering that I had nearly twice as many knockouts (23) as she had fights (13), he had a point.

In those days they weighed you twice, the day before the fight and on fight night. I was right at the lightweight limit of 135 at the weigh-in. Deidre was lighter, but I had no idea how much lighter until I read her memoir a few years ago.

Women's boxing was banned in the United Kingdom at the time, so her fights were underground affairs hidden from the authorities. It was also banned in Europe for what they claimed were "medical reasons." Without any evidence or scientific studies, they just announced boxing increased the chance of breast cancer. So Deirdre came to the States to train with Beau in Lafayette, Louisiana, which I imagine was as different from Dublin, Ireland, as Las Vegas was from Itmann.

Deirdre put up with the same sexist attitudes I faced, including once being offered a fight only if she agreed to box topless. She declined that "opportunity," but that's the type of women's boxing that was getting attention until Don King got involved.

Regardless of how she got there, here she was in Vegas trying to get as close to 135 pounds as possible. Williford had weighed her in unofficially two hours earlier, and she was only 124 pounds. There couldn't be a differential of more than seven pounds from the 135-pound limit, which meant she had to weigh at least 128. How could she do that in two hours?

According to Deirdre, Beau went to the casino cage and came back with rolls of quarters. They stuffed them in her bra, socks, and even her underwear to hide them from the commission inspectors. I noticed she seemed to be walking kind of funny on the stage at the MGM, but I didn't give it a second thought. It didn't matter to me how she walked, just how she fought.

The crowd at the weigh-in was pretty big because of Tyson, and they were loud when I got on the scales. Then Deirdre bent over to take off her shoes and she said eight rolls of quarters fell out of her sports bra into the tracksuit jacket she was thankfully wearing and got caught in the lining! If not, they might have spilled all over the floor, and we both would have had a problem.

As she stepped on the scale, her socks started to slide down from the weight of the rolls of coins stuck inside them, but she managed to hit 130 before anyone noticed. I didn't pay much attention to any of that. Fortunately, the commission supervisor didn't either.

He was a little more concerned on fight night when I was up to 142, but I told him I'd weighed in wearing a leather skirt and had just been drinking a lot of water. That seemed to pacify them, although the truth was I never drank much water before a fight.

As I walked into my dressing room, I noticed it was next to Tyson's, which was just amazing to me considering how this had all started. I was more nervous than usual knowing if I was going to make it as a legitimate attraction, this was the night I had to do it. The fight was being televised around the world. There were 1.37 million buys in the United States alone, and there was a nearly sellout crowd of 16,143 packed into the Grand Garden Arena at the MGM. It was the biggest event I'd ever been part of and, unbeknownst to me, it was fixing to become a lot bigger than I expected.

When Jimmy Lennon Jr. introduced me, he added something new. Now I was not only "the coal miner's daughter," but he said I was *recognized as the woman's pound-for-pound champion!*" I had no idea when that happened, but I wasn't inclined to disagree.

I looked across at Gogarty with a little smirk on my face. She looked small to me and not too formidable, and I went right after her and landed some big shots. All of a sudden she hit me with a solid counter left hand that snapped my head around. I wasn't hurt, but she got my attention, and we went at it toe to toe at the end of the round, and the crowd reacted.

Jesse told me in the corner that I was rocking the house, and that continued early in the next round when I dropped her with a right hand. It had some power but it wasn't perfect, because I was reaching to hit her, and I missed a left hook behind it as she was falling. If that combination landed that might have been the fight, but she got up. And that was the best thing that ever happened to women's boxing.

I decided to go in for the kill, and I started to whale away after I pinned Deirdre in the corner. I thought I had her in some trouble, but she hit me with a good, straight counter right hand flush in the face, and it broke my nose. It gave me a nosebleed that my cut man was never able to stop. Later one sportswriter said it was the most valuable nosebleed in history.

Deirdre said in her book the impact was so hard it sent a sting up her forearm. I surely felt it. When I realized what had happened, I was shocked. I stepped back, dropped my hands and took a couple more of her punches and then flurried to show the crowd I wasn't hurt. They loved it. Female version of macho, I guess you'd have to say.

I felt fine, but blood was flowing down my face and onto my pink shirt, so it looked a lot worse than it was. I hurt her again late in the round and really started to put it on her just as the bell sounded. When she got back to her corner, the ring physician, Dr. Bill Folliard, went to check on her and asked, "Are you all right, honey?"

What? He would never say something like that to Tyson or any male fighter. Honey? What did he think she was? A waitress? I didn't know he said that until I watched the replay later, but good Lord, it made me mad, because it just struck me as disrespectful to her as a fighter.

Her co-trainer, a guy named Abdulla Mohammed, told her, "Courage, D. Just a little more courage, D." She was not lacking in that area, so when Beau asked her to tell the doctor if she wanted to continue, she looked straight at him and said one word: "Yes." Boy, did she mean it.

Meanwhile, I'm in my corner with blood running out of my nose like a waterfall while my cut man, Johnny Tocco, was sticking Q-tips up my nose and using pressure to try to stop the blood flow. Johnny was a legend among boxing people. He was this grumpy little old guy who had a gym in a shady part of Vegas where every great fighter who came to town trained at some point.

I had first met him two years earlier when King rented his gym for Chavez and some of Don's other boxers to train at the week of a King promotion. I was on the card, so that's where I was supposed to go. What I didn't know was Johnny wanted nothing to do with women boxing or even women in his gym. When Jim and I walked in, it was like someone sucked the oxygen out of the place.

I asked three or four people where the dressing rooms were. Nobody answered. Finally, one of them said to ask Johnny. He showed me where to go, but I could feel what he really wanted to do was tell me where to go.

He watched me work for a few days, and I finally won him over because of the way I approached training. He could see I was serious about it. I came to love Johnny, and he treated me like I was his own daughter. Eventually he worked my corner several times before my regular cut man, Miguel Diaz, took over. On this night that was a blessing. I thank God every day that Johnny Tocco was my cut man that night and not Miguel. Miguel probably would have stopped the bleeding, because that man could stop a bullet wound from bleeding, but Johnny couldn't, and that bloody nose probably made me a couple of million dollars.

People saw a girl bleeding, and I guess they thought I'd quit, but I'd never do that. In a fight you keep fighting to the end. Does it hurt? Of course, but the thrill of winning is that much greater than the pain you're feeling. Pain is temporary. Glory is forever. I didn't want people to see me as a quitter, or a bleeder, or whatever. I wanted people to see me as a winner.

For the next four rounds, we pounded on each other, and the crowd was going nuts. There was blood all over my face, my shirt, and my trunks, not because she was hurting me but because she kept finding ways to land that sneaky counter. There was one stretch where for about 90 seconds in the fifth round, we went toe to toe exchanging punches as the crowd stood up and applauded.

When it gets tough like that, you find out if you can go to that dark place inside you that makes you keep fighting. She took me to a place I'd never gone before. I'm proud to say I responded like a fighter. I was winning every round, but she made me fight for them.

At the end of the fifth round, one of Showtime's commentators, the former light heavyweight champion Bobby Czyz, said, "You rarely see fights of any kind at this pace." He was right, and one reason why was that at that time men boxed three-minute rounds and women boxed only two. During my career, I did both, but I liked two minutes best because I wanted action bell-to-bell. I liked fighting three-minute rounds, too, but it's easier to keep the crowd focused on two-minute rounds, because you can make it almost all action, and that's what we did that night.

When they rang the bell for the sixth and final round, Deirdre knew she needed a knockout to win, and she went for it. I could have just gone defensive and coasted, but that's not me, and the fight turned back into a brawl. I had blood all over my face, and we were tearing at each other. The crowd was on its feet when the final bell sounded, and I threw my hands into the air and just let the noise wash over me. The way the two of us felt must have been the way the gladiators felt in the Roman Colosseum. It was amazing.

The scorecards came back very one-sided. I won all six rounds on two cards and five of six on the other. Deirdre thought it was closer than that. I didn't, but I knew I'd been in a fight when I got back to my dressing room.

When I got into the shower I just laid down on the floor. I was exhausted, dehydrated, and I'd lost a lot of blood. I didn't show any of that until I was alone. Then I just lay down on that shower room floor and thought I was about to die. I really did. That's a horrible feeling, but a lot of boxers experience it. At some point in your career, it's what the sport demands of you.

Maybe some of that was a result of the pressure I'd felt to perform. I knew if I was ever going to make it in boxing, this was the night, and I'd barely survived. My body started to shake, and I began convulsing. I was physically spent and emotionally drained. That night I gave all that I physically had. It was the pinnacle of effort. Later on, when I needed it, I couldn't dig any deeper than I had against Deirdre.

While I was lying on the floor shaking and shivering, Jim was out in the dressing room talking to people about what "we'd" done. We? Who hit him? You'd think he'd be looking after his fighter, especially because I was also his wife, but as usual he wasn't there for me when I needed him most.

Finally, I got myself together and got dressed. We still had a press conference to go to, and I always dressed up for those in as fashionable clothes as I had. I came into that one all smiles in a leather suit and heels, like nothing had happened. In her book Deirdre wrote, "Back at the hotel Beau convinces me to dress up to face the press but Martin outpoints me again by wearing a stunning leather suit and six-inch heels. I feel dowdy next to her in my modest skirt and sensible shoes in the outdoor media tent."

In the boxing world, you're always selling your product, which is yourself. That's what I always tried to do in the ring and with the media. The way things turned out, Bruno hadn't put up much of an effort against Tyson, and Tyson refused to go to the press conference, which only highlighted even more what Deirdre and I had done.

Bruno had literally crossed himself a dozen times on his way toward the ring. He looked like a guy going to the electric chair. He got knocked down early, and the referee penalized him for holding so much before he finally stopped the fight 50 seconds into the third round with Bruno squatting on the bottom rope with his hands over his head while Mike was raining down punches on him.

Some people said it looked like a purse snatching, which in a sense it was, because Tyson got paid $30 million for pummeling a guy who didn't want to fight despite being paid $6 million to do so. Meanwhile I got $15,000, and poor Deirdre's purse was only $3,000. After the people in her corner got paid, she took home $1,500 for being half of the fight of the night.

After we were done, Jim and I walked over to the café at the MGM. I had a tradition when I fought there of having a piece of their hot fudge cake when it was over. My eyes were starting to turn black like a raccoon, and my nose was broken. Sometimes after a fight where I had visible bruises like that, I'd say, "Don't hit me again, Jim!" in public just to see people's reaction. I thought it was funny. I don't know what Jim thought, but on this night, I was too tired to even do that.

It was only when I got back to my room that I realized what had just happened. The red light was flashing on my phone, and when I picked it up, there were so many messages my voice mail was full, and they weren't just from family and friends.

Suddenly, everybody wanted a piece of Christy Martin, so I called Seth Palansky, a PR guy who worked Showtime's fights and was assigned to me. I asked him what all these calls from national radio and TV shows were about. I'll always remember what he said. He told me, "Christy, you don't understand what the buzz is in the casino about the fight."

It didn't take me long to realize I certainly didn't. After what felt like a lifetime of fighting, Christy Martin was about to become an overnight sensation.

Bright Lights, Big City

Two days after the Gogarty fight, I was in New York City with my nose aching and my head swimming. My reaction at first was that I didn't get it. In my mind I didn't think I'd done anything special. I just thought, this is what happens when I fight. I get bloody, but I win.

I'd forgotten this was the first time more than a million people had seen me fight, so initially I was overwhelmed by the public's reaction and a little bit scared, to be honest. I was a long way from Itmann, and I knew it.

It seemed like my name was everywhere, including on the lips of radio shock jock Howard Stern, who was arguably the biggest name in radio at the time. At one point that Monday morning he asked his cohost, Robin Quivers, if she'd watched the fight, and then just went off the way only Stern could. Deirdre actually quoted their whole rant in her memoir, *My Call to the Ring*.

STERN: "Yeah, those two women got on and bashed each other's brains in. One of them had her nose broken. Her blood was running down her face. The one who won had her nose broken. I say, the one who bleeds the most should lose . . . You would not want to fight one of those girls."

QUIVERS: "And punching constantly. They never stopped. They never slowed down. There was no dancing around. They were beating each other from beginning to end."

STERN: "Like they threw a punch in someone's face, the other would clip 'em in the jaw. So, my wife and daughter were like visibly shaken during it. It really showed the brutality of fighting, because not only was it a brutal fight, it was GIRLS! The whole time you're sitting there going, 'A guy gets his face bashed, you can live with it. But a girl? It's her face.'"

QUIVERS: "When that girl started bleeding, I was like 'Oh my God!' It's funny they put one in pink."

STERN: "Yeah, to make it more feminine. The blood clashed with the pink though. It was pretty wild."

QUIVERS: "The other thing that cracked me up, the announcers at the very beginning when they were talking about the fight, they said there was a lot of controversy in this women's boxing field because of the damage that could be done to the women's breasts. I thought to myself, 'Men get their brains knocked out, but we're worried about the women's breasts?'"

STERN: "Well, the breast is an important part for a guy. I kept thinking about the breasts and that girl's face, because she looks like a pug fighter now."

QUIVERS: "Would you want the face of a boxer?"

STERN: "Not if you're a broad."

I knew I was a boxer and what that potentially meant for my face, but I never thought of myself as "a broad," although I have to assume a lot of America did. What was more on my mind was the worry that I was now a gay woman in a phony marriage suddenly under the microscope that is the American hype machine. Thankfully, it was the American hype machine before social media, which in my case very likely would have turned into antisocial media in a hurry had it existed 25 years ago. As I've always said, I have a lot of things to be thankful for, and the absence of things like Instagram, Twitter, Facebook, and the like back then are some of them. Had they existed, I would have been "outted" long before Jim put a bullet in my chest and destroyed my hiding place.

Celebrity often comes upon you like a tropical thunderstorm. It's a sudden downpour that can be blinding when you're in the middle of it. So it was with me in 1996. One night I was a little-known woman boxer on the undercard of a Mike Tyson show. The next morning, I needed help just answering my hotel phone, and 48 hours later I was staying in a hotel suite near Central Park in Manhattan that was literally larger than the apartment I shared with Jim in Orlando. Being an overnight sensation was great, but if you were hauling around the hidden secrets I was carrying, it's not all it's cracked up to be, because what came with the elation of it all was a cold fear that I'd be exposed by someone from my past who knew the other Christy. The real Christy Martin.

I was taping radio and TV shows, doing live interviews, and coming to understand what Gogarty and I had accomplished together. Things can change fast in boxing if you win in a way the fans react to. The two of us had created that kind of fight that night. I bled all over myself, but I kept coming forward. She got knocked down but got up and kept coming forward, too. I prevailed, and that's how my professional life was changed. It changed because there was blood all over my face, but the referee still raised my hand. Winners get paid in boxing. Bloody winners get paid better. Everyone can see they survived difficult moments, and they admire that because they're not sure they could do the same thing.

Why did that bloody but frankly one-sided brawl lift our sport when so many similar nights had not? First, because more than a million people saw it. But there was another reason, one that to me was best expressed by Alex Wallau. He would eventually become the president of ABC but at that time was the network's boxing analyst and commentator. When asked to explain why this fight caught the attention of so much of the non-boxing world, he said, "The reason the Gogarty-Martin fight captured everyone's imagination was because it displayed the one quality that boxing can test in a way nothing else does and that is courage. That fight turned in a matter of seconds from being an event that was being laughed at and ridiculed in the arena to one that absolutely thrilled people who were watching."

Of all the things that were ever said about me as a fighter, that one meant the most, because it summed up all that I ever wanted to be in the sport. I just wanted to be seen as a good fighter. Not a good woman fighter. Not a pioneer, or some sort of feminist revolutionary. Just a good fighter. I was finally being looked at that way.

The other side of what happened was captured beautifully by an old-school boxing writer from the Associated Press, Ed Schuyler. Schuyler had seen more fights than the commandant of the Marine Corps , so he looked at things from a very basic, bottom-line perspective. What he said summed up the reality of things for me: "That was the most lucrative bloody nose in the history of boxing."

He was right about that. That drippy nose and the uniqueness of the story of the husband-and-wife fighting team turned me into a national phenomenon. Over the next few months, I made around 50 appearances on network television and radio talk shows including the *Today* show, the *Tonight Show with Jay Leno*, Late Late Show with Tom Snyder, a guest appearance on *Roseanne*, *Inside Edition*, *Extra!*, *MTV* and *MTV Beach House*, CNN, FOX, the *George Michael*

Sports Machine, Good Morning America. I even did one of those ESPN commercials that they do with athletes at their complex in Bristol, Connecticut, that have become so popular.

It seemed like every major city in the country had a local version of the "Good Morning" show, and they all wanted to say good morning to the girl with the bloody nose. I tried to oblige them all. It was cool at first, but you get to the point you just want to go home. You don't want to do another show, or another interview, or get on another airplane. It's draining always having to be on, especially when as soon as the cameras are off Jim is telling me I should have mentioned this or what I said was wrong.

I also was troubled by an unsettling feeling. I kept asking myself, "Do you really deserve all this?" That was fueled by my lack of self-esteem and Jim privately telling me repeatedly that I didn't. He kept reinforcing that he'd created me, and without him it would all collapse. That made me mad, but it also made me doubt myself a little more than I realized. Even so, I kept doing everything they asked, because I understood when your moment comes, you'd better grab it.

At first, King had no reaction to it at all. I don't think he was ready for everybody to be interested in his female fighter. If he gave it any thought, he probably figured now he was going to cash in. Jim felt the same way, which immediately created a problem between them.

Jim and Jesse told me when I did those interviews, I had to tell people I'd only made $15,000 and wasn't getting what I deserved from King. We all want more money, but I didn't really agree with them. At least I didn't think it was the right time to be saying those kinds of things. Later on, I felt some of that, but before the fight I had no negotiating power, so I got what I was worth. That $15,000 was 10 times what Deirdre took home, so although the numbers were sure different, the ratio was better for me than Tyson's was for Bruno. Tyson got $30 million, and that was only five times what Bruno was paid. So how could I complain?

I didn't feel like it was the right approach, but the day after the fight I did an interview in Las Vegas and gave in to what Jim and Jesse were telling me. I publicly complained about my purse.

I didn't even bother to think for myself. I let Jim run the business side. I felt like he wasn't going to listen to me anyway, and I didn't want to argue with him. All I did was train and fight. Earlier in my career, I'd talk back and question him a lot, but the further along we got and the more he wore down my self-confidence outside the ring, the more I just went along. That's not a great way to run your life, but at that particular time it seemed like the line of least resistance.

The longer we were together, I just got beaten down and began to accept his thoughts as my thoughts. It was as if my thoughts didn't matter. That's what long-term domestic abuse can do. You don't matter anymore, even in your own eyes.

The truth was none of us had any idea what the right number was. I think Jesse was looking at it from the perspective of a male fighter after a big win. The difference was a woman fighter then wasn't in any position to make demands. King could make you disappear if he wanted to, and he wouldn't have to turn his pockets inside out because he would have gone broke if he had. Only our pockets would be inside out.

That was the only interview where I said those kinds of things, and by the time I got to New York, I was already publicly apologizing to Don. He was growling that "she thinks she's Mike Tyson!" I never said that, but it didn't matter what I'd said. Don wasn't happy, and I could feel his anger. Don can be a very intimidating guy, and the truth was he held my future in his hands. I didn't fight again for six months. Don never said a word to me about it, but the message was clear. I had gone into the deep freeze. It wouldn't be the last time.

Stories about me were appearing not only in all the boxing magazines of the day but, more important, in *TIME* on April 1, *People* on May 24, and in a feature that ran in the *New York Times Magazine* on November 3. I was on Clairol's list of the most fascinating women of 1996, although it wasn't clear to me what was so fascinating about getting punched in the face for a living. It seemed like the publicity was never ending.

The biggest hit of all came on April 15. Barely a month after the fight, I was on the cover of *Sports Illustrated*. That magazine was the zenith of sportswriting then, reaching millions of readers not only in the United States, but around the world. Never once had they had a female fighter on their cover before, and they've never had one since. You could not get any bigger in the world I was inhabiting than to be on a *Sports Illustrated* cover, and there I was, staring back at myself from every newsstand in America.

SI had already interviewed Jim and me before the fight for a small item that was going to run the next week if I won, but no photo shoot was planned. Then they said they might make it into a sort of day-in-the-life of a female fighter feature, but a few days after the fight, someone called and said, "If no one famous dies, you'll be the cover in a couple weeks." When I heard that, it was beyond my dreams. The cover of *Sports Illustrated*?

If you'd told me when I was fighting in arenas where my dressing room was a janitor's closet that one day *TIME* would do a story about me and *Sports*

Illustrated would put me on its cover, I would have told you that you'd been hit in the head more than I had. You dream about some things, but other things are so big you don't even think about them happening, because just the thought would be ridiculous. That's what being on *SI*'s cover was for me.

A writer and photographer came down to Apopka, where we had just moved into a new house, for the photo shoot. We were like the TV sitcom *The Jeffersons*. We were movin' on up! Yet although boxing was beginning to give me all this stuff, I was still trapped in an empty marriage and still hiding from an ever more-intrusive world outside the ring. It was a side of my life I just accepted because things were too much on the upswing professionally to jeopardize my career by trying to fix my personal problems. That would have to wait.

We had been looking for a house near Orlando for a while. I'd gotten a loan, but I didn't have the down payment, so someone else gave me a second loan to cover it. It was the same house where Jim would shoot me 14 years later. Because of the way my career took off after Gogarty, I paid it off in two years. Because of the way I let Jim run my life, it was foreclosed on not long after I got shot because he'd remortgaged it, and I didn't know a thing about it. There are both sides of my life during those years in a nutshell.

If you look at the *SI* photos today, Jim and I look like the loving couple. The perfect marriage between athlete and trainer, wife and husband, but it was all for show. We were never honest about our life together. Not to the public, the media, my family, and not even with each other. He knew who I really was, but we never talked about where our life was headed. We just lived day to day. Some good days. Many not so good.

It was the typical Christy and Jim Show by then. My head on his shoulder. Me in the kitchen bringing home the bacon and frying it up in a pan for my man. It was fake, but we'd told those stories so many times, you almost start to believe them. You've lied so many times about your life that it becomes easier and easier to tell the next lie. The only problem is it's hard to keep lying to yourself.

If you looked at interviews closer to the end of my career, you could see the distance between us, but not at this time. If we were doing a national TV interview, and Jim said something I didn't agree with, it just wasn't the place for me to dispute it. We'd fight about it later, but we had to show this strong team front, because that's what the public wanted. It had to be presented as if I felt it, which more and more I didn't. It was all just show for the public, but for a while it was a pretty good show.

Anywhere I saw that *SI* cover, I bought one just so the person who was running the newsstand had to look at me and down at that magazine cover and then back at me. Then I'd say, "Yeah, that's me." It was a great feeling.

Those were very heady times. My boxing career was taking off, and it became the greatest therapy I could have asked for. Maybe my personal life wasn't good behind the scenes, but I had a career that was on fire. Without it, I would have driven myself crazy with worry. Crazy with questions. Crazy with crazy. But I had boxing, and that was enough.

Back home in West Virginia, my family had no idea how life was changing for me. I was still "Sis" to them. By that time, I think they really believed I'd gotten over my "lesbian phase" and was a straight woman in a normal marriage. As far as they knew, I had straightened out, so to speak, from a sexual standpoint, so they were happy, although they often seemed bothered when I'd tell them I didn't have time to come home for birthdays or weddings and things. They had no idea how fast my life was changing, or how Jim kept me away from my family and friends more and more.

I really wanted to be happy, though, so around that time I decided I was going to try to love him. That may sound odd, but it was what I resolved to do. The truth is Jim was never going to be the kind of person I could be happy with, but I tried. I really did. Might it have come out differently if he were a different kind of man? I doubt it, but I don't doubt this: whatever that kind of man would have had to be, Jim Martin wasn't it.

Even though things were changing for me professionally, I realized the majority of the naysayers were still naysayers about women's boxing. I didn't think that one fight alone had changed people's thinking overnight, but it had made them more aware of me and our sport. People were taking notice, and some attitudes were changing. By the end of 1996, USA Boxing held its first women's national amateur championships, and women were allowed to fight in the New York Golden Gloves, which was one of the biggest amateur tournaments in the country. Progress was being made, but to some people it seemed like what we were doing was a threat to the men in the sport.

One of the harshest critics I ever read was a columnist at the *Irish Times*, Sean Kilfeather, who wrote a column after my fight with Deirdre ripping the whole idea of women boxing. She quoted that column in her book, where he said, "As someone who has been watching boxing in a professional journalistic capacity for some 20 years, I can only suggest that whoever allowed this so-called contest to take place should be in prison, and possibly sharing a cell with the convicted rapist Mike Tyson and his manager, the convicted killer Don King."

I couldn't tell if he was suggesting we'd committed a crime, or he just didn't like the thought of what we were doing. Either way, I didn't care. I was finally on the map, although Don made sure I wasn't getting a raise until he was good and ready.

It was six months after Gogarty before I fought again. Although I was busy doing appearances, I had begun to get antsy. I'd been scheduled to fight in July at Steve Wynn's casino, but King claimed Wynn found out there was a woman's fight on the card and refused to allow it. King pulled me off, so I didn't fight again until September 7. I wasn't quite sure if King was telling the truth. By that point my trust in people was in short supply.

I had been making a lot of money outside the ring, so financially we weren't too stressed, but I sensed King was still mad about what I'd said about my purse. I had no idea what he and Jim were arguing over, but there was a growing sense of stress building up when I got a call from someone in King's office in August telling me to come to New York for an open-air workout in Times Square with Tyson, who was preparing to fight WBA champion Bruce Seldon. They closed down Times Square and set up a ring right in the middle of Broadway. I was thrilled, but unfortunately that moment led to another quarrel with my mother.

I had her and my dad set to fly in from West Virginia to take it all in. New York had never closed down Times Square for a boxing workout, and I was going to be part of it. I was so excited. At least I was until my mom told me she wouldn't come unless she could bring along my young niece, whom she was raising almost like another daughter. This was one of the first big moments in my career after so much struggle, and for whatever reason she couldn't put me first. I tried to tell her what it meant to me for it to just be us, but she was insistent she wasn't coming unless my niece came, too, and I knew what that would mean. It felt like she was putting someone else ahead of her daughter again, and I ended up cancelling the arrangements and went alone. Well, Jim came, but that was the same to me as going alone. It was still a thrill, but it was a reminder, too, that I could never quite get things right with my family. Her decision hurt me a lot more than she ever knew or I let on.

A month later I was back in the ring in Las Vegas on Showtime pay-per-view on another Tyson undercard. That meant at least a million people were going to see my rematch with Melinda Robinson. I'd just outpointed her in January, but this time my purse had more than tripled to $50,000 plus a BMW Z3 convertible as a bonus, which was worth another $32,000 or so. That made the value of my purse more than $80,000, which was a fortune to me and the largest purse any woman had ever signed for. It made me feel like I owed Don and the public a spectacular performance.

Jim and Jesse still weren't happy with the numbers, but I was ecstatic to be on another card with Mike. I began to feel like King was using me as the appetizer for the Tyson entrée. I was there to get things heated up, which was great for my career.

Later that car became a bone of contention when Tyson sued King. At different times King claimed he'd paid for it, Showtime thought they'd paid for it, and Tyson's lawyers insisted it got charged against his purse. I have no idea who paid for it, but I'm glad someone did, because I still have it. It's one of the few things I got from boxing that I didn't eventually lose. The money would all disappear, but I still have the memories, the belts, and the car, so all my blood, sweat, and tears weren't totally wasted.

Before the fight, Robinson and I ended up in the same elevator and my sparring partner, Jimmy Maloney, was carrying my WBC title belt. He told her, "The next time you see this belt, it will be like this," and he held it over her head. After I stopped her in the fourth round, Jimmy jumped into the ring while she was still on the floor and held it over her. I could not believe he did that, but I can't lie. It made me laugh.

Unlike our first fight, I'd completely dominated her. I wobbled her in the first round, knocked her down in the third, and then finished her with a straight right hand in the fourth. She tried to get up but toppled over sideways and fell again. That was all the referee needed to see to end things.

In the main event, Seldon was so intimidated by Tyson he didn't get out of the first round. People were booing and screaming, "Fix," but they forgot all about that a little later in the evening because that was the night the famous rapper Tupac Shakur got shot.

After Tyson's fight, I went back to my locker room to grab my equipment bag, and I saw Tupac waiting outside Tyson's locker room. One of my guys pointed him out, but I was too shy to go over to him. Later I was on my way to my room in the hotel and Tupac's crew got into a fight near the elevators with some guys. It didn't concern me, so I went up to my room and went to bed without giving it a thought.

It turned out that there was some sort of East Coast versus West Coast rapper war going on, and I learned the next day the disturbance continued on in the valet parking area. Tupac jumped into a black BMW 750 driven by the founder of Death Row Records, Suge Knight, and left with a five-car entourage. Someone followed them. A few blocks from our hotel they stopped at a light, and a white Cadillac pulled up beside them. Someone inside opened fire and started shooting into the BMW.

Tupac got hit four times, including twice in the chest, and died six days later. He was just 25 years old. Knight was shot as well, but he survived. I didn't have much of a reaction when I heard about it, because I barely knew who they were, and there was always some crazy shit happening around Tyson and King. You got used to it and kind of took it in stride. Looking back, those were wild times; but when you're in the middle of it, your reaction is different. Nothing that happened around Mike in those days was a shock. It was just another big headline I found myself on the edge of. I had no idea at the time, but that began a run in which I kept finding myself in that same spot, which was sometimes exhilarating but often baffling.

While I was having my hand raised in the ring that night, Jim noticed the actress Roseanne Barr in the crowd and waved her up to the ring. She came in, and we took some pictures together. Next thing I knew, I was included in a segment of one of the most popular sitcoms in the country. For a while *Roseanne* was No. 1 in the Nielsen ratings. By 1996 it was into its ninth season and losing some momentum, but still more than 16 million people were watching when I proved I hadn't missed my calling. I was playing a boxer, but I was a much better boxer than I was an actress.

We spent a week in October taping a 22-minute show. The idea was Roseanne had a dream that she was fighting Xena, the Warrior Princess. That's the part I was playing, which was kind of ironic because that fictional character not only became a hugely popular television show by the same name, but also gained cult status in the lesbian community.

Xena, who was played by an actress named Lucy Lawless, had originally appeared in a couple of segments of the TV show *Hercules* but was so popular a character that a spinoff was created that was getting big ratings. In the show Xena had a traveling partner named Gabrielle, and it became a big debate in the gay community about whether they were lesbian lovers. It became such a thing that groups of women called The Marching Xenas began appearing in gay pride parades. That I ended up playing the role of a woman who became an icon in the lesbian community was pretty nerve-wracking for me, but not because of that. It was because Roseanne could be as intimidating as King on the set. By the way, at the end of the dream she killed me.

It was one of those cool experiences I would never have had without boxing, but I was just as happy when it was over, and King told me I would be fighting on another Tyson card on November 9. It was destined to become one of the biggest pay-per-view fights in history. Tyson was going to face Evander Holyfield, who was the most respected 25-1 underdog in the history of the sport and a lifelong rival of Mike's.

I fought the first fight on the pay-per-view portion of the card and was given an easy match. I got $75,000 for working less than three minutes. Who wouldn't love that? I knocked the woman out in the first round. Tyson wasn't so lucky.

The buzz all week had been unbelievable. What surprised me about that was I thought everyone was into Mike, but although a lot of people were not betting on Holyfield, they were quietly hoping he would win. The fight turned into a good versus evil promotion with Holyfield, an avowed Christian who wore a biblical verse reference on his boxing trunks, versus Tyson, the childhood pickpocket and convicted rapist. That wasn't fair for either guy, because it turned both of them into cardboard characters rather than real people. But good versus evil sells, and nobody knew that better than King.

King blew the fight up as if Tyson were going to annihilate Holyfield, but Evander had boxing skills that were better than Mike's, and he could take a punch, which if you were in with Tyson was pretty damn important. He also had something even more important. He believed he would win. You couldn't say that about most of the guys I'd seen fight Mike before.

I understood how important the fight was for Tyson and King and everyone else who was fighting for King. My career rise was directly tied to Mike, so there was no bigger Mike Tyson fan in the house that night than me. My future was tied to his, and I knew it.

Early in the first round I saw Evander get hit a big shot. The crowd went wild, figuring this would be another rapid-fire knockout of a mere mortal, but if you watched closely, you realized Holyfield wasn't hurt. Instead, he hit Mike back, which frankly I think shocked Tyson. That was the first hint of what was coming.

As the fight went along, you could feel what was happening. Evander was taking over. He was asserting his will over Mike. He was physically stronger, his skills were better at that stage of their careers, and he was mentally stronger.

A lot of Mike's power came from his aura. He knocked a lot of people out before he even hit them. They were so convinced of his superiority they were just waiting to lose. Evander Holyfield was not waiting to lose. He was there to win. He was an underdog with a sharp bite.

A lot of knockouts are a result of speed more than pure power. Sure, you have to have the gift of punching power, which I was blessed with, too, but it's how quickly the punches arrive that gives you power. Mike at his best was really, really fast. He would hit guys with combinations that came so quickly it was really the second punch that got them out of there, but against a guy as skilled as Holyfield he could never land that second shot. Evander would slip it or block it, then smother Mike and push him back, which was also shocking to me. Holyfield, I could see, was the stronger man.

By the fourth or fifth round, you could feel the vibe changing inside the arena. All those Tyson fans were beginning to get anxious. Something was in the air, and after Holyfield finally knocked Mike down in the sixth round and sliced open his eye after a clash of heads, it became a Holyfield crowd. He was winning them over by working Mike over. Because it was Tyson, I kept thinking he'd get him eventually, but he never did. Evander got him instead.

I was surprised when Tyson got knocked down, but I wasn't surprised when they stopped the fight 37 seconds into the 11th round. Mike had been beaten up pretty badly in the 10th round and was still dazed when he came out to answer the next bell. It didn't take long for Holyfield to finish the job, hitting Mike with 12 unanswered punches before the referee stepped in. Later Mike told me that he didn't remember anything about that last round. I'd been in the same kind of situation back in Bristol when I fought DeShong, so I knew what he was talking about. It's like someone pulled the shades down, and you're sitting in a dark room. Your instincts keep you going, but you don't have a clue what's happening.

After it was over, I was worried about Mike. This was a man with a lot of responsibilities and pressure on him. How was he going to bounce back from this? He hadn't just lost. Evander had manhandled him. When they call you Iron Mike, how do you recover from that?

I didn't go back to see him after the fight. I just went to the MGM café and had my piece of chocolate fudge cake. There was nothing I could do for him. When you win in boxing, the people are all with you, but when you lose, you lose alone. If you fight long enough, we all end up in that spot one night. It's what you do next that will tell your story, and I wasn't really sure what he would do.

What I did know was that my purse had gone up to $75,000, and Jim told me that pissed off a lot of the men on the card because they made less. I was stunned to learn that Ricardo Lopez, who was the undefeated strawweight champion and considered to be one of the top 10 fighters pound-for-pound in the world had only been paid $50,000 to defend his title. He was 43-0 and would end up in the International Boxing Hall of Fame. Jim told me other fighters resented that and hated me for it. I didn't really see that or feel it from male fighters, but when you hear it all the time from your husband, it's hard not to start believing it, which I began to do. The process of isolating me from my athletic peers as well as my family and friends had begun.

In two fights my purse had gone from $15,000 to $75,000, but Jim and King were still arguing over a new contract, and Jesse was pushing hard for me to sign with someone he knew who was willing to buy out my contract. At one point Jesse showed up at my house with $80,000 in cash. The guy wanted to pay me directly, and then after my deal with Don was up, he'd take over as my promoter.

When you see $80,000 in cash, believe me when I tell you it's a big pile of money. That's especially true if you come from Itmann, but I wasn't comfortable with it. I deposited the cash in the bank and then wrote the guy a check back for the money and said, "No thanks." Jesse thought I'd lost my mind.

Jesse's friend wasn't the only one interested in promoting me now. Bob Arum, King's biggest promoting rival, was talking to us. So were other people. King got wind of it all and had his lawyers send out cease-and-desist letters claiming tortious interference with his contracts. I didn't know all that was going on, but it was pretty uncomfortable to feel trapped in the middle of it. Jim was afraid to push too hard, thinking King might dump us, and we had no assurances really that any of the other people would do better by me. So, we were unsure what to do next, or where to turn. At the time, the most comfortable place in my world was when I was inside the ropes with someone trying to take my head off, not negotiating a contract with Don King.

One day at a press conference Tyson told Jim he should never leave me alone with Don. I didn't really understand what he was implying, but Jim never forgot it. Meanwhile, I was asking Mike for advice on how I could get more money from King. He told me, "Go in and tell him what you want and then walk out." I reminded him that might work for Mike Tyson, but it wasn't going to work for Christy Martin.

After I said that his whole demeanor changed. He looked really concerned and asked if I needed money. He told me he'd give it to me if I needed it. You know how many fighters would have said to him, "Yeah, can you spare $10,000?" I told him that I was fine and just wanted to get paid fairly. Money just didn't seem to mean as much to Mike as it did to everybody else.

I'm the kind of person who doesn't care what other people say about you. I go by how you treat me, and Mike was always very kind and respectful. He could have stopped my career at any time. All he had to say was he didn't want me on his shows, and that would have been a big step backwards, but he never did. He was supportive of me and women's boxing and ready to help me if I needed it.

There's nobody who has been used and abused and taken advantage of more than Mike Tyson from what I saw, but he still has a good heart. He did a lot of crazy things, and he rightfully had to pay for it, but he certainly made a difference in my career, and he didn't get anything out of it for himself.

I know he gave away a lot of money to people. I know he bought computers for kids at a number of gyms and other things like that. Mike Tyson did a lot of kind things, but it seemed like nobody wanted to hear about that. They just wanted to hear about Crazy Mike. He and some of the people around him, like Tupac, didn't disappoint them. Little did I know at the time that as profitable as those days were for me, the Mike Tyson Gravy Train was about to be derailed and take me with it.

By fourth grade, I was the only girl on the Itmann Falcons' boys' basketball team. I'm number 12. *Photo courtesy Christy Martin.*

I was an All-Star catcher on my town's boys' little league team. Catcher put you in the middle of the action, and I loved it. *Photo courtesy Christy Martin.*

My senior season of high school in 1986, I was an All-State basketball player who never passed up a shot. *Photo courtesy Christy Martin.*

The belt on the left is my first-ever "world" title. I didn't even know I was fighting for a title until they handed me that belt. *Photo courtesy Christy Martin.*

My dad, Johnny Salters, after a hard day in the coal mines. *Photo courtesy Christy Martin.*

The day I signed my first contract with Don King in 1993 was one of the biggest thrills of my life. *Photo courtesy Christy Martin.*

My first win for Don King was at the MGM Grand in Las Vegas. That's Sue Melton behind me and referee Kenny Bayless raising my hand. *Photo courtesy Christy Martin.*

Together with my trainer/ husband/abuser Jim Martin. Notice even then only one of us was smiling. *Photo courtesy Christy Martin.*

My career-long nemesis, Andre DeShong (left of Don King), and me. We fought four times, starting in a Toughman contest promoted by the man on my right, Jerry Thomas. *Photo courtesy Christy Martin.*

I shared a lot of podiums with Mike Tyson (center). My career would not have been what it became without his support. *Photo courtesy Christy Martin.*

Deirdre Gogarty gave me the most valuable bloody nose in boxing history in our 1996 fight. It made me millions and legitimized women's boxing to the public. *Photo courtesy of Tom Casino/Showtime.*

Deirdre Gogarty and me fighting at close quarters. This is how the whole fight between us went, and the crowd loved it. Me, too. *Photo courtesy of Tom Casino/ Showtime.*

After they announced that I'd easily outpointed Deirdre, there was elation in my corner but no idea how that fight would change my life. *Photo courtesy of Tom Casino/Showtime.*

Autographing a mock-up of my 1996 *Sports Illustrated* cover at the All-Star Café in New York a few months after the Gogarty fight made me famous. *Photo courtesy Christy Martin.*

I was thrilled to share the first public outdoor workout ever held in Times Square with Mike Tyson. Having two of New York's finest by my side didn't hurt either. *Photo courtesy Christy Martin.*

I got to do a lot of cool things during my career, including "boxing" Chris Rock on his TV show. *Photo courtesy Christy Martin.*

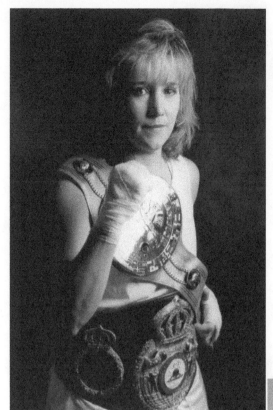

This is what you fight for: to win world title belts, especially that green WBC belt across my shoulder. *Photo courtesy Christy Martin.*

Boxing can sometimes be a glamorous occupation, except when you're actually fighting. *Photo courtesy Christy Martin.*

With my parents after winning the WBC championship. *Photo courtesy Christy Martin.*

The Salters clan back home in West Virginia: my mom; my brother, Randy; and my dad. *Photo courtesy Christy Martin.*

What a thrill to meet the original coal miner's daughter, country music legend Loretta Lynn. She gave me good advice before my fight with Laila Ali. I should have taken it. *Photo courtesy Christy Martin.*

This was the worst moment of my professional life, when I took a knee and let myself be counted out against Laila Ali. *Photo courtesy Pat Orr.*

This right hand stunned me and was the beginning of the end against Laila Ali.
Photo courtesy Pat Orr.

Lucia Rijker and I with our hands on a million dollars at the press conference announcing our Million Dollar Ladies showdown fight, promoter Bob Arum standing between us. It was the first million-dollar payday in women's boxing history, but a week before the fight Lucia pulled out, claiming an injury. *Photo courtesy of Chris Farina.*

It's all about the fans. They supported me all the way to the top. *Photo courtesy Christy Martin.*

Firing a right hook at Mia St. John with bad intentions. *Photo courtesy Pat Orr.*

It's never a good sign when a boxer is wearing sunglasses at midnight, even if she won the fight. *Photo courtesy Christy Martin.*

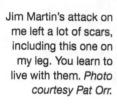

Jim Martin's attack on me left a lot of scars, including this one on my leg. You learn to live with them. *Photo courtesy Pat Orr.*

I had a lot on my mind while preparing for my comeback after being shot and stabbed. Having Muhammad Ali's image in the background reminded me what I was fighting for—to be the best. *Photo courtesy Pat Orr.*

I always believed that I was fighting to be the best and tried my best to prove it. *Photo courtesy of Pat Orr.*

My friend and loyal trainer, Miguel Diaz, brought me back to boxing from the brink of death. *Photo courtesy Pat Orr.*

The day I married Lisa Holewyne was the biggest win of my life. *Photo courtesy Christy Martin.*

CHAPTER ELEVEN

Big Fights, Ear Bites

Everyone faces challenges, whether or not the world knows about them. Life is a struggle for all of us. It's something we must learn to accept and fight to overcome to avoid becoming a victim. Yet sometimes, for me at least, things could turn into a fight in the most unlikely places. Like in the middle of a parade route.

One of my biggest thrills after the Gogarty fight was being invited to serve as the grand marshal at the International Boxing Hall of Fame's annual induction parade in June. I'd never been to the Hall or thought much about it until I arrived in this little Upstate New York town of Canastota. It's an unusual location for a Hall of Fame, because it's not like that's where prizefighting began in America or that any big fights were ever contested there.

Logically, you'd think it would be in New York City, where so many historic boxing matches have been staged at Madison Square Garden, or Las Vegas, for equally obvious reasons. Actually, there is a Nevada Boxing Hall of Fame in Vegas, and there's the World Boxing Hall of Fame in Los Angeles, too, which is typical of boxing's unregulated nature. Unlike our other sports, boxing has more than one of everything, from champions to ratings organizations to Halls of Fame.

The most recognized of them, though, is the one in Canastota. If you get your name on the wall there, you'll never be forgotten by boxing fans, even though the Hall was originally started by some people who really only wanted to honor a local legend, the great middleweight fighter Carmen Basilio. He was the local boy who made good.

Basilio had some hellacious fights with Sugar Ray Robinson, who is considered the greatest fighter who ever lived by most experts, and he was world champion several times. He was known as "the onion farmer," because that's what they have a lot of in that area, although I don't think Carmen pulled many onions out of the ground. He was too busy knocking people to the ground for that.

I didn't know much about Carmen at the time, but when Seth Palansky, the publicist Showtime had assigned to me, called a month or two after the Gogarty fight to ask if I'd be willing to be the grand marshal in June, my first reaction was to say I wouldn't do it.

I've always been shy in that type of situation, but that wasn't the only reason I was hesitant. Jim had told me so many times by then that boxing people hated me because I was stepping into their space and making too much money that I just didn't want to put myself in that kind of situation. He'd created the idea in my mind that everyone was against me, that it was us against the boxing world. It was another way to isolate me, but I didn't understand that. I just believed him even though I had a lot of experiences that showed me it wasn't the case. I'll say one thing for Jim Martin. He could be a very convincing guy, especially if you had some emotional weak spots like I had.

I told Seth the boxing public hated me and I wasn't going to put myself in the middle of them if they felt that way about me. I just wasn't going to do it. He couldn't believe what he was hearing.

Jim didn't tell me we should or we shouldn't do it, though, and fortunately Seth was able to convince me that going up there would keep my name out front with the ticket-buying public. It's one of the biggest boxing events of the year and one of the few times other than at a fight where everyone you meet is a fight fan. He reassured me I'd find out that I had a lot of fans in my corner.

Even after I agreed to do it, I was a nervous wreck. To be around so many great fighters was just overwhelming to me. I didn't want to be a distraction. I didn't want them to think I was up there trying to take over their show. It was their day, not mine. It was an honor just to be among them, so when they asked me to ride in the parade, I jumped at the chance. It turned out I wasn't going to be the only woman fighter jumping into a car that day.

To my surprise, one of my oldest rivals, Andrea DeShong, was in the crowd and pretty steamed over my success. Her manager, Jerry Thomas, had advised her to go home to Ohio and retire after I beat her six years earlier because he saw no future for her in the sport. She took his advice, but I guess she wasn't happy about it.

I didn't realize she'd started a comeback a few months earlier. She'd had a couple fights with mixed results when she saw my face on the cover of *Sports Illustrated* and called Thomas the same day madder than a hornet.

She told Thomas she'd beaten me twice (including our Toughman fight when I barely knew how to lace up my gloves) and claimed she got screwed out of the decision the last time I beat her. She wanted him to get her a rematch with me, and Jerry was up for it, because I was becoming where the money was in women's boxing.

I wasn't aware Jerry had called King's chief matchmaker, Bobby Goodman, trying to pitch a fight between us, or that Don decided he had no interest in matching me against a woman who had barely fought in six years. It seemed like that would be the end of it, but Jerry was persistent in the same way he had been when he first started promoting Toughman contests, and so was Andrea, but in a more hands-on fashion.

So now it's a beautiful early June day in Canastota, and I'm riding down Main Street in a convertible, waving to the crowd. I could hear people yelling, "That's the girl who won with blood all over her face!" It was really fun until this woman came out of the crowd yelling at me. I recognized her right away. It was DeShong.

I wasn't sure what she was yelling, but it was pretty clear she wasn't congratulating me on my success. In an instant, she ran up to the car and jumped in as we were rolling down the street and tried to start a fight right in the backseat.

She was saying she was coming out of retirement to kick my ass. I was trying to act like I had a little dignity and class, even if I didn't, so I didn't hit her. I just kept yelling, "Get this bitch out of my car!"

The former heavyweight champion Ken Norton was in the car behind me, and he jumped out and was going to go after her. That struck me as pretty funny, because Ken and I had just worked a card show in California a few months earlier, and a fighter named Gina Guidi had come up to me at the autograph table and thrown a rubber chicken at me!

Guidi's nickname was "Boom," but don't ask me why, because she couldn't break an egg with a hammer and had a phony record. She'd fought the same girl four times, and the first three times the other girl still hadn't won a fight. This girl was challenging me?

I was really mad about it and jumped up and took it to a place it should never have gone. I hollered, "Get away from me, you dyke bitch!" Not the nicest thing I could have said. Regardless, once again I'd used a homosexual slur to demean someone. Don't ask me why. Maybe I'd just become conditioned to do it, but that's a pretty lame excuse. In fact, it's no excuse at all. I said what I said, and I should never have done it. Period. But I did.

Ken jumped up from where he was sitting to defend me, and the incident ended pretty quickly. When I thought about it later, she had to pay $20 just for the chance to insult me. I tell young fighters today they have to let those kinds of things roll off their backs, because people who do that are only doing it because they're jealous and want what you've got. Like most people, I find it easier to give advice than follow it. What I should have done was ask her if she wanted to pay me another $20 to sign her chicken.

Despite that incident, I never expected someone to jump in my car and start throwing hands at me in the middle of a parade. Fortunately, the police got there pretty fast and grabbed DeShong. I was so mad about it, she got what she wanted. I called Don and asked him to make the fight.

It actually made a lot of sense. At that point I was 31-1-2, and DeShong was the only woman who'd beaten me. Still, King didn't jump on it. DeShong had had nine comeback fights, and frankly lost against the best opponents she faced, before he finally made the match.

She was 5-3-1 in her comeback by then and had just been stopped by Jane Couch in the seventh round of a WIBF super-lightweight title fight, so she had both the veneer of being a legitimate opponent and a long history with me that we could sell. Still, Don waited more than a year from the parade incident before he put her across the ring from me. It's the only time I was happy to see Andrea DeShong.

While that was all percolating, DeShong was the least of my worries. Several months after I beat Deirdre, King signed her to a three-fight contract offering her the possibility of a rematch with me. I had no problem with that. I was certain I was the better fighter and felt like he'd just signed her to stick it to me and give himself a little leverage in our contract negotiations.

Along with signing a promotional deal with Don, Deirdre also had to sign a managerial contract with King's son, Carl, meaning he would be her comanager along with Beau Williford. She probably didn't have any choice in that. Regardless, it wasn't long before King used her against me, but not by putting her in the ring with me.

Deirdre had fought for him in September in Florida, but I wasn't concerned. I knew I had a fight coming up in Nashville in January, and the negotiations for a Tyson-Holyfield rematch in June were already taking place. I was pretty sure I'd get a spot on that card, too, so my career was in good shape. Even though King and Jim hadn't hammered out a new contract for me yet, we were in the midst of ongoing negotiations. At least I thought they were negotiations. I guess King thought they were demands.

King knew we were talking with other promoters, and he thought we were threatening to walk out on him. Maybe Jim was threatening him with that, but I had no interest in leaving Don. I always thought he was the best promoter

BIG FIGHTS, EAR BITES

for me. I still do, to this day. But I wasn't really involved in the business side. I just kept training and doing appearances and let Jim take care of the rest of it.

Everything came to a head in the weeks just before the show in Nashville. It was supposed to be a huge 13-fight card with something like five world title fights on it, and I was scheduled to be part of it.

A few weeks before I was to arrive in Nashville, someone from Don's office called and said he wanted me to appear with him at the Grand Ole Opry during fight week to promote the show and ourselves. That was a big shot in my opinion. I'm from West Virginia. Grand Ole Opry was a huge thing to us, and I wanted to do it.

I was in my gym in Florida when they called to explain it would just be me and Don. They didn't want Jim included, and he got angry about it. He was so sure he was the creator of Christy Martin that he'd begun to believe he was the show, not his fighter. King felt the same way, and in his case, maybe most of the time he was right. But Jim Martin? Please.

Jim didn't want me to go, so we argued over what to do. Without my knowledge, he called Don and told him I couldn't come, because I'd cut my mouth in sparring, which wasn't true. Don thought we were holding out for more money and pulled me off the card, just like that. I was so mad at Jim. I asked him why the hell he would do that. Even if I had been cut, that was no big deal. I was always bleeding anyhow, plus fighters fight with small injuries all the time. If you only boxed when you were 100 percent healthy, there wouldn't be many boxing matches.

I called my dentist and had him send King a letter saying I was fit to fight, but he never responded. Instead, he announced I was being replaced by Gogarty. King was paying her $10,000 to take my place. That was a big raise for Deirdre, but it was $65,000 less than what I was supposed to make, so he'd saved money and flexed his negotiating muscle at the same time.

When I heard about it, I released my dentist's letter to the media, so Don changed his story. He said it wasn't a cut that was the real problem. He said I'd refused to live up to my side of our contract, because I'd refused to do a promotional appearance at the Grand Ole Opry. The truth was I hadn't refused to do anything. That was Jim Martin who said no, not Christy Martin.

Once I released that letter, things between Don and me turned into a media fight as much as a contract negotiation. King said I thought I was worth as much as Tyson and claimed other promoters were trying to interfere with his contract. I was angry and blamed Jim for the whole mess, because it was clear Don had only reached out to Deirdre to stick it to me. We'd just blown a big payday, Don was mad as hell at us, I was mad at Jim, and Jim was mad at me for telling the media my mouth was fine.

This was the same media that only a few months earlier was praising me. Now it was ripping me for being selfish. Many of the writers said I didn't want to fight because I thought I was worth more than I actually was. Maybe I did, but I would never have blown a $75,000 payday and a chance to appear at the Grand Ole Opry to prove it.

Jim kept telling me it wasn't because of what he'd done. He blamed King. The more he talked, the madder I got, because that problem was all his doing. I wanted to go to Nashville. I wanted to go to the Grand Ole Opry. I wanted that $75,000 purse. Are you kidding me? To think that all blew up over who was going to be on the stage with me was ridiculous, but what I realize today is I should have stood up for myself and just gone to Nashville, whether or not Jim liked it. That was my real problem. I'd let someone else control me again.

I lost some fans over that incident, because they don't like that kind of stuff. Fans just want fighters to fight each other, not fight over money. Maybe they understand that it's a business to a degree, but they quickly run out of patience with fighters squabbling over their purse. They hear Christy Martin was offered $75,000 or $100,000 and isn't fighting, and compare that to their paychecks. It pisses them off, and they start to sour on you. I understood that, because as a fan I'd felt the same way about other fighters who refused a fight I wanted to see.

That's the chaos I was living with. I was finally starting to move up and being pulled back down by my own husband. It was like we were crabs in a bucket. One's trying to get out, and the other is pulling her back down. It was nuts, but I wasn't strong enough at the time to do anything about it but get mad.

When I learned Don had replaced me with Deirdre, it didn't sit well. It fed into my underlying lack of self-esteem. I could act pretty cocky in public or in the ring, but on the inside, I never thought for a second it mattered to Don whether I was on his shows. Putting Deirdre in was confirmation of that to me. Other people thought differently and tried to convince me I was worth more than I thought, but I never totally believed it.

Inside the ropes I believed I was the best female fighter in the world, but I had no confidence that I had any real value to anyone. That's what abuse does to you, whether it's physical or psychological. It corrodes you from the inside out, and it takes more to reverse that than winning some boxing matches.

I learned later that Don had only called Deirdre a few days before the fight to replace me, so it wasn't like he had it planned all along. He gave her a soft touch whom she stopped in 43 seconds. After it was over, he told her she was going to be the next female sensation.

Don started saying Deirdre was the most powerful puncher in women's boxing, which all three of us knew was bullshit, but that is what Don does best. He could bs the public and the media better than P. T. Barnum, and he got very rich doing it. That kind of sales job is a skill that requires some boldness, and Don certainly had plenty of that.

After I missed the Nashville show, he put her right back on his next show as well, but as far as I knew, there was never any talk about a rematch with me. I'd won every round in our first fight, so there was really no competitive reason to do it, although it would have made a lot of business sense. It had certainly been a compelling fight, and it would have gotten a lot of publicity if we'd done it again. I would have jumped at it, because in my view it was a safe fight for me. Deirdre didn't have the punching power to keep me off her. She might make my nose bleed, but she was never going to hurt me. Of course, in those days I didn't think anyone could hurt me but Don . . . and Jim.

This tug-of-war between King and me went on for nearly six months, but we finally came to a new agreement. I signed a five-fight per year contract with him that guaranteed me a minimum purse of $100,000 a fight for three years. That's $1.5 million at a time when most of the women were lucky to make $1,500. Despite all those disagreements, in the end I was still "the man" in women's boxing.

After I signed, I said, "If I can hold up, he'd probably fight me every month. The business side of this sport is very tough, but I've come back much more focused, much stronger physically. It's a tough, brutal sport, but just because you're in it doesn't mean you have to take that macho-type attitude on outside of the sport. You have to keep your femininity about you."

That was me selling myself in a way the people around me wanted and in a fashion I was convinced the public wanted to hear. It didn't matter that keeping your femininity might have meant something entirely different to me than it did to my audience. It was just another sales job.

The new contract would go into effect for my next fight, which was set for June 28, 1997, on the undercard of the biggest boxing match of the year: the Tyson-Holyfield rematch. That was the fight that was on the mind of the public, but my mind was on a different fight. Not the one King originally made for me against Dora Weber. It was focused on the opponent who replaced Dora a week before the bell rang. Standing across the ring from me was going to be the girl who crashed the parade route. Andrea DeShong was back, and I was happy to be paid for the opportunity to punch her in the face.

Like Deirdre replaced me in Nashville, DeShong took the fight on short notice. King didn't call her until six days before we were going to meet, and it nearly didn't happen because Jerry couldn't find her. She was off camping, according to Jerry, and hadn't been training. Maybe so, but she'd just fought for a world title three months earlier, so as far as I was concerned, she should have still been in fighting shape. If she wasn't, that was not my problem.

Friends of hers finally located her, and DeShong signed. I couldn't have been happier. This was going to be the fifth time we'd faced each other going back to our Toughman days, but this promotion had an edge to it, and not just because she'd rained on my parade the year before.

At the final prefight press conference the week of the fight, Andrea stood up and said, "The canary just died," and I about lost my mind. Maybe people in the crowd didn't get her meaning, but if you were a coal miner's daughter you did. She had just said she was going to kill me.

Down in the coal mines they used to carry a canary with them inside a cage, but it wasn't for entertainment. That bird was an early warning system, because it would drop dead if noxious gases started to build up. That would be the sign to evacuate, because the bird would die before there was enough gas built up inside the mine to cause an explosion and a mine collapse if so much as a spark went off. All my family had been inside those mines, and most of them got hurt, so I didn't think what she said was funny. She was saying she was coming to kill me, and that put me in a bad frame of mind.

Athletes in other sports can say that type of stuff and get away with it, because they're playing games. Nobody plays boxing. Inside the ring people get hurt. Sometimes they die. Every fighter understands that and either learns to cope with it or quits and gets a day job. I wasn't about to quit.

I was so angry when I got to the podium, and with King egging me on, I grabbed the microphone and said, "I'm going to put something on you that your girlfriend can't get off." There it was again. Another homophobic insult further endearing me to the gay community.

King loved it because he thought that stuff sold tickets. Jim loved it because he was a homophobe. Certainly, I knew there were a number of gay women fighting, and I was one of them, which was part of my problem. I wasn't being real with myself or the public, and I was more and more feeling the strain from trying to bury who I really was and be someone I was not.

I didn't like saying those kinds of things, but I'd done it again and said it with conviction. It was all part of the show to Don and Jim, but inside me it was another part of my self-destruction. I paid a price for those kinds of statements, and still do, to this day, with some people in the gay community, but short-term it was DeShong who paid the price for what she said that day.

When there's true dislike between two fighters, you expect the other person to bring it on the night of the fight, and she did. I was so fixated on hurting her, I didn't box well at first. The fight was the first live show on the pay-per-view portion of the card, and the first four rounds were more competitive than they should have been, because I was just trying to hurt her instead of boxing, and she was trying to do the same to me.

She head butted me once and broke my nose early in the fight, and I got so angry I tried to backhand her, which is illegal. That was one of the most embarrassing moments I ever had in the ring. It was such an unprofessional response. It still bothers me that I reacted like that, but it shows how little control of myself I had in the early rounds of that fight.

Once I settled down, I began to wear her down, landing more and more flush power shots. She wasn't able to do anything about it but take them. After I'd hit her with my best shots for a while, I thought I'd try using my jab and see what would happen next. She was so tired and beaten up by then, I found I couldn't miss her. She'd become a punching bag. A tough punching bag, but a punching bag all the same.

In the seventh round I drilled her with four consecutive hard jabs that had her head moving around like a bobble-head doll. That's when the referee came in and stopped it. He didn't really have to, but he knew she was exhausted, and all the fight had been beaten out of her. If it went on, she was just going to take a lot of unnecessary punishment. I definitely took some personal satisfaction when he raised my hand. I knew Andrea wouldn't be jumping into my car again after that.

After it was over, I went back to my dressing room, which was again next to Mike's. I was nervous for him, because I knew he had to make right what had happened in the first fight with Holyfield.

When Jim and I went to find our seats, they were five rows from the top of the building. You needed a telescope to see the ring! Fans were stopping me to take pictures and saying, "Your tickets are up here?" All I could do was laugh, sign some autographs, and say that's life with Don King.

The rematch seemed to start right back where their first fight had ended. Holyfield was in charge from the opening bell, and before long he and Tyson had clashed heads. Mike was badly cut over his right eye and irate about it. After having suffered through the same kind of thing six months earlier, he didn't think that butt had been an accident.

When Mike came out for the third round, he didn't have his mouthpiece in, which was kind of odd. Little did I know, Mike had a method to his madness. As the round was coming to an end with Holyfield manhandling Mike again and smothering his punches, Holyfield suddenly jumped up in the air like he was literally hopping mad, pawing at his right ear. From where I sat, I had no idea what was going on. After a stern lecture from referee Mills Lane and a two-point deduction taken from Tyson, they went back at it. In seconds, Holyfield was jumping back again just before the round ended.

I could see the referee talking with people from the athletic commission and then he waved his hands and said the fight was over. Lane had disqualified Mike. I had no clue what had happened, so I called home, and my dad told me, "He bit him! Twice!" I was so shocked all I kept thinking was, "Did that really happen?"

It seemed like Mike had lost total control of himself after they clashed heads and his right eyelid split open. He had mayhem on his mind after that, not boxing. Once he realized he'd been disqualified, Tyson charged toward Evander, who was surrounded by a wall of security guards and Las Vegas policemen. They held Mike back until they could clear the ring, which took a while, and the longer it took, the worse things got inside the arena.

The crowd was as angry as I'd ever seen one, until finally someone threw a water bottle at Mike as he was walking toward his locker room. He and a couple of his handlers tried to climb into the stands after the guy, and then some more things were thrown out of the crowd at him. It was getting crazier and crazier, so we went back to my locker room to grab my stuff and get out of there.

By the time I got backstage and walked down the long hallway to my locker room, I saw Don sitting all by himself in a folding chair. I think it may have been the only time I ever saw him completely alone. He looked like he'd just lost his last dollar. He had a look on his face that seemed to be asking, "What do I do now?"

I didn't even want to talk to him. What could you say? It'll be better tomorrow? No, it wouldn't. There were no words. I think King and I both understood that you could survive a lot of crazy things in boxing but not something like what had just happened.

Boxing is a brutal sport. Fans accept that. It's naked violence on display sometimes. Fans want that, too. But there's a difference between that and cannibalism. That they don't want, but it was how a lot of the world was going to view what Mike had done. Almost immediately the tag name for the fight went from "The Sound and the Fury" to "The Bite Fight," and it's stayed that way ever since.

We headed over to the MGM café for my usual chocolate fudge cake, and you could hear a lot of commotion as people came into the casino from the arena. It kept getting louder and louder. Fans were pushing and shoving and arguing with each other depending on which guy they favored. Then you heard it. BANG! It sounded like a gunshot.

People started running and diving on the ground. Big Jeff jumped on me to protect me. Jim was there, too, but he didn't jump on me. He dove on the floor to protect himself. At least my husband was consistent. He was covering his own ass, not mine.

Now it was like a stampede from the arena onto the casino floor. People were knocking over blackjack tables, slot machines, and roulette wheels. People were running away from what they thought had been gunshots. It had basically turned into a riot spilling into the casino.

There were a lot of bad dudes in the crowd that night. Someone said later the crime rate in the country dropped to nearly zero all weekend, because any perpetrator worth his salt was in Las Vegas for Tyson-Holyfield II. I don't know about that, but I know I saw more pairs of purple shoes and red suits than I'd ever seen in my life.

It's hard to describe, but you could feel a brooding sense of violence just below the surface building up all week, and now it was spilling out right in the middle of the MGM Grand. Crazy as it was, not everyone was running. Casino cameras caught people stealing chips from off the floor after the tables went flying. It got so bad they completely shut down the casino for the only time in the history of the MGM.

In the middle of it all, someone from the restaurant who knew me came over and took us out through the kitchen to a service elevator. They told us to go to our rooms and stay there.

Later that night, all you heard in the casino was the sound of vacuum cleaners. Not another sound. It was another first for Don King. He'd promoted a fight that totally shut down one of the biggest casinos in Las Vegas.

A day or two later, I began to understand that there would be serious fallout from this. Something had happened that was changing how people looked at my sport. The ride on Tyson's coattails had been great, but it was over.

Mike was suspended indefinitely and fined $3 million, but Vegas being Vegas, they reinstated his license to box on October 18, 1998. He was back in the ring on January 16, 1999, but I wasn't on that card. He kept making money, but now it was more like he'd become a carnival act than an athlete. People paid to see if he'd go berserk again more than just to watch him compete. He didn't, but he never won the heavyweight championship again, and I never appeared on another Mike Tyson card.

Something got broken that night that couldn't be fixed. I would still have some big paydays, but generating them would be up to me now, and that meant they'd be harder to come by.

Chasing a Million Dollar Payday . . . and Not Getting It

It wasn't long after "The Bite Fight" that I realized I was alone again. It was a feeling familiar to me, something I'd known many times in my life.

Mike Tyson had been like a magic carpet ride for me, providing a platform to show my skills and a huge audience that turned me into someone I never thought I could be. I wasn't the sun in boxing, but I was a star. Now he was gone, and I was unsure what the next step would be.

For most of my life, I'd felt this sense of loneliness, even in a crowd. Because of the conflicts resulting from my sexuality, there was a gulf between my family and me that I couldn't quite bridge. I was hiding in plain sight from many of the people who thought they knew me and was trapped in a loveless marriage of convenience that was becoming ever more inconvenient.

Even after I signed with Don King, and my boxing career took off, I understood there was no loyalty there. I was a commodity to Don, as all his fighters were. To be fair, that didn't make him any different from all the other promoters I encountered during my career. Frankly, he was the best of them for me, but I was still just something to sell, and with Mike suspended for Lord knew how long, I feared it would be a harder sell now.

Would Don even bother with me anymore? The fear of being devalued, or perhaps having no value at all, had been a driving force in my life for a long time, but it was also a corrosive one. If you always feel like you have to prove your worth to the world, how sure are you really that you truly have any value? Not so sure at all.

I knew I had become a good fighter, and I realized I was doing things no other woman had ever done, but I also knew a lot of what Jim, Don, and I were selling was a fiction. Not the fighting part, but the rest of the package wrapped in pink boxing trunks. So where were we headed now?

Surprisingly, where we went just two months later was to New York City to make history again. Like Frank Sinatra sang, "If you can make it there, you'll make it anywhere," and I did. Almost.

Once I got back to Florida, I kept wondering where King would go from here, because where King goes is where Christy goes. I had no illusions about the business side of boxing. I knew I got paid what I got paid, which was not only a lot for a woman but for most male boxers as well, because of what Mike had been generating. All our eggs were in that basket if we fought for King, so you had to give Don credit. He went back to Felix Trinidad and Ricardo Lopez and a bunch of middleweights he maneuvered into all holding pieces of the title and made it work. Not like when Tyson was fighting, of course, but he made it work.

I'd begun to hear rumors I might have to renegotiate my contract, and I knew that didn't mean for a raise, but Don never came to me with any of that. Did he and Jim work something out where Jim skimmed a little less off the top that I knew nothing about? I have no idea. I just know Don didn't try to change my contract. He paid me what he promised and sometimes more than my promised $100,000 minimum per fight.

So, when someone from King's office called to tell me I'd be fighting in two months at Madison Square Garden, I was relieved to be coming back quickly and incredibly excited. Vegas was big and everyone wanted to get there for the glitz and the glamour and the payday, but to me the Garden was the mecca of boxing. True fighters understand that the history of the Garden is unmatched. Since 1925 nearly every great boxer has fought there, and everyone who hoped to be great was striving to get there, too. No woman ever had. I was about to become the first.

Jackie Tonawanda did compete in a mixed martial arts match against a male kickboxer named Larry Rodania on June 8, 1975, at the Garden and won, but some people believe the event was tainted. They think the outcome had been predetermined the way pro wrestling is. As hard as Jackie fought in the 1970s to break down barriers for female fighters, I was the first to box in the most storied arena in the sport.

My opponent was a girl named Isra Girgrah, and I was worried about her. Not because her record was 9-1-1, but because she was being managed by Debbie and Carl King, Don's daughter and son. Isra was more in bed with Don's people than I was, and that concerned me.

Don turned it into a very big pay-per-view show with three world title fights plus appearances by Trinidad and a former champion named Edwin

Rosario, who were both very popular with the large contingent of Puerto Rican fight fans in New York. The place was packed that night.

When I came out of the locker room, I could not believe the reaction I got. The place went crazy. As I walked down a dark aisle toward the ring, I had that crowd. Everyone was standing and cheering for Christy Martin!

What a feeling that was. All I had to do was perform, and I started out hot. I knocked her down early in the fight, but for some reason I ran out of gas. I'd had a little trouble making the weight and caught a cold the week of the fight and was having trouble breathing, but every fighter has excuses when they don't perform up to par. Those were mine. I also hadn't gone eight rounds in five years, and once I began to tire, she took advantage of it, as she should, and took me the distance. At some point she also took the crowd from me.

The fans expected me to knock her out, and with good reason. I'd had 26 knockouts in 35 fights and three straight since my brawl with Deidre Gogarty, so when I didn't finish her off early, they got behind the underdog. I understood that. I'd done it many times myself when I was watching a fighter doing better than I thought he or she would. It didn't mean I thought they'd won, but you start pulling for them, and that's what happened.

Two of the three judges were women, which was highly unusual then and a sign we were making small inroads in the sport. All three had me winning easily. Two had it scored 78-73 and one had it 78-74, meaning I'd won at least six of the eight rounds in everyone's opinion. Everyone but the crowd.

When they announced a unanimous decision, the fans started to boo. That hurt me to my soul. All I had to do was knock her out and I would have been a hit in New York, but in the end, they booed me. If someone went the distance with Christy Martin, people thought it meant they'd won. I knew I had, but I lost the crowd. I was 33-1-2, but 18 months later King put Isra on a Tyson card, not me. She lost that night, too, by the way.

I finished the year with a fight in Pompano Beach, Florida, on December 5 against a girl I'd run into under unusual circumstances a few months earlier. I'd been invited to do a week of appearances in Argentina for $25,000 in cash plus expenses. That little girl from Itmann was seeing the world on someone else's dime, so off we went.

I did a lot of interviews, went to some fights, and was asked to appear on a morning television show that was their version of Good Morning Argentina or something like that. Of course, I agreed but when I got there, they had a ring set up, and that surprised me.

They said they wanted me to wrap my hands and put on some gloves, which I was willing to do, but then they asked me to show another woman how to punch. It felt like something wasn't right about that, so I refused, but Jim said, "Oh, just do it." So, of course, I did.

By the time I walked onto the set, it had turned into a full-blown sparring session with a young woman named Marcela Acuna. She supposedly didn't know how to box, but the truth was she'd been a South American martial arts champion at 14 and made 16 title defenses before she got pregnant in 1995 and retired. Now she was coming back and training to make her professional boxing debut.

I knew none of that at the time. I just thought she was someone they wanted me to move around with until she hit me. She hit me so hard I was instantly incensed and drilled her in the face, and her head snapped back. The whole thing was a setup, I think, to get her a fight with me, and she got her wish. Her pro debut came against me a few months later, and I was still mad about what had happened.

Marcela took an ass whipping for 10 rounds that night in Florida, losing every round on one judge's card and nine of 10 on the other two. Nine months later she was fighting for one of the light welterweight titles against a woman who would become my nemesis for many years, Lucia Rijker. Rijker knocked her out with a body shot, and Marcela didn't fight again for two and a half years. To her credit, when Acuna came back, she'd put in the time and the work to learn what boxing was all about, but that's how unregulated women's boxing was in my day. Nobody was really looking out for us or our safety. If you couldn't fight, you could end up in a dangerous situation like that. Poor Acuna. Here was a girl who had never boxed facing two of the best female fighters in the world in her first two fights. It was ridiculous.

Eventually, Marcela turned into a very good boxer. She fought for 22 years and ended up winning several world championships as a featherweight and super-bantamweight and became a national hero in Argentina. Props to her, but she never should have been in the ring with me that night.

That fight ended the greatest two-year stretch of my life. I had been doing all kinds of cool stuff. I was traveling around the world at other people's expense, winning fights and making more money than I ever dreamed possible. I had big cars, real estate, money in the bank, and a reputation as the face of my sport. The biggest promoter in boxing was making my fights. So why didn't I tell Jim then, in the middle of all that success, that I didn't love him and was unhappy with the way he was always trying to control me? Why didn't I just say I was tired of living a life of hiding who I really was from nearly everyone in my world and was ready to come out of the closet and move on?

I've asked myself those questions many times. What I know is a lot of women end up in situations similar to the one I was in. We stay out of fear, out of obligation, out of believing it's all we deserve. The brave ones don't stay, but would an openly gay female fighter in 1997 get the same chances I got if I wasn't hiding who I really was? I didn't know, but I hadn't seen anyone who did, and I wasn't about to risk it all to find out.

By this time, people in boxing and in television had begun to talk about Rijker. She was a former kickboxing champion from the Netherlands who had come to the United States and reeled off nine straight wins by the end of 1997. She was tall, strikingly attractive, and had a fantastic body, one that always made me wonder exactly how it was constructed.

By the middle of the year, I was often being asked about fighting her, because eight of her wins were by knockout, and she was being trained by one of the best trainers in the sport, Freddie Roach. Around that time, I was scheduled to fight Dora Webber, who had taken Rijker the distance. I was looking forward to it, but the fight never came off, and I ended up in the ring with DeShong the night Tyson bit off Holyfield's ear.

I did an interview at the time with the *Boston Globe* and told them honestly, "I don't mean to be arrogant but at the same time I don't think any of the other female boxers bring the same intensity and skill that Jim has taught me. I only get hit a lot because I'm careless. I take chances. That's my character and my style. I think that's what the crowd likes.

"The Weber fight will be a war. Dora is very durable and she can punch. She went the distance with Rijker, so I want to go out there and knock her out and show Rijker how it's done. Hopefully, that lifts us up in the fans' eyes.

"For the rest of my career, I will be in competitive fights. I want to fight the best. When I walk away, I don't want people to say, 'Christy was good but she didn't fight so-and-so.' If Rijker is a fight the public's interested in seeing I'm sure it will happen. I spoke to Don about it. He promised me it would be made. Bob Arum and Don King are both interested in making money."

So was I, and it appeared the way to make the most of it was to fight Rijker. Once she came along, I told Jim and Don over and over to make that fight. I never ran from her, because I knew we were both going to get paid big-time if it happened. In the end I signed to fight her twice, so people who say I didn't want to fight her have no idea what they're talking about. We didn't have to fight for a million dollars. By the end, I would have fought her for 100 bucks, but I don't believe she ever wanted to fight me.

She turned pro five days after my fight with Gogarty. Seven fights into her career, Arum added her onto an Oscar De La Hoya-Hector Camacho pay-per-view show in the fall of 1997 against DeShong. I'd just stopped DeShong three months earlier, and Rijker did the same in three rounds. Andrea was damaged goods by then, and I'd had a lot to do with that. But Lucia was a fresh face, the good-looking woman with the muscular body, and that seemed to fascinate people. She did look good. The only problem is boxing is not body building. How you look is a lot less important than how you fight.

People began accusing me of deflecting talk of the fight, but the truth is I never once said no. I did raise issues about how she looked, and how she got to look the way she looked, because I suspected she was on steroids. I couldn't prove it, because she wasn't willing to take a test, but what other woman fighter looked like that? No one I'd ever seen before or since.

At one point she met with both Don and Arum about signing a promotional deal and opted to go with Arum, which she had to know would make it a lot more difficult to make a fight between us because those two guys hated each other. They refused to do business together regardless of how much the public wanted their fighters to meet. They only did it when the money was so big they couldn't pass it up. Our fight would be big, but it wouldn't generate the kind of money those guys would have needed to agree to it.

One of Don's guys told me once that he was in the room when King and Lucia met to negotiate a promotional contract. When she left, Don turned to him and said, "This bitch don't want any part of Christy Martin. She don't want to fight."

Rijker later said that King wasn't offering her a fair deal. Certainly Don wasn't famous for that, but he did right by me, so why wouldn't he do the same with her to make the biggest fight in the history of women's boxing happen? He would have had both ends, so it wouldn't have mattered to him who won, which is how he liked to do business. To me, the only reason to sign with Arum was to avoid me.

I'd just made more than $300,000 in 1997 boxing for King and a lot more from the outside opportunities that kept coming my way, so I felt no pressure to fight her for money. But I needed a rival, and women's boxing needed a mega-fight, so when they anointed her, it was fine with me. What made it even better was for once we were both in the same weight class, junior welterweights.

I wanted to do it to prove I was the best. That's how I'm wired. If someone thinks otherwise, there's one way to settle it. But it seemed to me like all the people around her wanted to do was talk about fighting me, not sign to do it.

The more the media asked me about her, the angrier I got. She was supposed to be a very smart woman. If she was, then she knew she'd killed any chance of us fighting by signing with Arum, yet the media began blaming me for the fight not being made. It started to make me crazy when I'd read someone say I didn't want to fight her; and when I get crazy, I usually start saying things that are crazy. It's part of my "charm," I guess. I've learned to control that better, but I'm stuck with it, too. You are who you are.

One thing that was a driving force in my life—but also a weakness of mine for a long time—was if there were 100,000 people in a venue, and 95,000 were cheering for me, I heard the 5,000 who weren't. I tended to hear the negative more than the positive, which was one of the reasons Jim, and later Sherry, were able to manipulate me emotionally.

It's a character flaw, I'm sure. I've been working on it all my life. I've gotten a lot better about it, but it certainly made life more difficult for a long time. I'm not sure why dwelling on the negative was so much a part of my personality, but I think it's partly because I'm a perfectionist, and a perfectionist is never satisfied. That's all well and good in some areas of life, like inside a boxing ring, but you have to find a happy medium. I didn't have that ability during my boxing career, and really for much of my life, because there had been such a negative reaction to me and to women's boxing for so long. But I was part of the problem there, too.

I didn't just let the negative come to me. Oftentimes I was looking for it. And when you're always looking for something negative and expecting it, you'll find it, whether or not it's truly there.

It's true that for a while I said I wouldn't fight Lucia unless she took a chromosome test to prove she was actually a woman, but she was just so muscular and lean it was a legitimate thing to wonder about, in my opinion. If people didn't like it, or didn't understand it, or wanted to twist that into something else, I don't care. But people claiming I turned down $750,000 to fight her was, as usual in boxing, only half true.

We were offered a $1.5 million purse, but it came with a 50-50 split. I wasn't Don King smart on business, but I wasn't Gomer Pyle dumb either. She didn't have half the drawing power I had at that time. I would never have turned down three quarters of a million dollars under a normal 60-40 or 70-30 split, which would have been appropriate. I'd been carrying the sport for three or four years. She'd only had nine fights, and she thought she deserved purse parity? If I'd agreed to that, someone should have made me have a CAT scan. I'd been hit in the head a few times, but I could still count.

While all that talk was circulating, King didn't put me back in the ring for nearly nine months after the Acuna fight. When he finally did, I told him I could have had a baby between fights . . . which was never a consideration, in case you're wondering. I could sense things weren't quite the same now, but I'd anticipated that, so I wasn't too bothered. King ended up using me three times again in 1998, so once again I'd made more than $300,000 in purses alone.

I only fought in Las Vegas once, but I couldn't complain, especially when he scheduled a fight for me the week before Christmas in Fort Lauderdale, which was only a few hours' drive from my home near Orlando. I wasn't happy about the growing fascination the media had with Rijker, but I had knocked out my last two opponents and now was 36-1-2. I hadn't lost a fight in nine years when King matched me with Sumya Anani, who had a reputation that made a lot of people nervous. I wasn't one of them.

Two years earlier, in her fourth professional fight, Sumya put a girl named Katie Dallam in the hospital with severe brain injuries. Dallam was a novice who had gotten her boxing license only one day before the fight and never should have been matched with someone as strong as Anani, who was a former weight lifter and a more experienced fighter. That's not how you make your boxing debut if anyone cares about you.

It was a four-round fight, and they claimed Anani hit her in the head 119 times. I don't even know how that's possible without it being stopped long before 1:12 of the final round, but that's what happened. After the fight Dallam collapsed in her locker room and was rushed to a local hospital in St. Joseph, Missouri. She needed emergency brain surgery. It was a sad story but those things happen in boxing. It's why fighters say you play other sports, but nobody plays boxing. It's a potentially deadly endeavor, and we all know it and accept the consequences.

My friend in King's office, Donna Westrich, was worried. Maybe any normal person would have been, but your average, normal person wouldn't choose to get hit in the face for a living or want to hit someone else for a living either. Fighters think differently. We're wired differently. I didn't ever go into a fight thinking I was going to get hurt. We all know what can happen, but we dismiss it. Once a fighter has that fear in their mind, it's time to stay home. My only thought was she may have done that to someone else, but she couldn't do it to me.

The only thing I did was remind the referee, Tommy Kimmons, to watch her head, because Sumya was known for head butting. She could be like a billy goat if they let her get away with it. I knew Tommy pretty well, but that night he didn't listen, and I paid for it.

The fight was originally supposed to be in Las Vegas in August, but I got sick, and it had to be postponed. Don thought Jim put me up to that to get more money, but I would never get to a city and pull out. That's not me. I was legitimately sick, but we were already in Vegas, so Jim and I decided to go and watch the show anyway. That turned out to be a fight in itself after someone from Sumya's camp got up in my face, hollering that I was afraid to fight her.

He got the shock of his life when he found out he couldn't get away with that. I grabbed him around the throat and started pushing him backwards. A friend of Jim's, a guy named Nate Hallet who had been a college football player, grabbed me and pulled me away. I told him I was calmed down so he could let me go. He made the mistake of believing me, and the minute he put me down, I made a beeline back toward the guy. Scared of Anani? I wasn't scared of anybody in the ring, and I wanted this guy to know it. Nate scooped me up, and this time he literally carried me away.

So, there was already a little bad blood between us by the time the fight actually came around on December 18. That altercation in August set the tone for what became a long night for me. When I first entered the ring, I bounced around until I put myself right in front of the same guy I'd gone after before and gave him the choke sign. Then I just bounced off toward my corner feeling pretty pleased with myself.

It was one of those fights that was just brutal. I wasn't wasting much effort on defense, and she was stronger than I was and very aggressive from the outset. She landed some hard shots with her fists and harder ones with her head.

She butted me on my left cheek in the opening round, and it began to swell immediately. I told Jim in the corner between rounds that she'd got me with her head, but there wasn't much he could do about that.

As the fight progressed, I hurt her several times, but she was stronger than I was and stayed in close, which made most of the fight a toe-to-toe brawl. It also gave her ample opportunity to put her cornrows in my face. Kimmons didn't seem to notice until he finally warned her in the sixth round. By then I had a bruise on my right eyelid, both eyes were closing, and I was in trouble.

My face was taking a beating, and I knew the fight was close and I wasn't performing my best, but I kept attacking, and she kept using her head for more than thinking. To be fair, she also kept windmilling punches at me and landing plenty of them, especially once I began to have trouble seeing them coming through the slits my eyes had become. It was like peeking through the closed slats of window blinds, which means you're not going to see everything coming at you too clearly, if at all.

I needed to use my jab, and box more, but she made me fight her fight. Jim had no other strategy, and neither did I. I was used to being the one who put the pressure on, and this time she was doing it, and I didn't have a counter. I circled and used the jab some in the middle of the fight, but I didn't stick with it, and Jim didn't have any adjustments for me. He just kept looking at me between rounds like he was in shock.

Early in the fight she actually knocked me out on my feet for a second or two when she hit me solidly on the jaw. I fell back against the ropes and just blanked out. Fortunately, she came and hit me again, and I woke up. Damndest thing you ever felt. Who gets hit in the head and wakes up? Only a boxer. That kind of thing happens more than you might think in boxing. Maybe in life, too.

I just didn't have it that night, and I knew it, so before the 10th round I made a conscious decision. I made a gesture I knew people would eat up regardless of how things ended. I got up off my stool for the final round, exhausted and with my eyes half shut from swelling, and I kissed Jim in the corner and said, "I'm sorry." That was all bullshit.

It was good marketing on a bad night, and I understood that. I should have been thinking about her, but I wasn't. By that time our public life was a TV show for both of us, so I played it out. He knew it, too.

When they announced the decision, I thought maybe a draw would have been appropriate, but she got a majority decision. She won on two cards, and the third judge had it a draw. The thing I believed was in Florida if Don King wanted me to get a close decision, I would have gotten it. I saw Don sitting at the officials table during the fight, which is illegal. I'm not saying he did anything, but you didn't usually lose a close decision in the situation I was in. But I did.

It was my first loss in nine years, and I was really busted up. After the fight my cut man, Miguel Diaz, was putting ice on my face to keep the swelling down, and it hurt so much I finally told him I couldn't take it. I was halfway crying and didn't know if I'd ever want to fight again. Later I'd learn that's how you feel after you lose a tough fight, but it had been so long since I'd lost I wasn't really thinking straight.

This was one of those fights that changes you. You leave a little piece of yourself behind in that ring that you can never get back. It's how young fighters become old fighters. How many times can you go through something like that and still be the same? I wasn't too sure, but I knew it was less often than most fighters think.

After it was over a friend of mine brought me a McFlurry from McDonalds. The reason I remember it is she got stopped by a cop driving to the hotel and told him she was bringing me that McFlurry. He was a fight fan and he let her go. I may have lost, but at least my name still had a little cachet.

When we got back to our room, Jim didn't even stay with me. Maybe if I'd loved him that would have been enough for me to walk away from the relationship. But because I didn't, in a weird way it was excusable—except that he was also my trainer, and I expected my trainer to look out for me after taking that much punishment. At least I had my McFlurry.

We left the arena to go back to the hotel when I saw King as we were walking toward my car. I went up to him and said, "I promoted myself up to here. Now it's your turn."

That was pretty bold of me after a devastating loss like that, but I was hurting and half blind and didn't care. He just cackled that Don King laugh and said, "My champion! I still love you, baby! We'll be back."

Jim wasn't as encouraging. He had a look on his face that said more than words. It said, "What are we going to do now?"

I don't remember much being said. I was in a lot of pain, and mentally I felt terrible. I was busted up, not only on the outside but also on the inside. It was more than it being hard to accept losing. It was scary, because financially you didn't know where you'd be next. I kept wondering what Don was going to do now. Would he release me from my contract? Was Sumya going to become his new star female fighter? A lot of negative thoughts were running through my head.

By the time we got back to the hotel, my eyes were so swollen my dog wouldn't even play with me. He didn't recognize me. He hid in another room. I looked like a purple gargoyle. For a few days I did a lot of sleeping and pouting. All I had at that moment were my doubts, which always seemed to be lurking just below the surface, waiting for the chance to come out and torment me.

I wondered if I still had it, if I could really fight any more. Did I even want to? That was a good question. But before I could come up with an answer, Jim and I headed to West Virginia for Christmas.

While I was there, I went to see an eye doctor, because two weeks after the fight there was still blood in the whites of my eyes. He told me I'd be all right, but it would take time for my eyes to heal. That made me feel a little better, but my emotions were still pretty raw when we went to visit my dad's parents. One of my aunts, his sister Mary, kept asking to see my eyes, because I was wearing big, dark sunglasses everywhere I went.

Finally, I snapped, "For what? So you can go tell everyone you know how bad I look?"

The room went silent. I lowered my sunglasses so she could see my half-shut eyes. Then I turned, marched out the door, and walked home.

The only good thing that came from that loss was I forgot about Lucia for a while. I needed to take care of myself, and I began to. By the time I got back to Florida, I was over it and ready to get back into the gym.

I wasn't angry. I was just disappointed in myself. That fight—and the way some people acted after it was over—taught me an important lesson that applies not just to boxing, but often to all aspects of life. You win together, but you lose alone.

On Boxing

It's Not about Violence; It's about Self-Control

B oxing is the most misunderstood sport. People think the bell rings, and you just walk out there and fight like it's a barroom brawl, when it's really not like that at all. Not if you're well-trained and know what you're doing, at least. You train for years for it to not become what most people outside the ropes think it is.

Despite its elemental nature, boxing isn't really about violence. It's about harnessing your emotions and solving a puzzle. The puzzle is your opponent. Controlling your emotions is your problem, one you have to learn to master or you will never be successful. Inside the ring or out, uncontrolled emotions will doom you to a difficult life. They may even lead you to a place where you have lost all control of your environment, as happened to me and happens to victims of domestic violence every day.

To box successfully, you must learn to keep control of yourself under pressure and to gain control of your opponent and the real estate in which the two of you are working. This is true inside the ring and just as true in your home and in your life. For too long I didn't have control of anything but the 20-by-20-foot area inside those ropes. Maybe that's why I loved it in there so much.

To establish control in the ring, the boxer first has to control him- or herself. Then the boxer must find ways to control the terms of engagement and the distance in which the fight will be contested. Is it best to be in close to your opponent, or do you need to be on the outside, using your jab and movement to keep your opponent at bay? This you must determine and then execute a plan to make that your work space.

Last, you must control your opponent as much as possible. Make her go where you want her to go. Avoid situations that don't favor you. You determine when to fight and when to retreat. That's the kind of control you hope to establish.

For most of my 23 years in boxing, I had no control of my life outside the ring. Maybe that's part of the reason I was so aggressive inside it. This was the one place where I felt in charge of my life. For 30 minutes or so every few months, Christy Martin got to be in nearly total control of what would happen to her. I had that inside the ring, but I didn't have it anywhere else. That makes me angry to this day. Angry at myself for letting some of the things happen to me that happened. They happened because I was unable or unwilling to control my environment and do the things that were safe and best for me. Thankfully, I was finally able to change that in the years after Jim tried to murder me but, like learning how to box, it took time to learn how to live my best life.

When I climbed outside the ropes, Jim knew how to push my buttons. So did my mom, although to be fair maybe she didn't always realize what she was doing. The same was true with Sherry when she and I were together. They did to me what I did to most of my opponents. They controlled me.

Jim would create a sense of animosity toward my opponents by telling me they were all jealous of my success and that everyone in boxing hated me for it. He'd do the same thing in my private life, and slowly I lost control of who I was and who I wanted to be. I allowed myself to do things I didn't want to do and to become someone I knew I wasn't. When you lose that kind of control of yourself in boxing, you pay for it. When you lose that kind of control in life, you pay a higher price, which is why you have to stop that from happening however you can.

A journeyman named Randall "Tex" Cobb, who once went the distance with heavyweight champion Larry Holmes and paid dearly for doing so, described the difference between boxing and all other sports better than anyone I've ever heard. He said, "If you screw things up in tennis, its 15-love. If you screw things up in boxing, it's your ass!"

That, to me, is the dilemma of losing control of yourself, whether it is inside a boxing ring, inside your home, or inside your head. You have to maintain some control over your environment and your emotions to survive.

I started to box in Toughman contests for two reasons. People said I couldn't do it, or I shouldn't do it. That always motivated me. The more people said that, the more I thought, *"I'll show you."* That was the fuel for me at first.

As things got more serious, I felt I had developed good skills and wanted to show those skills to the world. I was learning how to solve this unique problem that an opponent poses inside a boxing ring. I loved training, because I loved mastering something as difficult and challenging as boxing. As time passed, I began to believe the ring was where I could be me.

I could be physical. I could be aggressive. I could be Christy without anyone saying, "But you're a girl." In the gym, after a while, I was just another fighter, and that's how I wanted it. I loved the atmosphere of the gym and the people who went there to learn what it takes to box. I still do. It was a safe haven for me. It was home.

Boxing became my only connection to who I really was. I didn't want anyone to know about my sexuality. In the ring, who I chose to love didn't matter. I didn't want them to know about my problems with Jim or my family, and in the ring, they didn't matter either. I just wanted to be a boxer. It became all that mattered to me.

Boxing gyms are really like little families. There are different people there with different personalities and from different backgrounds with different problems in life, but all of us are working toward the same goal. We're all trying to master a dangerous trade, and you learn to respect each other and appreciate each other's efforts.

In my mind, boxing is actually one way to break the cycle of uncontrolled violence in society, because it demands you control yourself no matter the circumstances or the pressures you're facing. It's about self-control, not acting like someone out of control.

There's an art to boxing, too. It's ballet with bruising added. A great journalist named A. J. Liebling used to write about the sport in, of all places, the *New Yorker* magazine back in the 1950s. He's considered one of the best writers who ever wrote about boxing, and that covers a lot of writers—from the ancient Roman poet Virgil to novelists like Ernest Hemingway, Norman Mailer, and Joyce Carol Oates, to a lot of very literate newspaper reporters. Liebling called boxing "the sweet science."

I don't know if it's exactly science, and I'm not sure how sweet it is, but I do know it was always chess in pink boxing trunks to me. It's the chess part that is so interesting and so hard to master. What you are trying to create in both disciplines—boxing and chess—is a scenario where your opponent thinks they have you when, in reality, you know you have them.

Patience is required to be a good boxer or chess player. Isn't that true in life, too? Impatience gets you into trouble. Patience works.

Most people may not see the connection between patience and boxing, but it's essential. You have to be patient to set traps, create openings, and lure your opponent onto unsafe ground while keeping yourself free from harm. The best hunters are patient. So are the best boxers. They'll both wait all day to land the perfect shot.

If you watch some of my fights on YouTube, you might not look at what I'm doing and have patience immediately come to mind, because I was always aggressive. I was always trying to put as much pressure on my opponent as I could so they'd make a quick mistake I could capitalize on and be out of there. I wasn't patient like the great pure boxers, but I always understood what I was trying to accomplish. I was patiently aggressive.

I won't sugarcoat what boxing is about. You don't find too many well-adjusted prizefighters. We all have our demons, something driving us to run toward pain when human nature says run away. That's usually a result of being broken somewhere deep inside. They say you don't find fighters sleeping in silk pajamas, and that's true. But you also don't find many fighters who weren't spawned out of some kind of dysfunction.

If you're normal, whatever that means, you're not likely to choose a sport that involves getting hit in the face. At least you won't choose it for long. You can't be totally normal and love to fight the way I did. That's just a simple fact.

In my case, I did have some inner rage over living a double life from the time I was 12 or 13 and first realized I was gay, and I needed an outlet to let those emotions loose. If I hadn't had to hide that and deal with all the tension and the psychological pain it caused me, maybe I would have ended up as a basketball coach or even a detective dealing with forensics, because that became an interest of mine. But it was in the boxing ring where I found the release I needed.

Looking back on it, my inner rage often spilled out at press conferences and weigh-ins, where I'd get into scuffles and say things I sometimes regretted. But in the ring the rage that fueled me was very controlled. I was aggressive, but I knew it didn't benefit me to get angry.

When you fight with my kind of aggression, it's pretty logical to assume there's some sort of rage inside you. In a twisted way the fight itself becomes an outlet, a legal place where you can lash out at how the world has made you feel about yourself. Inside those ropes you can develop a confidence in yourself you don't otherwise feel. You begin to believe you are more than you thought you were capable of being.

You might think you would ask yourself where that aggression comes from, but you don't. You already know. You know why you want to hit the person in front of you as hard as you can, and it usually has nothing to do with them. It's very seldom personal inside the ring. If it becomes that, it's probably not to your advantage.

A lot of controlling your emotions comes from your training. You train so hard and throw the same punches in different situations so many times that it becomes instinctual. You see the opening, and you react to it without thinking. See it. Hit it. See a punch coming. Slip it and fire back. It becomes just survival instinct once you're properly trained.

You see the scenarios, and you respond to the stimulus. If she does this, I'll do that. This is what to do if this happens. This is how to respond if that happens. When those situations actually appear, you don't think, *"Now I have to punch her in the ribs."* You just react to what you see.

That's why it takes so many years to develop into a good boxer. You have to put in the time and pay the price, and the price is quite often pain. Muhammad Ali once explained the process of becoming a fighter this way: "The fight is won or lost far away from witnesses—behind the lines, in the gym and out there on the road, long before I dance under those lights."

A fight is won by hard, consistent training, mastering self-control, and one more thing: the ability to accept pain as a consequence of the path you've chosen becomes essential. That applied to me inside the ring and out. People often ask me how you don't feel pain when someone hits you. The truth is at first you're like everyone else. You do feel it. When you first start out sparring, you get hit in the nose, and your eyes start to water. You feel that punch, and your mind reacts to it. You aren't in control of that part of yourself yet.

After a while, when you get hit like that, your eyes don't water any more. You get to the point where if you get hit, you don't think of what you're feeling as pain. Not when you're in the middle of it. Your body and mind get conditioned to being hit. You learn to accept what happened not as pain but as a problem to be solved.

The craziest thing is you don't really feel any pain until after the fight is over. As a fight goes on, and you get hit a bit, it ups your awareness and your concentration. It's like a lot of situations you face when you're being abused emotionally. You don't feel the real damage until later. You'd think a punch in the face would be different, but it's not. The pain comes later. I boxed for so long getting hit became normal. I never thought, "Wow! Do I really want to do this?" If you hit me, I wanted to hit you back. Frankly, I wanted to do all the hitting, but unfortunately it doesn't work like that too often.

Now, if a body shot is perfectly placed, that's a different story. A pain comes with that that is hard to describe, but there is nothing you can do when it happens. You go down involuntarily, because you can't breathe. Your mind is clear, but it feels like you may never breathe again, and you can't make your body work right. It only happened to me in sparring a couple of times, but it's a very frustrating feeling. Your mind is clear, but your body won't listen to you. It won't respond to your commands. It wants to sit it out for a while.

That feeling only lasts for 14 or 15 seconds, and then you're fine, but it only takes 10 seconds to be counted out. If a body shot hits you perfectly in the right spot, it is just not something you can be mentally trained to overcome. Fortunately, very few of them do; and the rest of them, a punch in the belly or on the ribs, you condition yourself to accept.

You learn not to fight the pain, because that's when you feel it. Instead, you tell yourself, "That was a good shot." You accept it as part of the job and move on, or you're not a fighter for very long.

Most people run away from pain. That's a natural survival instinct. Fighters, like firemen, run into the fire. We run toward the pain, which defies human nature, so you have to train yourself to do it. It's a matter of training yourself to be comfortable in uncomfortable circumstances. If you can learn how to do that in life, how to find a way to be controlled when you're in uncomfortable moments and let yourself see what's really happening, you can overcome anything.

Because of the hazards of the occupation, the boxer has to learn to face his fear. Fear is an emotion we all have to deal with. Fear is one of the common denominators in life. There is nobody who doesn't know fear. The question is, can you control it, or will you let it control you?

In my life, I did both. In the ring, I controlled it. Outside the ring, I let it control me until my life became chaotic. I submitted to my fears and the world's pressures and became lost for a long while. You don't have to do that. You don't have to remain that way. You can learn how to take care of yourself, and you don't have to become a boxer to do it. You just have to understand that being afraid in a bad situation is a normal emotion. It doesn't mean you're weak. It's what happens after you feel fear that defines who you are.

The old boxing trainer Cus D'Amato used to say, "The coward and the hero feel the same thing but the hero uses his fear, projects it on to his opponent, while the coward runs. It's the same thing, fear, but it's what you do with it that matters."

This is so true. A boxer sitting in the locker room as the clock is ticking down feels every emotion there is, including fear. Whether or not you think you can win, you know there is an opponent in another room who is waiting to try to damage you. To embarrass you. To beat you in the most physical, elemental way. You must face that reality and not try to hide from it, because soon it will be in front of you. You must deal with it or give in to it.

That is the same feeling a domestic violence victim feels. The difference is the boxer figures out how to control herself and solve the problem. Those of us who survive domestic violence must take the same approach. It may take longer than it should, but the survivors survive because they find the strength to face the truth of their situation and do what they must to escape it. The survivor becomes willing to face the fears of an unknown future and fight for themselves. It's not easy, but those of us who want to be survivors and not victims eventually find the strength to do it. It can be done, because it is done every day.

You may need help to win your fight, but so does the boxer. The boxer needs a trainer, cornermen, sometimes a good cut man to control the bleeding and the bruising. The boxer needs all of that, but in the end what the boxer needs most to win is control of his own fear and the will to face his problems with a clear mind. Not a fearless mind, because fear is a part of being human, but a clear mind. Don't lie to yourself. See your situation for what it is. It is what it is. Nothing more and nothing less.

Waiting for that moment when you're told its time to leave the dressing room is one of the worst parts of boxing. Before a fight, while I was sitting there acting all confident, underneath I kept asking myself, "Did you run enough? Did you spar enough? Did you prepare yourself hard enough?" I never cut corners in training. Even Jim gave me credit for that. But in those final minutes before someone knocks on the door, and it's time to head toward the ring, there's so much anxiety that you keep questioning whether you're ready for the challenge. This is normal. What you don't understand is the person in the other dressing room is feeling the same way you are.

When I fought on Tyson's cards, I always knew exactly when I was going on because it was early in the evening, but later in my career it was different. I was closer to being the headliner, so I fought later, which meant I had to wait longer. Waiting to act is the hardest part. Waiting to act is always more difficult than acting, which is something you come to understand.

When I was boxing, I never feared my opponent or getting hurt. I never thought about getting knocked out. What I was afraid of was the shame of losing. For me, losing meant I had to go back to reality. Boxing put me into a life that wasn't real to me—a life I never could have imagined once my career took off. I wasn't the real Christy when I was boxing. It was almost like I was a character in a movie. I was playing a role, which was easier than being who I really was; but if I lost, I'd have to go back to being just Christy from Itmann with all her problems. That was my fear, and it was a legitimate one, but never as big a problem as I let it become in my mind. The demons your imagination creates are always worse than the actual ones you have to face.

I never thought much about losing a basketball game. Not in the same way as I did a fight. I wanted to win just as much, but I wasn't upset as much if we lost a game except for my final one in high school. We lost the county championship, which meant we didn't go to state. That bothered me, but still not in the same way a loss in the ring bothered me. It was just so much more personal in boxing, I suppose, because I was alone in the ring. There are no teammates to share your defeat. There is no asking out because you need a break. It's just you and your problems, which are the fighter across the ring and the ones you create inside your head.

Once, when I was visiting the International Boxing Hall of Fame, I had the honor of meeting Floyd Patterson, who was an inductee, a former heavyweight champion, and a 1952 Olympic gold medalist. He was such a soft-spoken man you'd hardly think of him as a fighter.

Floyd was a very sensitive guy who had grown up a lonely, troubled child who ended up being sent to reform school in Upstate New York when he was 10 for perpetual truancy and petty theft. He said that saved his life, because there he learned how to box, and boxing became his way of expression. In some ways, the same was true for me.

He became a very popular fighter in New York to whom many writers took a liking. One of them was Gay Talese, a well-known journalist, novelist, and magazine essayist. Floyd once explained to Talese the fear fighters carry with them for an article in *Esquire* magazine. It was about as perfect an explanation of the fear of losing as I've ever heard.

"We are not afraid of getting hurt but we are afraid of losing," he told Talese. "Losing in the ring is like losing nowhere else. People who lose in business—get fired from their job or lose a client or get kicked upstairs—can still go down with some dignity and they might also blame their defeat on an ungrateful employer or on the unfair competition.

"But a prize fighter who gets knocked out or is badly outclassed suffers in a way he will never forget. He is beaten under the bright lights in front of thousands of witnesses who curse him and spit at him, and he knows that he is being watched, too, by many thousands more on television and in the movies, and he knows that the tax agents will soon visit him—they always try to get their share before he winds up flat broke—and the fighter cannot shift the blame for his defeat on his trainers or managers or anybody else, although if he won you can be sure that the trainers and managers would be taking bows. The losing fighter loses more than just his pride and the fight; he loses part of his future . . . and is one step closer to the slum he came from."

Those words come with a lot of thought and, I feel, from a lot of pain. He expressed what the boxer goes through so well. That is what fear is for most fighters, especially the accomplished ones. Everybody is scared in the locker room with one exception. The only boxer who isn't scared before a fight is the one who doesn't care anymore whether they win or lose.

Early in my career I never looked my opponent in the eyes when we'd come to the center of the ring for final instructions. I'd look down at their feet. I didn't want them to see any fear in my eyes. Your eyes don't lie. Later I would look them in the eye, and I could see whether they believed in themselves. The eyes will tell you everything you need to know about your opponent and yourself.

One fact about boxing is it's the loneliest sport ever invented. When the bell rings, everybody climbs out of the ring but you and your opponent. There's a referee in there, of course, but he's way off in the distance. So when you're standing in the corner waiting for that first bell to ring, it can feel like the most desolate place on the planet. Looking back on it, the only lonelier place was in my marriage.

What keeps you going is you've trained for this moment. Some fighters, the great ones like Sugar Ray Leonard or Marvin Hagler, were born for that moment. The rest of us have to learn how to deal with it, and that's where controlling your emotions comes in.

It's logical to assume if someone smacks you in the face, it will make you angry. In boxing, where that's what the sport is, you have to control that feeling most of all.

A boxer can't go into the ring angry. And you can't get angry if things start to go wrong, because that's when you make mistakes, and mistakes are fatal in boxing. What Tex Cobb said about the price of making mistakes in the ring is so true. It's the essence of the difference between boxers and other athletes. It's the level of risk the boxer is taking and what is at risk. In boxing, it's you who's at risk. It's not a goal, or a line, or a net, or a lost golf ball. It's your ass that's at risk. It's a beautiful description of the fighter's dilemma. It's your life that is at risk, and you're the one who has to take the actions necessary to save it, because you're worth it. Isn't that the same decision everyone who becomes a domestic violence victim must make? Are you worth saving? The answer is yes, you are.

You can't simply get angry about the predicament you're in. That won't solve your problem. You get angry, and you'll get hit a second time. Instead, you have to stay focused and figure out why you're getting hit. You have to think your way out of trouble.

Use your mind to solve the problem. Correct the mistake that allowed it to happen. That's boxing. It is problem solving, not violence.

I've noticed over the years that quite a few boxers play chess. Good chess players are sort of like good counterpunchers. They are illusionists. They make you think a move is leading to one thing when it's really trapping you in another direction entirely. It's seeing where things are headed before it's too late and acting to control the outcome. You can't just get angry because someone took your bishop and expose your queen just to get his bishop. Control the heat of emotion.

I wasn't a chess player or much of a counterpuncher. I wanted to take your king right away, but I was still a thinker. I was a more complicated boxer to fight than people outside the ropes realized. I was always looking to set you up and then make you pay dearly for your mistakes while trying to limit my own. It took me many years to do the same thing in life.

To be a successful boxer, I think you have to be two people. Certainly, I was. I still am. When I'm promoting a fight card or speaking at a fund-raising event for my foundation or for domestic violence awareness, I become "the coal miner's daughter," again. I'm walking around, shaking hands, thanking people for coming, telling them my survivor's story. Christy Salters from Itmann, West Virginia, could never do that. But Christy Martin the fighter? Sure can. I slip into a different persona.

It was the same when I was boxing, but even more so. It would start a week or so before the fight. I would become a real asshole as the fight got closer. I began to become someone who was coming to hurt my opponent. In real life, I'm not that person. Not at all. I don't want to hurt anyone. But when I walked out of the locker room and began to make my ring walk, I was someone else.

If you watch videos of my ring entrances, you can see the look on my face change as soon as the sound of "Coal Miner's Daughter" comes on. You can see it in my eyes. I could feel it inside as I moved down the aisle toward the ring up ahead.

When I'd see the arena dark, and those lights off in the middle of the building shining down on the ring, it fueled me. That was where I wanted to be. It was where I was fully alive, because it was the place where I felt I could show the world I was the best. I felt blessed to be in that position. I imagine it's what a Broadway actor or a great singer feels when they go on stage. You're there to shine, and you know you can, because you've prepared yourself for this moment.

You know why you're there. You know why those bright lights are shining on you. You know you're in the hurt business at that point. A fighter named Jimmy Doyle once died from injuries sustained in a fight with Sugar Ray Robinson. Robinson had tried to get out of the fight after having a dream the night before that Doyle would be badly injured, but the show had to go on.

After Doyle's passing, an inquest was held. During it the local coroner in Cleveland asked Robinson, "Did you intend to get Doyle in trouble?" Robinson replied, "It's my business to get him in trouble."

That's the other side of the boxing trade. Not the sweet science side. The hurt business side. A boxer's job is not to just touch the other person more times than they touch you. That's amateur boxing. Prizefighting is about pain. It's about how much you can dish out and how much you can take. That's the bargain you make when you decide to become a prizefighter. It was a bargain I was willing to make to win a fight. Isn't fighting to win over the pain in your life worth more?

Despite its harsh realities, I will always argue boxing is not about violence. It's about problem solving. My sole focus was to be rid of the problem in front of me. You're thinking in there all the time about that, not about hurting someone. It's not a brawl.

Inside the ring I felt like I was bulletproof, which, in a sense, I guess I've proven to be. Heading toward the ring, I became someone who didn't believe I could be hurt. I didn't believe I could be beaten. I believed I was willing to pay a higher price to win than you were. I knew I was in charge of myself, and that made me confident that I would react appropriately when the challenge came.

Once I left the locker room, I was not the same person I was in the rest of my life. I wanted to dominate. There are a lot of reasons for that, but I think the biggest was that outside the ring I was the one being dominated. By Jim in life, and by Don King on the business side, because he controlled my career and where it was headed. In the boxing ring I wasn't going to allow anyone to control me. No one was going to be free to give me a beatdown, physically or mentally. In there, no one was going to make me do anything I didn't want to do. At least that was my goal.

Outside the ropes I gave in to my fears for too long, but you don't have to. You can change that the same way I finally did. You don't have to become a boxer to do it. You just have to find the help you need and the willingness to fight for yourself.

That won't happen overnight, like you don't just run down the aisle and jump into a boxing ring. One thing every fighter has to face is the three steps you must climb to get into the ring. You're making a choice when you take those three steps. You're making a choice not to be part of the crowd below you. Not to be part of the world on the other side of the ropes. You're making a choice when you go up those steps to test yourself in a harsh environment.

Each step meant something different to me. You're a little brave if you can take that first step. You're a little braver, and maybe a little crazy, if you take the second. And the third step? If you take the third step and slip under those ropes, you're a little bit closer to finding out who you really are.

There are rules and a code of behavior inside the ring, but it is a warrior's code that would not be accepted by the outside world. Some look at boxing and see legalized assault and battery, but what the boxer sees is different. Boxers are willingly trapped inside four strands of rope with no exit door. They're in there facing their fears and their doubts, armed with a belief in their ability to survive. Once the bell rings, you control yourself, or you don't. Win or lose, you learn a lot about yourself.

Everything, really.

All Done with Don King, But Not with Fighting, Inside and Outside the Ring

It's been said that you learn more from losing than you do from winning. I've never really been convinced of that. Frankly, I'd rather be a blissfully ignorant winner than a smart loser, but I learned at least one thing from my first loss in nearly a decade. I learned that Christy Martin had more value in the marketplace than I thought.

Every successful athlete wants to be paid well. The more successful we are, the more we think we deserve. I was no different, except that unlike my male peers in boxing, I always feared that many of the people who ran the sport would have gladly discarded women fighters without a thought the first chance they got. Although a lot of fans supported me throughout my career, for a long time the people in power seemed to just wish I'd go away and take women's boxing with me.

So, imagine how surprised I was when someone from King's office called several months after I lost to Anani to tell me I was booked on a big card in Washington, D.C., on April 24, 1999. King had put together a show in which three boxers from D.C. would all be fighting in separate world title fights, and I would open the televised part of the show. I was glad to hear I was going back to work and happier still when Donna Westrich, who ran Don's KingVision pay-per-view operation, told me after the fight that the main reason I was on the card was the people at the MCI Center insisted on it. That was surprising to me and good to hear.

I was so ready to fight that night. I wanted to get the bitter taste of losing out of my mouth, and Don had given me a soft touch named Jovette Jackson, a young fighter with hardly any experience. When we came out for the first round, she put her hand out to tap gloves, and I drilled her with a right hand that dropped her. It wasn't exactly the best form of sportsmanship, but in boxing the referee instructs you to protect yourself at all times. She didn't, and she paid for it. She got up, and I hit her with about eight unanswered punches. The referee ran in there so hard to stop it that he knocked me down in the process.

I didn't care. The crowd was cheering wildly, and it gave me that same feeling I'd felt when I scored my first knockout in Toughman. It just lifted me up, but it didn't take Jim long to bring me back down.

Some people I knew from West Virginia were living in D.C., and they'd come to watch me fight. As I was walking back to my locker room, they tried to pull me up into the stands with them. I was ready to go, but Jim stepped in and ordered me not to even talk to them.

I tried to explain they were people I knew from home, but he wouldn't have it. He didn't care about them or me. I did what he told me to do and walked away, but it was a lousy thing to do. I was afraid for a long time that those people left the MCI Center thinking I'd gone "big-time" on them and blown them off. Once again, I'd done what someone else wanted me to do instead of what I knew was best for me.

Why did I do that that night? That's the kind of question I've asked myself off and on for a lot of years. Sometimes I have an answer, and all too often I don't. Either way, I still feel bad about it all these years later.

I fought once more in 1999, and this time I was back in Las Vegas at the Hilton. Julio Cesar Chavez was on the undercard, and he stole the show for all the wrong reasons. He was upset by a journeyman named Willie Wise and lost nearly every round in the process. I felt bad for him, because he was starting to fade, like all aging fighters do, but I was more concerned about my own opponent, a big, strong former kickboxer named Daniella Somers.

Early in the fight I thought I was doing all right until the crowd started booing. It was so loud I heard it in the middle of the round, which is unusual because normally you don't hear anything when you're in there boxing. Your focus is too sharp to notice crowd noise, but it was so loud you couldn't ignore it. It bothered me so much I felt I had to go for a knockout to please them, and I got one in the fifth round. I landed a right hand so hard it stunned her, and she turned her body away. She was out on her feet.

Somers ended up draped over the ropes with her back to me, and before I could move in and finish her, the referee had stopped the fight. It was only after it was over that I realized the crowd hadn't been booing us. The booing started because King had walked into the arena, which I found pretty funny.

Ever a bottom-line businessman, Don never seemed to care if the fans booed or cheered as long as they bought tickets. I wish I could say I felt the same, but I never did.

I was always trying to please someone. The crowd, Don, Jim, my family. I could be selfish and arrogant at times, but people pleasing was always a priority in my life, and that can wear you out. It eventually happened to me. But at this point of my career, I'd done it well enough in the boxing world that by the end of the following year I was on a five-fight win streak, and the World Boxing Association had named me Female Fighter of the Year. That allowed me to grab a small piece of another dream I'd carried for a long time.

There was a dinner in Philadelphia for the WBA's honorees, and a fight card was held as part of the weekend at a famous old venue called The Blue Horizon. The Blue was like a movie set of what people think a small fight club should be. It only had 1,346 seats. It was a classic, smoke-filled building perfect for boxing.

The balcony literally hung over the ring so it seemed like every fan was on top of the fighters. The place was always packed, and it was so loud in there that you would have thought 21,346 seats were filled with Philly fight fans. *Ring* magazine once voted it the number one boxing venue in the world, and *Sports Illustrated* called it the last great boxing venue in the United States. I surely would agree with both of them.

I used to see fights from there on television and always hoped I'd get to box at the Blue one day, but the man who promoted most of the matches there then was a guy named Russell Peltz. He was a great matchmaker, and he promoted more fights at the Blue than anyone else in boxing history. But he hated women's boxing. If there was one person he was not going to promote there, it was me, but that weekend all the honorees went, so he couldn't keep me out, even if he wanted to. Jim and my mom and dad went with me, and I was so excited to be in that building . . . until they introduced me.

When they did, most of the people cheered, but one section of fans just booed me like crazy. Being booed in front of my parents hurt. Whether or not people thought I could fight, I was giving boxing all I had, and I was representing the sport well. I never wanted anyone to put that "pioneer" label on me, but I certainly was one, and I didn't think I deserved to be booed. All you can do is try your best to be the best. I knew I was doing that but, as they say, haters gotta hate, and that night some of them in Philadelphia hated me.

You learn to get over things like that when you're in the public eye, but it's been more than 20 years, and I still remember what it felt like to be booed in front of my parents in a building where I'd dreamed of fighting. Maybe you don't quite get over everything, I guess.

A lot of good things happened during those years, though. One came when I was asked to do one of those "milk moustache" ads, one of the most popular print and television ad campaigns in history. It had been created for the California Milk Processors Board, and the advertising company that came up with the idea decided they'd have all these famous people wear a "milk moustache," the assumption being they'd gotten it drinking milk. The idea just took off. Today you'd say it went viral. The crazy thing for me was I didn't even like milk. Nobody asked me my opinion, though, and I didn't offer it up. They just wrote me a check, and I was happy to take it. I liked milk a little more after that.

If I recall it right, I got paid $20,000 up front, but I never actually did the ad. When I asked King's people why the photo was never taken, someone said "Christy, Don is only going to let you get so big." I have no idea if that's true. I never asked him about it, but the funny thing was when I got my check for the ad, I wrote Don a check for his percentage. His lawyer, a guy named Charlie Lomax, called me and said Don didn't know what to do with the check. He said no fighter had ever sent *him* a check. I don't know about that, but I figured I'd gotten the money because of him, so he should get his cut. Too bad they never took the picture.

The relationship between Jim and me at the time is hard to describe. We were together all the time in public but not all that much in private. He was out every night, and I wasn't venturing too far from my home in Florida except for training and public appearances. Despite the problems between us, we no longer argued much, so there was no physical threat. I understood there were boundaries, and I could pretty much do what I wanted as long as I stayed within them and didn't push the edges too hard.

Somehow, I stayed faithful to him the entire time we were married. Much of my time I was around only men, and I was all right with that. I always felt more comfortable hanging around with guys, and that's all Jim allowed in the gym anyway unless he brought someone in to spar with me, so it was easy. It was good, too, because if I was around a lot of women, either I'd feel uncomfortable because I wouldn't be interested in the things that interested them, or I might be attracted to one of them.

I didn't want to make someone feel uncomfortable, and I didn't want to do something to tip anyone off that maybe I was gay. Hiding who you are at the supermarket is hard. Hiding it in a locker room setting is harder. It involves a lot of mental gymnastics and denial and feeling sneaky, so it was just easier to stay home or with my boxing guys and Jim, which is mostly what I did.

When we first got married, I was still a little confused about my sexuality. For a time, I kept trying to figure out that part. Most people believe you're either gay or straight, and that's it, but it's often not that simple. At least not back then it wasn't. Deep inside I knew I was gay, but I spent a lot of years trying to figure out how I felt about that. It was exhausting.

When I chose to marry Jim, it had been more to save my family and my boxing career than to cover up a gay lifestyle. But the longer we were together, and the better I understood who I really was, the more it weighed on me. Part of the boxing sell for us was that I wasn't a gay woman athlete. I was a married woman trained and managed by her loving husband, so how could I be gay? By this time, I had no questions about my sexuality, so I limited situations that would leave me alone with women and concentrated on other aspects of my life.

Occasionally Jim and I would go out or to events together, such as the races at Daytona and things like that. People would often recognize me in those settings, because we'd had so many stories written about us in newspapers and general-interest magazines such as *People* and been seen on television so often. I always felt Jim resented it. I know he did for sure one time when we went to a rodeo in Florida.

It was like a country fair set up with the rodeo in one area and a midway with all kinds of games and food booths in another. We were walking along with some friends, and a guy in one of the booths said he could guess your weight and your age. Jim always thought he looked a lot younger than he was, so he started telling everyone how the guy would never be able to guess his age.

The man in the booth finally looks at him. Then he looks at me and back at Jim and says, "I don't know how old you are, but you're too old to be with her!"

I laughed my ass off, and so did everyone who was there, with the exception of my husband. By the standards of our relationship, that was a good night for me.

Every now and then, I'd get kind of a shock in public when someone famous would recognize me. It would remind me that I really was accomplishing some things I'd never dreamed possible. That feeling never came over me in the ring, because by now I expected to win, and I understood that I had become where the money was in women's boxing. It was things that happened outside of the ropes, like the time I saw a magazine interview with Charles Barkley, the Hall of Fame NBA basketball star. One of the questions he was asked was if he came back in his next life as a female athlete who would he want to be? He said, "Christy Martin." I was dumbfounded he even knew who I was.

By this point, for the most part notoriety wasn't really a problem for me anymore. Neither was money with the exception of one thing. My problem had become finding an opponent the public felt would be a big enough challenge that we could make big money together in the female version of a "Super Fight."

No matter how great a fighter you are, you need an opponent the world believes is your equal. Someone they think truly has a chance to beat you. That is how all great fighters are measured. Great as he was, even Muhammad Ali needed Joe Frazier to confirm his greatness by testing him in ways no one else could. I was still looking for that kind of opponent, but in the meantime, Don was paying me well every fight, and I kept picking up regular outside money that was adding up.

I fought three times for King in 2000, and I also got paid once just for shadowboxing. EA Sports decided to do a women's version of its popular boxing video game, and they paid me well to get involved. It was probably the easiest money I ever made in boxing.

I flew to Los Angeles for a taping, and they hooked me up with electrodes all over my body and had me throwing punches with a green screen behind me. There was a male fighter named Fernando Vargas there that day doing the same thing. He was a world champion already and none too friendly. I didn't bother to ask him what he thought of women's boxing. My guess was he wasn't onboard with it, and with all the phony rumors about how much money I was making, I could understand why. I see him around now, and we're cool with each other, but at the time he was pretty frosty to me.

Once one of King's fighters, a tough guy named Angel Manfredy, asked if it was true. A little nervously I said, "Is what true?" I figured here it comes. I'm out of the closet. Instead, he said, "You make $1 million a fight."

I burst out laughing and told him, "Trust and believe, I don't make anywhere near that. I damn sure am not making $1 million a fight."

When I asked where he heard that, he said someone in King's office told him. I never found out if that was King's way of driving a wedge between his fighters by paying some of them less than they wanted and then blaming me for it, or what was going on. I have no idea where the idea came from, but I know it created some jealousy among some of the fighters, both women and men, because they thought I was being paid a lot more than I was.

After Jim tried to kill me, I wondered about what Manfredy said. Was it just someone lying to Angel, or was I really getting money like that, and Jim was skimming it all those years? It's among a number of questions I'd love to ask Jim.

I actually wrote out a list of questions for him a few years ago. Part of me wants to have one last conversation with him. I don't know what I'm hoping for. I know he'll lie, but I feel I know him well enough that I'd be able to fish through his answers and get to the truth. Is that realistic? Probably not, but I have that list on my cell phone. It's always with me.

I told Deb Barra, one of the prosecutors in the case, that I wanted to go see Jim. She didn't think it was a good idea and asked why I'd give him the satisfaction of knowing he still occupied space in my head. I didn't really have a good answer.

I see her point, but then I think, what if I get a call one day saying he's dead, and I never asked those questions. I know I'd probably get his version of the truth, not the real truth. He's lied for so long he probably doesn't even know what the truth is anymore. Yet I still have questions for him, ones that will probably never be answered.

What I do know is at a minimum of $100,000 a fight, I was well paid, not just by women's standards, but by industry standards at the time. Even though my paydays couldn't compare to people like Mike Tyson or other top male stars like Oscar De La Hoya or Julio Cesar Chavez, I was earning more than a lot of men who were world champions. But why would anyone think I was making a million dollars a fight? Women had made some strides in the sport by the early 2000s, but nothing close to that, and I knew the only way it would change was if we could somehow make that fight with Rijker, which was still being talked about.

The situation between us had continued to percolate even after I lost to Anani, and it finally boiled over a few days before I was to fight at Caesars Palace on March 3, 2000. I was finishing up training in Las Vegas for a fight with a 21-year-old woman named Belinda Laracuente. She was 10 years younger than me and had put together a decent record, but I knew she couldn't punch as hard as I could. So I was confident about the outcome and excited to be on the show, because it was a pay-per-view card in which the main event was welterweight champion Felix Trinidad moving up from 147 pounds to 154 to face a young American Olympic gold medalist named David Reid, who held the WBA super-welterweight title even though he'd only had 14 professional fights.

Felix was very popular, and David had become an American hero after he came back from looking like he had no chance to win and knocked out heavily favored Cuban fighter Alfredo Duvergel with one punch in the final round of the gold medal fight. It was the only gold medal in boxing won by a United States fighter at the 1996 Olympics in Atlanta, and it led to Reid being called "the American dream."

Considering the popularity of both fighters, and the controversial fact that many felt Reid was too inexperienced to be facing someone as formidable as Trinidad, I knew the card would be widely watched, and appearing on it could only enhance my career. What I didn't expect was a fight before the fight would make bigger headlines for me.

To hype the Friday night show and drive up pay-per-view sales, King had David and me fly to Los Angeles for a public workout on February 28, the Monday before the fight. We'd train lightly and then do some interviews and fly right back to Vegas, which is a short hop. As it turned out, Rijker was also in Los Angeles waiting for me.

I went over to the LA Boxing Club with David, and who walks in wearing a big, floppy hat like she's trying to hide who she is? Lucia Rijker. One of the publicists working for King noticed her standing against the back wall and asked her when she was fighting next. He told me later she said, "In about five minutes."

Rich Marotta, a longtime Los Angeles television sportscaster, was also there. He knew Lucia and went up and asked her what she was doing there. Later he said she kind of smiled and told him, "You'll see."

As soon as I saw her, I started to get agitated. She wouldn't fight me, but she'd come to my workout? For what?

Next thing I knew she was in my face. She leaned in close to me but didn't say anything. I pushed her away, and then she sucker punched me. She hit me twice and then started pulling my hair, and I hit her back. I was screaming and calling her a bitch and a lot worse. Some of my guys jumped in, and we all ended up on the floor. I think it's fair to say I can be a little volatile at times, but this time it wasn't me starting anything. It was her.

After they got us apart, I kept screaming at her, and she just walked right over to Don and then out the door with a cut under her eye. At the time I believed either Don or Bob Arum put her up to it, but maybe it was all her idea. Regardless, we were the lead story on ESPN Sports Center that night, and I remember one of the broadcasters saying our fight had to be legitimate, because there weren't any cameras rolling when it happened. He had a point.

That made me laugh, but it also pissed me off, because when it came to boxing, there wasn't anything that wasn't legit about Christy Martin.

Later Lucia sent a writer named Katherine Dunn an e-mail about the whole incident. Dunn had just written a *New York Times Sunday Magazine* piece about her and women's boxing, and I guess they'd developed a friendship of some sort. Dunn wrote about the whole incident on a website titled "CyberBoxingZoneNews." If you Google it, you can still find it.

Dunn claimed Lucia had written her, saying, "Monday turned into a cowboy movie. I went to a public training session of Christy Martin and we ended up in a fist fight (not just with her but with her whole team). I got in some good shots but against all those guys it was pretty tough.

"This woman is an unfair player. She attacks me and then screams that I hit her, which I did as a reflex on her attack. And the media (channel 2-7-10 in Los Angeles) love her dirty mouth. Now she's calling me a steroid dyke. First she was calling me a man and now she's screaming dyke and more wonderful filthy stuff.

"I am really sorry that it had to go like this, but let me tell you that this is the dirtiest business that I have ever had to deal with."

Dunn said Marotta reported seeing Rijker whisper something in my ear, after which I pushed her and screamed at her, and Rijker "reacted" with a left hook. Dunn wrote that I'd tackled Lucia, and I later said on television that she'd sucker punched me and still couldn't put me down. I did say that . . . because it was true.

Lucia claimed I'd walked up to her and pushed her, and that's why she threw the first punch, which wasn't close to the truth, because I was in the middle of doing interviews with a bunch of reporters, and I sure wasn't going to walk away from them to go up to her. She came to me looking for exactly what she got.

Dunn quoted her in their e-mail exchange saying, "Afterwards I saw Don King and I shook his hand and said I was sorry. He said, "No you're not. You wanted this." And I said, "You know you're right. I did.'"

Dunn said Rijker told her, "I regret lowering myself to her level because it's not my style. But it happened. The fighter in me got challenged."

That last part was completely ridiculous. She's the one who came to my workout. She's the one who came up to me and got in my face. Like she told King, she got what she wanted . . . except for the punch in the face.

Initially Don thought it was great publicity, but later in the day he got pretty mad about it. He started to think Lucia had been trying to hurt his show on Friday in Vegas. In a sense, he was right.

That incident affected how I fought that night, because I hurt my right foot during the scuffle when my assistant trainer, Jeff Bailey, stepped on it. Jeff was a heavy guy, and after he stomped on my foot, it got really swollen. The problem with that was Laracuente was not only 10 years younger than me, but she was a runner. She had no interest in going toe to toe. She wanted to move all night, and she did it well. Not well enough to win, but well enough to claim after the fight, "I beat up the old lady."

Not hardly. I won on two of the judges' scorecards and the third had it a draw, but that was close enough for the Christy haters to come out of the woodwork claiming she'd been robbed. One of them, a promoter of women's fights named Rick Kulis, said at the time, "Once again the judges saw a payday not a fight. . . . Las Vegas is a money town and once they see a payday in the works they usually come down on the side of the cow with the milk. Tonight that cow was Martin, since they know Rijker is ready and both are willing. Belinda meant nothing to the Las Vegas crowd so goodbye Belinda."

Did he really call me a "cow?" Yes, he did. Imagine the firestorm if someone did that today?

Another of my critics wrote that the two women judges had voted for me, and the man voted for Laracuente. I had to remind him that Belinda was a woman, too. What the hell was he talking about?

Other people saw it differently. They saw me chasing a woman all night who didn't want to engage and punishing her to the body when I caught up to her. I was the one trying to make a fight of it. What Rick Kulis forgot to mention in his post-fight comments were two things: he promoted Belinda, and Rijker was the farthest thing from willing to fight me unless she could do it at a press conference.

Around this same time, Lucia left Arum, claiming he'd "decided he enjoys chick boxing (a reference to his having signed the former Playboy model Mia St. John) more than women's boxing." To be fair, she had a point. Arum was more about the spectacle than the fight, and he became fixated on showcasing Mia over Lucia, even though Lucia was by far the better fighter. That says more about Bob's mind-set when it came to women's boxing than it does about Lucia or Mia, especially because he often paired Mia on cards with Butterbean Esch, the 340-pound four-round fighter I first met back in my Toughman contest days.

Lucia said she'd left to find a promoter who believed in women's boxing, but instead of signing with the guy who was paying the biggest paydays in history to a woman fighter, she signed a four-fight deal with a company called

America Presents. If she really wanted to fight me, she was doing all she could from a business standpoint to prevent it.

By the time we had our confrontation in LA, she had begun to fade from view to a great extent. Her last fight had been in August 1999 and, as things turned out, she wouldn't fight again until February 2002. She'd stopped a girl named Diana Dutra, who was nothing special, and came away with a bloody nose and, I was told, a broken eardrum. She backed out of a fight a few months later and seemed to me to have become a reluctant warrior.

Everyone in boxing wanted me to test her, or for her to finish me, depending on which camp you were in. That makes for an exciting promotion and a big event. I was 31. She was a fresh face. That's the classic boxing matchup. It was also the first time in boxing history that a woman's match was really being talked about. If you're a fighter, that's the kind of test you live for. If you're not, you don't fight for two and a half years.

Fighters all have layoffs, injuries, and periods where they just can't get a fight. I understand that. But I find it interesting that at the same time people kept saying she wanted to fight me so badly, and I allegedly was avoiding her, I was the only one who was actually doing any fighting.

Rijker was 14-0 with 13 knockouts against essentially nobody when she walked into that press conference and ended up on the ground. Then she didn't fight for two and a half years. Meanwhile, I won five straight fights over the next 18 months after our run-in. Who didn't want to fight?

I was not only still winning, but King was giving me some bigger paydays. Although I liked the money, it was secondary to me. Not to Jim, but to me. I don't mean to suggest it was meaningless to me, because it wasn't, but I just didn't think all that much about it.

I knew the money was rolling in, and when it does a fighter seldom thinks it's going to stop one day, because all your life there's always been another fight somewhere. The future never seems farther away than your next boxing match, and there'll always be a next one, right? Wrong.

That kind of thinking, or lack of thinking, was never more obvious than after I won a majority decision from Kathy Collins at Madison Square Garden in 2001. I actually thought I might have another night like the Gogarty fight because Kathy was tough, had skills and a good record, and was from Long Island, so she had a lot of local support. I thought she'd bring a lot of energy to the fight, but it turned out it wasn't close.

The one thing I was worried about was that Larry Hazzard Jr. was one of the judges. I knew my contract with Don was fixing to run out at the end of the year, and I thought he might try to influence Hazzard's judging to get me beat. So, when I heard "majority decision," I thought Don had gotten to the judges and stolen the fight. But Larry had me winning big, 98-92, and so did Tom Kaczmerck, who gives seminars on how to judge fights to commissions all over the country. He had it 97-93. The third guy called it a draw. How can two judges have you winning big and the third see a totally different fight? I'll never understand judging, and the fans don't seem to either, but in that case two had me winning seven and eight of the 10 rounds while the third had it split, 5-5. I think somebody needed an eye test that night, and it wasn't me.

The card was on HBO pay-per-view, and I was part of the televised portion, which was another first for me. I had become the first woman to box on HBO, which at that time was the biggest name in televised boxing, although technically they could say I hadn't, because this was not part of their regular premium cable shows.

I learned later there was a split among some of the executives at HBO Sports. Some wanted to put me on as the most popular woman fighter in the world, but others wanted nothing to do with women's boxing. They felt the competition was too uneven and not up to their standards. Sure, there were some problems with some women's matches, but HBO still televised a lot of mismatches in the 45 years it broadcast boxing. And they weren't in women's fights, because for years they refused to put a woman on their network.

HBO didn't televise a woman's boxing match on its regular air until May 6, 2018. Seven months later two women's fights would headline the final boxing broadcast on HBO. By then, they were no longer the industry leader, but at least after 45 years, 865 fighters, 1,116 fights, and 9,447 rounds, HBO had discovered women's boxing. It was 29 years after my first professional fight.

By the end of 2001, I was tired in the way you get at 33 after 47 professional fights and a dozen years fighting the lords of my sport and the man living in my house. I was tired in a way you aren't when your 23 and starting out; but even though I was tired, I was still anxious to continue showcasing my talent. Don had paid me $250,000 for the Collins fight seven months before my contract was going to run out, so I figured if he didn't want to keep me, what sense did it make to pay me like that?

A month or two before that fight I received the kind of news that can change how you think about money. I received my monthly bank statement and when I opened it up it said I had more than $1.1 *million* in my account! That was a wow moment for sure. Everything we owned was paid for. My house, our cars, and the gym we owned in Apopka. We owned everything we had, and I was still fighting for Don. I felt, no matter what, I should be OK.

I figured if you have no mortgage, and your cars are paid off you, can work at Wal-Mart and pay your living expenses. We'd moved to Apopka right after the Gogarty fight in 1996, and by the end of 1998 my house was completely paid off thanks to boxing. Now I'd just earned a quarter of a million more in one night on top of that $1.1 million in the bank. So why complain?

The truth of it was Don had paid me that $250,000 because he owed me $100,000 or so from a fight he'd shorted me on the year before. I had a guaranteed number of fights a year at a minimum $100,000 each that he had to make for me, and he'd missed one, so it wasn't like he was giving me a raise. But there are always two sides to things, as there were in this case.

He owed me the money, but he didn't really have to pay it, because what was I going to do? Sue the most powerful promoter in boxing? No, I wasn't, and Don knew that. I wouldn't say he paid me $250,000 out of the goodness of his heart or to make things easier to negotiate a new deal with me, but I also have to admit he really didn't have to do anything but pay me that $100,000 minimum for Collins. Legally, I had a right to the extra money but was I in a position to sue Don King? Only if I didn't want to fight any more.

Obviously, I should have been paying more attention to the business side of my career, but I thought that was Jim's job. And, to be honest, maybe I just didn't want to take on the responsibility for that side of boxing, too. It was easier to just be an athlete, train and fight, and let somebody else worry about the business of boxing. I know that was both unwise and somewhat irresponsible, because you have to take care of your own business in life. You have to be responsible for yourself, but after the Collins fight, I even left the Garden without picking up my check.

We went back to my hotel to celebrate and I finally asked if anybody had it. A quarter of a million dollars, and I don't know who has my check? It's crazy to even think about now. I'd forgotten all about it, but Jim hadn't. He had it in his pocket.

That same week an old fear that was always in the back of my mind resurfaced. We were staying in a very nice hotel in Manhattan and a friend called me and told me that a big story was about to come out about me in the National Enquirer. I was immediately scared to death. I knew this was it. It was all going to come out about my sexuality and my phony marriage, and my career was going to disappear. I was convinced that this was not another positive story about the rise of the coal miner's daughter.

I was worried all night, but it turned out that's exactly what it was. Just another story about a Christy Martin who only existed in people's minds and PR executives' imaginations. I was never happier to read a story than I was reading that one.

Even though behind the scenes things were coming to an end for me and King, I didn't even know we were having contract issues. I knew there were arguments over money, but that's pretty common in professional sports. It had been more than eight years that Don and I had been working together, and I was still winning and still getting a lot of media interest. I knew the contract was running out at the end of 2001, but I never thought I wouldn't sign another one with Don. I was sure I was going to finish my career as a Don King fighter.

At the time I was pushing him to make a fight for me with Laila Ali, Muhammad Ali's daughter, who was becoming a hot commodity. I kept thinking Don would eventually do that fight, because he'd promoted so many of Muhammad's biggest fights that it seemed like a natural.

I was sure we'd come up with some sort of agreement, but I should have known something was up after the Somers fight near the end of 1999. That's when Jim first came to me in our house in Florida with a very strange suggestion, even by his weird standards. He acted like he was asking if I wanted steak for dinner when he said he had an idea for me.

I said OK, and he looked at me funny and blurted out, "Would you sleep with Don King for a million dollars?"

I went out of my mind because I realized immediately he was serious. I'd done a lot of things by then that I wished I hadn't, but is my husband really asking me if I'll have sex with my promoter for a million dollars? It was hard to believe what I was hearing.

Even after Jim realized how mad I was, he didn't try to say he was kidding or just teasing. He brought it up a few other times, but that was the only time I really felt he was serious. To have your husband—even in as twisted a relationship as we had—say something like that is pretty stunning. If he'd said Don wouldn't renew my contract unless I slept with him, I would never have done it, but at least that would have been something I could understand. But it wasn't presented like that.

The reality is Jim was always pimping me out the entire time we were together. Pimping me out to promoters to fight and bleed on their shows. Pimping me out to guys who wanted to box me in hotel rooms for weird reasons. He was always selling my body in one way or the other.

Don did try to proposition me once in Venezuela at a WBA function, but we laugh about it now. As the #MeToo Generation is making clear today, that kind of stuff in the workplace is hardly new.

We were at a function. I asked him to go into another room, because I needed to talk to him, and he came on to me. After he made his pitch, I laughed and told him I only wanted to fight my way to the top. He started cackling and said, "You're already at the top!" Then he came to hug me and poured his drink down the back of my dress.

It didn't offend me. I didn't feel like he was pressuring me or threatening me. It was just the kind of stuff women have had to face in the workplace for too long. It seems like that's finally changing, and it's a welcome change. It's also a hell of a lot different when it's your husband who brings it up, I'll tell you that.

I didn't value myself a lot then outside of a boxing ring, but I wasn't about to devalue myself in that way. Don and I were talking recently about my helping him with a promotion in Florida. He reminded me I'd said if he ever tried that again, I'd tell my dad, and he might kill him. We got a laugh out of that, but it's interesting I didn't say "my husband."

As it turned out my last fight for Don came on November 17, 2001, back in Las Vegas at the Mandalay Bay casino. It was against Lisa Holewyne, a woman I didn't know but who would become a major part of my life some years later when she became my wife.

Yes, I actually fought my future wife. I'd seen about a 45-second video of her knocking somebody out with a straight right hand, which was something I was vulnerable to, so I asked King's people why they would want me to fight someone like her.

I knew that this was the last fight on my contract. I wasn't sure if that meant it would be my last fight promoted by Don, but I did fear that he would have already re-signed me if he still wanted me, so I was feeling kind of uneasy. I kept asking Jim what was going on and why they wanted me to fight someone whose best punch was the one that gave me the most trouble. He didn't have any answers.

At the weigh-in Lisa said, "Good luck, Martin." As usual before a fight I was pretty surly and overreacted and said, "Good luck getting knocked the fuck out!" She looked at me like I was crazy, which I was at the time.

I took her saying "good luck" as being arrogant, like she thought I needed luck to beat her. The truth was all she meant by it was a sportsmanship-like thing. To me at that time, my reaction was normal. I had to win. I see now that maybe it wasn't as normal as I thought.

The beautiful part about the fight was for once I didn't go out there and just try to pressure her and go for the knockout. She expected me to come out very aggressively as usual, but I didn't. I outboxed her for ten rounds.

One judge gave me nine of the 10 rounds, and the other two gave me eight. I like to tease Lisa about that because she was supposed to be the boxer, not me. She was a very good boxer, so good she was inducted into the Women's Boxing Hall of Fame, but that night I was better.

Looking back, I think I could have boxed like that a lot of times, but too often I trusted my chin. I just wanted to try to land the big punches to please the crowd, and I was willing to get hit to do it. When I look back on my life today, I realize that was a choice I often made outside the ring, too.

I always had a hard time transitioning from offense to defense and back to offense smoothly. I usually had to do one thing or the other. Most of the time, I chose offense. That was my personality. Offense sells. It hadn't taken me long to realize that.

After my fight with Lisa, I was 44-2-2 and had two possible big fights on the horizon with Laila and Rijker. People were actually talking about a woman's fight so important it could sell tickets on its own.

Showtime's boxing analyst in those days was a former light heavyweight champion named Bobby Czyz. Every time I fought, it seemed he'd bring up Rijker at some point and say my career would never be complete until I fought her. He implied I was the one preventing it from happening. Bobby Czyz knew boxing, but he had no clue why that fight wasn't getting made.

Despite that kind of constant criticism from some corners, at least people in boxing were talking about two women in a potential big fight. That had never happened before. There were two fights the public wanted to see and were ready to pay to watch. My name was on top in both of them, so I figured I'd just wait to hear from Don about a new contract. Maybe he'd make me sit for a while, but I was sure he'd call.

Twenty years later I'm still waiting.

Down for the Count and Ashamed of How I Got There

There have been a lot of turning points in my life, and it's clear one of them was no longer boxing for Don King. When I would climb into the ring knowing he was my promoter, I felt like I was carrying his reputation with me, so I had to perform. It gave me an edge that I lost after I was back on my own and having to fight not only in the ring but outside it as well just to get a chance to climb back in.

Jim knew long before I did that we were done with Don. I don't know how he knew or what he knew, but he started trying to sell me on the idea we had other opportunities and didn't need Don any more. He kept talking about big fights with Rijker, Mia St. John, and Laila Ali being available, and he halfway convinced me we'd be all right and make a lot more money on our purses. Our purses? Who was hitting him for the money?

I wanted to believe it was all true, but I never totally did. Suddenly Jim thought he was a lot smarter businessman than he was, and I didn't share his inflated view of his business acumen. He figured being a free agent, we would be able to go in any direction we wanted unencumbered by contractual obligations. I went along with it, but I wasn't comfortable with the idea, not that Jim ever asked my opinion. He just did what he wanted, and I followed.

Maybe I was the most popular female fighter in the world, but I knew that was not that big a deal outside of boxing circles. I was well known and living a remarkable public life, but the truth was I'd never been the main event on any of Don's cards. I was always underneath Tyson or Chavez or Trinidad or one of his other main event fighters. I understood what that meant, but I wasn't sure Jim did.

We were back rolling the dice, but I wasn't a 22-year-old kid any more. I was a 34-year-old fighter with a lot of mileage on my body and my mind. Starting over is scarier than starting out, because now you know how long the climb can be to the top and what you have to do sometimes to get there. At the end of the day, though, I only had two choices: quit or do what I had to do, and I was never too good at quitting. The fact of the matter was Don King wasn't walking through my door with a new contract. It was time to move on.

Once we split, it felt like I'd fallen from grace. I thought I might have blown my career, because I wasn't going to be on the biggest cards in boxing any more. Fighting for Don King at that time was like having the Good Housekeeping Seal of Approval. The best promoter in boxing wants the best fighters, so if I was fighting for him, by definition I was one of those great fighters. Now who was I?

I fought 27 times for Don in eight years. I made several million dollars, was on the cover of *Sports Illustrated*, won two world championships and worldwide recognition as the No. 1 female fighter in the world and was seen by millions of people on Showtime and on pay-per-view. I would fight 11 more times after we split, but it would take me a decade to do it. I never again signed a multiyear contract with any promoter. The worm had begun to turn.

For more than eight months, I didn't fight, but Jim kept talking with various smaller promoters, including a guy named Peter Klamka, who I believe had been promoting beauty pageants before he got involved in boxing. That was about right, because he was now promoting Mia St. John, who was trading more on her looks and her time as a Playboy model than she was on her boxing skill. She may have thought a fight with me was about a boxing match, but the truth is it had less to do with boxing and more to do with everything I had tried to avoid since the first day I turned professional.

Mia didn't start boxing until she was 29, but after Arum signed her, he began billing her as "the queen of the four rounders." It was the same approach he'd taken with Butterbean, the 340-pound "king of the four rounders." He often put them together on the same cards, like a circus act. I've been told Mia hated that, and by 2001 she'd left Arum and begun managing herself.

She also started being trained by Robert Garcia, who was a former junior lightweight champion who knew what he was doing. He'd made her better, but we were still not on the same level. What we shared was the fact we were two women fighters at the same point in our careers. We were both on our own and looking to cash in on our name and reputation, so from that point of view the fight made sense.

I felt this was an easy one for me. I had far more experience and was a much bigger puncher and better boxer than Mia. The fight was the most money for the least risk, because in my mind the only risks for me were getting hit by a bus on the way to the arena and Jim's dealings with an unknown promoter.

Every time I thought we had a date and a venue, something seemed to go sideways, and it didn't happen. Mia and I were both promotional free agents, so in theory it should have been easy to make a deal, but Klamka never seemed to come through. He kept saying he was taking it to a different city for a bigger site fee or whatever, and Jim bought into all the crazy stuff he was feeding us about how much we'd make. Me, being the naturally negative person I was, thought it would never happen, and that began to affect my training. The fact I didn't take her seriously as a fighter only made that part of it worse.

Mia and Klamka did finally bring us a deal to fight on December 6, 2002, at the Silverdome, outside of Detroit. I was to be paid $300,000, which was bigger than any payday I'd gotten from Don. It sounded good, but my cut man, wise old Miguel Diaz, warned me I couldn't go into a fight like that with someone we didn't know without a guarantee in writing, so I asked Jim to be sure to get me a letter of credit to ensure my purse.

It was simply good business when you're dealing with a promoter who had no track record in boxing, but Jim never got it. We argued over it almost daily, but Jim never got me the protection I needed. I eventually assumed it was taken care of, and in a sense, it was. Mia got a letter of credit for her purse. All I got was a worthless contract and a date to fight.

I knew there were problems as soon as we checked into our hotel and the girl at the reception desk recognized me. Normally that would be a good thing, but she said, "You're Christy Martin! What are you doing here?"

The host hotel for the fight didn't know what I was doing there? If they didn't know, who did? The answer was not many paying customers.

In the weeks leading up to the fight, there were a lot of rumblings that it wasn't going to come off, and that affected my preparation. I was unfocused and only did 13 rounds of sparring. That was a bad omen and a bad business practice for a prizefighter.

I don't think I had two good weeks of training, but I figured it wouldn't matter, because the fight wasn't likely to happen. If somehow it did, I didn't see any way she could beat me. That's not the right way to prepare for a fight where everyone is expecting you to knock the girl out in a hurry.

I'd been out of the ring for more than a year, and Jim and I were arguing more and more, especially once I found out we didn't have that letter of credit. I'd asked him for a divorce several times by then and even tried to convince him he could still train and manage me if he agreed, but he refused to even consider it. I wasn't bold enough to just up and leave on my own.

Jim still had a lot of psychological control over me. I wasn't going to move out of the house I'd bought and paid for and risk losing it. I wanted him to leave me, but he wouldn't, and I couldn't get out of my head how he'd threatened so many times to kill me if I left him. So, I stayed.

I was tired of being bossed around. I was tired of training for what seemed like a nonexistent fight. I was tired of feeling like a prisoner in a cell. I could only go so far forward before I ran into the walls Jim had put up around me. The only positive thing I had was working with some young amateur kids and a few young pros in my gym in Apopka, which I loved being part of. Still, I stayed.

By the week of the fight, Klamka was laying the groundwork not to pay me. Tickets weren't moving, so he and Jim wanted me to appear at a strip joint to try to get some publicity for the fight. I didn't have to take my clothes off, just try to convince the men in there to come and watch a fight between a Playboy model and "the coal miner's daughter." I refused.

Jim was furious, and we got into quite an argument over it, but I was not going to do any more of that kind of stuff. The promoter claimed I'd refused to do media for the fight, which wasn't true. Mia and I had done a lot of appearances and interviews to promote the show together, and I actually had come to enjoy being around her. The only thing I'd refused to do was appear at that strip joint, but I could see what was coming. Klamka was going to use that to say I'd voided my contract.

I thought about not fighting, but Klamka told me if I didn't, I'd get sued, and Lucia would step in and fight Mia. I knew she was in Detroit already, and I wasn't about to let that happen. A few days before the fight, I realized I was probably fighting for nothing. But I also realized if I refused to fight, it would be a bigger problem than if I went through with it and got stiffed. I figured we might get paid if I fought, but we'd never get paid if I didn't.

I'd convinced myself this was going to be so easy I would knock Mia out with a body shot. That was total arrogance on my part, the idea that I'd show her I didn't even have to hit her in the head to knock her out. Considering that I was coming off a 13-month layoff, had barely trained, wasn't getting paid, and wasn't thinking like a professional by respecting my opponent, it was no surprise I didn't fight well.

The night of the fight it was so freaking cold I couldn't believe it. I was freezing all week, and when we left for the Silverdome, it was 22 degrees. It felt like Antarctica to someone who had been living in Florida for years. When we got to the building, I don't think there were 200 people inside this massive NFL football stadium. They could have introduced everybody in the crowd, not just the fighters, and it wouldn't have delayed the start. In one night, I'd learned the difference between having Don King in my corner and having no one. It was a depressing atmosphere, and that did nothing to improve my mood.

I rocked her early, but she was tougher than I expected, and she fought back. I beat the dog out of her, but she went toe to toe with me a few times. Garcia had taught her how to cover up and hold so she could survive. I knew Rijker was sitting at ringside watching, and I wanted to knock Mia right into her lap, which is no way to box effectively. Knockouts come from execution and timing, not by running in and throwing wild punches. But as the rounds passed and my frustration grew, that's exactly what I began to do.

I won a 10-round decision and barely broke a sweat. No bleeding that night. One judge gave me 9 of the 10 rounds, and the other two gave me seven. It was a lopsided victory, but because I hadn't knocked her out, a lot of people believed I was no longer who I'd once been. The fact she went the distance was taken as a sign I was slipping.

I didn't see it that way, but I was disappointed with myself. I knew people expected a lot more from me than I'd delivered. I was still bothered that Jim hadn't protected my purse, too, but by this stage the mental beatdowns in my life had brought me to a point where I wasn't as likely to stay angry about things as I once had been. I was more worn down than I was mad, especially after my accountant told me not to worry too much about it, because I was making more money in interest than a lot of people earned working.

I have to give Mia credit for being a better businesswoman than I was. She made sure she was covered. I was the bigger name, but in the end Klamka refused to pay me, and because I had no letter of credit, the Michigan Boxing Commission told me I'd have to sue him if I wanted my money.

By Monday morning a lawsuit was already starting. One fight after leaving King, and I hadn't gotten paid a nickel and was suing the promoter. It took a year of legal battles before we eventually went to arbitration, and I settled for around $110,000 or $115,000. You get to the point where you just take what's on the table and move on, because between the attorney's fees and going to Detroit to argue about it it was costing me more than it was worth.

That was the beginning of a downward spiral in my life, although I didn't know it yet. All I was fixated on was getting back in the ring and showing my critics I still was the fighter I'd always been. I knew who I wanted to prove that against. I wanted Muhammad Ali's daughter for the same reason I'd agreed to fight Mia. That's where the money was, even though there was an obvious problem that was evident from the start: Laila was three weight classes bigger than me.

I was fighting at between 140 and 147 pounds. Laila was six inches taller and outweighed me by at least 20 pounds. In boxing, that kind of size difference is a huge disadvantage for the smaller fighter. I don't care who you are, you don't just jump up 20 pounds and give up nearly seven inches in reach (arm length) without consequences, but I hadn't worried much about consequences all my life, so why would I start now with nearly a half million dollars on the table?

Laila didn't have her first professional fight until she was 22 and publicly said that her inspiration to box had come from watching me on a Tyson under-card on television, not from watching her father. She was four years old when her dad fought for the final time, so all she really knew about his boxing career was what she'd read or seen in old fight films. He wasn't totally damaged yet from Parkinson's disease the way he would become later, so she didn't really understand the hurt this sport could put on you until she'd already committed to doing it.

Like most dads, Muhammad was opposed to the idea of his daughter boxing when Laila first brought it up. But she ignored his pleadings and, I guess you could say, followed the path I'd blazed into an unforgiving sport. By the time we agreed to face each other on August 23, 2003, she was 15-0 with 13 knockouts and at 25 was viewed as the young lioness of boxing. No one had to tell me who the old lioness in the female pride of the sport was. It was 35-year-old me.

A young guy named Brian Young brought us the deal. He had a company called Prize Fight and had become a hot promoter for a little minute. He and Laila's husband at the time, former light heavyweight champion Johnny "Ya-Ya" McClain, put it together. But it had first begun being talked about not long after Laila beat Joe Frazier's daughter, Jackie, a couple of years earlier.

Laila was athletic, but she didn't really know how to box at that stage, and at first, I disrespected her a lot. I thought she was just living off her daddy's name. But as time went on, she went to the gym and hired Roger Mayweather, Floyd Mayweather's uncle and a former world champion himself, to train her. Roger was hard-core boxing, and she worked hard to learn how to fight. I knew she could get a fight with just about anyone because of her name without spending much time training, but she was working hard at it, and I came to respect her for that.

I'm a fan of Joe Frazier, who was her father's great rival. His style of boxing was my style of boxing. Come in hard and fast and be willing to pay any price to do some damage. I liked Ali, too, but not the way I liked Joe, so the media played up that angle, although there was another angle they made more of.

My dad had volunteered for the Vietnam War. Her dad fought the draft and beat it. I didn't begrudge him that, and I don't think my dad did either, but it became one of the issues during the promotion because it would sell tickets.

I had one of my dad's army patches sewn onto my trunks with his name, Salters, underneath it. At the same time, I had the utmost respect for her father. He stood up for what he believed, and my dad stood up for what he believed. We understood her father lost a lot by doing that.

So many people were against her father back then. He's a saint now that he's gone, but that's not the way a lot of Americans viewed him back in 1967. People forget that a lot of people hated her dad. He ignored it all and did what he thought was right. I understood that and admired him for it. I remember at one of the press conferences before the fight, when I was asked about the difference between the decisions our dads had made, I said, "She's no more proud of her dad than I am of mine." I meant that, but it was never an issue between Laila and me or my dad and her dad. There was nothing but respect.

Muhammad's presence loomed over the promotion, but he had zero effect on me. I didn't train with the idea I was fighting Muhammad Ali. He wasn't going to be in the ring, and it wasn't going to help her whose daughter she was. She was just another opponent to me, but I did get a little tired of hearing Muhammad Ali questions. I finally told one reporter, "My dad will be at ringside, too, and he can't help me any more than her dad can help her. If I was fighting both of them it would be different. But I'm not."

Most people thought Laila was too big for me. I know Laila thought that 100 percent. She didn't take the fight because of the way I'd looked against Mia. She wanted to beat the biggest name in women's boxing. Even though size wise it made no sense, it was the one women's match that was about both fighters, not just me versus whomever. It was a fight that made sense because it was going to make dollars and cents, and a lot of them.

I agreed to the biggest purse of my career, more than $400,000 once you included my share of the upside on pay-per-view sales after expenses. I was also guaranteed $1 million for a rematch if I beat her. Big as she was, if I did beat her, why would Jim put me in there again against someone 10 years younger and 20 pounds heavier? Why would you give her a second chance to beat me? Protecting his wife never factored into his thinking. I was just a human ATM machine to him.

By the night of the fight, we'd attracted a record crowd for boxing at the Mississippi Coast Coliseum in Biloxi, Mississippi, down on the Gulf Coast where they'd built a lot of beachfront casinos. The place held more than 10,000 for boxing, and they added extra seats because the demand was so high. We had outdrawn Roy Jones Jr., who at the time was considered the best fighter pound-for-pound in the world. He lived not too far from Biloxi, in Pensacola, Florida, and was considered their homeboy, but two women outdrew him.

I'm very proud of that. Laila and I broke every record in that building. That part of the fight still makes me feel good, but not much else does.

The contract was for 160 pounds, which is called a catch weight, because she had to come down from her normal 168, and I had to come up from my usual fighting weight, which was around 144 pounds. That's a big difference, and by the time they rang the first bell, I knew it would be even bigger once she rehydrated after the weigh-in, but that didn't faze me. I had no fear of her, even though she was so much bigger. My only fear was the same one I always had. I was afraid of letting people down.

I still had a lot of rage on the inside about how my life had gone, and Jim knew how to push those buttons whenever he wanted to make it come out. On New Year's Day that year, while we were still negotiating the Ali fight, I got into an argument in the parking lot at Sears in Orlando. I'd just parked, and when I went to get out of my car, another car came barreling into the spot next to me and nearly ran me over. The woman driving jumped out and started yelling at me. I started to walk away until I heard Jim whisper, "I knew you wouldn't do nothing."

It was like a put-down or a dare. He was pushing my buttons, and I took the bait. I was driving a Cadillac Escalade then and slammed her against the car and started hitting her like we were in a title fight. Jim should have told me to walk away, but he thought it was funny to watch me lose control of myself.

The police came, and things settled down until the cop said to the woman, "You know who that is? That's Christy Martin, the boxer." It didn't take her long to sue me for $100,000. A small incident in a parking lot ended up costing me $30,000 in a settlement, but it was a reminder of how easily I could be manipulated by Jim. How I reacted was ridiculous, but so was the life I was living when there were no reporters around.

A few months before the fight there was a press conference to announce the show, and I arrived with a bigger chip on my shoulder than I usually had, which was saying something. I knew she was bigger than me, but I'd never been in the same room with her until then. When we stood face to face, and my eyes were about up to her chin. I remember thinking, *"This is a damn big woman!"* She wasn't just tall. She was wide in an athletic way. Broad shoulders. A big, strong woman. Because of the obvious size difference, I felt like I had to show her I wasn't afraid of her if the opportunity presented itself, which it did.

When it was my turn to speak, I said she wasn't her father and she hadn't proven she was the best out there. In an earlier interview, I was asked about her being the future of women's boxing, and I told the reporter, "I'm the past, the present, and the future. I'm everything about women's boxing." Laila didn't like that.

When she got up to speak, she kept looking down on me and calling me "little momma," which pissed me off, even though I'd been called a lot worse by my own family. She finally turned to me and said something, and I stood up and said, "Don't give me that phony ghetto bullshit! You don't scare me." Then I pushed her backwards. I got the party started, which was what I wanted.

She grabbed my head with both hands and started pulling out handfuls of my hair as I was pushing her and trying to hit her. Her husband jumped in and grabbed me, but all Jim did was go behind Ya-Ya and try to hit him in the back. By the time they broke us up, she'd pulled out a lot of my hair, but I'd made my point. Afraid of her I was not.

This wasn't some kind of staged thing. I can't say it was spontaneous, because I was looking for a fight from the moment I got there, but it was real. Emotions were running high by then. Someone tried to claim it was staged, but if they knew me, they knew there was never anything staged about me when it came to boxing. The rest of my life? That was a different story.

When we got back to my room, I started to comb my hair and big chunks of it came out. I put it all in a baggie. I still have it somewhere in a storage locker in Charlotte.

I never gave any thought to the size difference between us when I first signed the contract. I fixated on the fact it was a big moment for women's boxing and for Christy Martin. I was getting older, and people were starting to have doubts about whether I was still the top woman in the sport, so this fight was where I could reestablish that in the mind of the public, and I believed I could do it. That's how much confidence I had, but after the press conference, I'd be lying if I said I didn't think about that size difference.

You couldn't ignore it. It had to be dealt with. I felt I could use her size against her, because I moved better than she did. Speed would be my edge. I expected she'd start cautiously, trying to use her length and her jab to keep me away rather than come to me and fight. I'd try to tire her out by making her follow me around and potshot her when I could. It didn't end up that way.

I believed I was going to hit her like she'd never been hit before. I was playing the Tyson card. He used to say, "Everyone has a plan until they get hit in the face." That's the way I was thinking, but Wednesday of Fight Week I stopped thinking completely for a minute, and it cost me any chance of winning.

When we arrived in Biloxi, I didn't feel quite right and told Jim I wanted to spar on Wednesday, which I normally would never do three days before a fight. I would just move around a little to stay loose. All the work had been done by then. If you aren't ready by the week of the fight, no amount of sparring in the last few days is going to help you.

I never sparred after Friday the week before a fight. That was always the last day. So why did I change my routine? Did I have some doubts deep inside? I guess I needed reassurance that I was ready. I'd never had to do that before, so why did I need it that time? Credit her. She'd made me doubt myself and my preparation.

As my trainer, Jim never should have let that happen. He should have reassured me by saying I was ready. Looking back on it, the odd part is he never had a problem saying no to me in so many things. But in an important moment like that, he said, "All right" and put me in with my usual sparring partner, Jimmy Maloney.

Maybe Jim thought it wouldn't matter, because he didn't believe I could win. Maybe he didn't give it a second thought. I'll never know why he said yes, but I know that sparring session is when I lost the fight to Laila.

That day, for some reason, Jimmy and I went to war. He'd been my sparring partner since 1992. We'd sparred hundreds and hundreds of rounds. We both knew what we were doing and how it should be done this close to a fight, but Jimmy told me later I hurt him with a hard shot, and he saw an opening and just retaliated on instinct. I can understand that, but when his right hand landed, I was out on my feet.

They stopped the session, and Jim started belittling me. I believe I lost the fight right then. Getting wobbled like that shook my confidence. I probably was concussed. I'm not making excuses for losing. Laila was too big for me, and at some level I suppose I knew that, but getting hurt in sparring so close to the fight just eroded my confidence.

The day before the fight I weighed myself in our room and was 147 so I wore full combat fatigues when I got on the commission scales. I weighed in at

159, but it was phony. We'd already been told Laila couldn't make 160, so they had to buy back a couple of pounds from us, or the fight was off. I agreed and got $5,000 for the extra two pounds but that money did me no good.

We should have forced her to make 160, because it would have drained her and taken away some of her strength advantage. She was totally baked out, which is why she couldn't get any lower. She had no water weight left inside. But Laila understood the truth of the situation. The contract weight didn't matter, because there was no way I was going to refuse to fight with nearly a half million dollars on the table. She could have said she was 10 pounds over, and it would have been the same answer from me, so why waste time with the charade of a threat I wasn't going to follow through on?

By the time they rang the opening bell, and Laila had rehydrated, Lord knows what she weighed. She might have been 175. Boxing has weight classes for a reason. Size matters when someone is hitting you in the head. As you move up into a higher weight class, you lose some speed or some power. Sometimes you lose both, but you almost always lose something. I was hitting with the power of a junior welterweight or welterweight, but she was a super-middle-weight. My knockout power didn't carry up three weight classes. Neither did the resilience of my chin. She hit like a mule, and I say that with all due respect to mules and to Laila.

The morning of the fight, Jim found me looking out the window of our hotel room. I told him I didn't feel right. I still thought I'd find a way to win, but I didn't feel like I expected. I didn't have the "big moment feeling" I always had the day of a King card, even though I knew it was a packed house and a pay-per-view event headlined by two women. It was surely a big moment in my career and in the history of women's boxing, but inside I didn't feel that way, which was unsettling.

Two things bolstered me a little bit. The first was when one of the maids in the hotel, an older black woman, came up to me the day before the fight and took my hand. She told me, "I'm black, but we're for you. That girl is so arrogant. You go out there and kick her uppity ass!"

Laila was arrogant then, but most top athletes are. If you're not, you won't reach the top in a sport such as boxing. Hopefully you can control it, but it's harder to keep your ego in check when you're young and undefeated in a confrontational sport. It's just how it is, but I was happy to have the woman's support.

The other thing was around that time I met Loretta Lynn, the legendary country singer who made "Coal Miner's Daughter" a hit. She was touring in

Gulfport, Mississippi, and she brought me onto her bus and treated me like we'd known each other forever. The first thing she asked me was, "How's your dad?" She didn't know him, of course, but she knew he was a coal miner, and that was enough. She was from Butcher Hollow, in eastern Kentucky, which was coal country just like Itmann. She knew what that meant, and so did I. It meant a hard life of dangerous work deep inside a dark hole. Coal country is all the same that way.

She took the time to call me before the fight to wish me luck. I'll never forget what she said because, unfortunately, I didn't take her advice.

"Make sure you get the first lick in!" she told me. She was so right, but unfortunately, I didn't. Laila did.

Even if I was suppressing my doubts, I was excited when we got to the arena. The place was packed. It may be the only women's fight ever where the arena was sold out. The paid gate was announced at 9,888, but the rest of the seats were filled with people who got comped. Once they counted the receipts, it was the highest paid gate in women's boxing history.

There's a lot of gamesmanship that goes on leading up to a big fight. Because boxing is such a mental game, many fighters believe the fight is decided long before you enter the ring. People are always trying to get an edge somehow if they can, and Laila's people were good at it.

People kept coming in and out of my locker room, which I didn't like. That wasn't how I normally operated. It was disconcerting for me at a time when I needed to be focused. The only person I was happy to see was Gogarty, who came in to wish me luck.

Jim was intimidated by Ya-Ya and his crew and wouldn't stand up to them. He was afraid to go to their locker room to watch them wrap Laila's hands. He sent Jeff Bailey instead. I noticed that. Those little things prey on a fighter's mind and create more doubt.

Who would walk in first became a big issue that night. I was the champion even though we weren't fighting for the title I held, so that shouldn't have been an issue. The champion walks last. That's the tradition of the sport, but there was an argument over it. She finally walked first, but when it came time for me, they didn't start playing "Coal Miner's Daughter." I always came in to that. It was part of my identity as a fighter, so I refused to walk. I told them I wouldn't go out until I heard my entrance music. That was the only time I ever had that problem. Eventually they played it, but it put me in a mind-set that wasn't ideal. It made me mad in a place where anger is not your ally.

When the fight began, Laila surprised me by not staying on the outside. She walked right to me, trying to overwhelm me with her size, and we went at it toe to toe for the first 15 seconds of the first round. We were blasting each other. I landed solid but didn't hurt her. She landed solid and hurt me with her first flush right hand, and kept hurting me.

I should never have gotten caught with that first big punch. I needed to box like I'd done against Lisa, but instead I stood there and slugged it out with a woman who towered over me. Just another in a long line of bad choices I'd made.

She hit me so hard near the top of my head that I don't remember much about the fight after that. I'd thrown out a lazy jab, and she countered right over it, and I was really knocked out right then. In the final seconds of that first round, she clubbed me with six or eight hard right hands to the head, and I was out on my feet and holding onto the ropes to keep myself upright. She didn't realize it until I told her that 20 years later, but from that point on, I felt like I was walking sideways. I'd taken punches my entire career. I wasn't afraid of anybody's power, but that first big right hand stunned me, and I never was clearheaded again.

The pattern of the fight never changed, because I couldn't change it. I landed some solid shots, but nothing that made her think twice about attacking me. The referee, a guy I knew well named Fred Steinwinder III, started keeping a close eye on me, getting closer and closer in the way they do when they're waiting for the moment to bail you out. I knew what was happening, so I tried to catch her with something that would hurt her the way she'd hurt me, which, of course, makes you more vulnerable to getting hit yourself.

She finally hurt me again with 70 seconds left in the third round, and all I could do was cover up. I could not get her off me, so I did something I'd never done before and never believed I would. I reached back with my right leg and took a knee. It was like I was genuflecting to find some way to clear my head and get my bearings. It was the first time in my career I'd been knocked down, except by my husband.

I knew why I did it. I took a knee to get a breather and start over, and I got a break when one of Laila's cornermen, a guy named Cassius Green, thought the fight was over and jumped into the ring. Fred saw him and went over and threw him out, which gave me a few extra seconds to clear my head, but I needed a lot more time than that.

Technically Fred should have disqualified her. If someone in your corner comes into the ring during a round, that's the rule. It's automatic, but I understand why he didn't. The fight was so one-sided, there would have been a damn riot if he'd done that, and deservedly so.

In no way did Laila or anyone in her corner think I was getting up, but they didn't know me. I still wanted to fight. That's why I took a knee. To collect myself and rethink the situation. I got up and fought back, but by the end of the round I was desperate and, for the first time in my career, wary of what was coming next.

My nose was bleeding, and I had a swelling under my left eye. I can't tell you a thing that was said to me in the corner, if anything was. I have no memory of it. I just sat there on my stool, buzzed, until the bell rang again, and I pushed myself up on instinct.

The television commentators were speculating that my corner should have stopped the fight after the third round, but Jim never gave it a thought. He sent me back out there, and she nailed me again immediately. I was in big trouble.

Less than a minute into Round 4, she was teeing off on me like she was taking batting practice. I was so exhausted and hopeless I took a knee again and looked over into my corner. My cut man was ready to throw in the towel, but he didn't have the authority to do it, and Jim refused to stop it himself. Instead, he brought his thumb across his throat, the signal for me to stay down. Jim could have saved me from having to quit. He could have preserved a little of my pride and dignity by stopping it himself and at least giving me a chance to claim I wanted to go on, but he wouldn't even do that for me.

Jim could have protected his fighter from that sorry ending. He could have protected his wife from it, too, but he made a different choice. He protected himself. He didn't quit. He made me do it. He left me out there alone to quit on my knee. By that point in my life, it didn't surprise me.

Now understand this. I'm the one who didn't get up. I'm the one who quit. If I say that it was Jim, I'm passing the buck, and I won't do that. I was the one who let the referee count me out 48 seconds into Round 4. That's the choice I made. I accept that. Bitterly, but I accept it. But my cornerman, my trainer, my husband could have protected me a little bit, and he didn't.

The one memory of that moment I have is looking down at the floor as Fred was counting and thinking, "Can't you count faster?" I just wanted to be done with it, but the minute it was over my first thought was, "What did you just do?" I knew the answer. I'd quit. It's the worst thing I ever did in boxing but it's the truth.

I don't remember walking back to my locker room. I know I laid down on a couch feeling like a loser. Roland Bryant, who was one of my young fighters at my gym in Florida, was among the people in there with me. He was so kind. He unlaced my boxing boots for me and took them off.

My mom and dad, my brother and his wife, my grandmother were all there, but nobody knew what to say. Finally, my dad came and told me he'd be at every fight I had from then on. I think he saw for the first time I could get badly hurt inside the ring. I don't think that ever dawned on him before that night.

If I didn't have a concussion, I don't know anyone who ever did, but I didn't go to the hospital. I went to the post-fight press conference, because it's what I'd done all those nights when my opponent was on the side I was now. I was dressed in pink, as usual, but the most significant part of my ensemble was that I was wearing the eternal symbol of a losing fighter. I was wearing sunglasses at midnight.

That was to hide the damage. My right eye was swollen, my left cheek had a plum-colored bruise, and there was a glint of tears in my eyes. I didn't cry, but I wanted to. When someone asked me if I could have gotten up, I told him the truth.

"I could have," I said. "I was fully aware, but what was going to change? There was nothing more I could do."

One thing about boxing: there's not much sense lying about what happened. It's written all over your face. At least it is when you lose, and I'd just been massacred. There are no teammates to blame, so why lie? Everybody saw what happened.

That fight was the biggest payday of my career, but no amount of money could buy back what I lost by quitting. After it was over, all I wanted to do was leave the country. I already had a vacation planned to Aruba, and I couldn't get there fast enough.

I wanted to erase the memory, not of losing but of quitting, something I'd always told myself I'd never do. I always believed if I was up against it, I'd go out on my shield, but it wasn't what I did. So, what happens in Aruba?

I wasn't there 10 minutes when we ran into someone who said, "Hey, you're Christy Martin! I just saw your fight with Laila. Sorry you lost."

I was totally embarrassed and ashamed. I'll never get over it. I'd be more accepting of losing to her if I'd been knocked out or taken a beating for six more rounds. To quit on my knees is not who I am. It troubles me to this day. The worst thing I ever did in boxing was to quit that night.

I've never watched the whole fight. You can find it on YouTube easily enough, but I know what happened. I didn't even watch clips of it for a long time. Some memories you don't want to revisit, and I've got a lot of them. But only one or two are worse than that night.

There actually were people who asked me if I'd taken a dive. Taken a dive? I'd bet $20,000 on myself to win. I think I was a 6-1 or 7-1 underdog. I thought I was going to fatten my paycheck. It really irks me when people ask me that.

Jessie Robinson, the guy who first brought me to King, said later I should never have been put in that situation. He said, "You have to protect your fighter, any fighter but most especially a great fighter, from what was happening that night. Jim didn't know what he was doing. It was a sad situation.

"Christy fought on pride and guts. If you do that long enough you'll regret something and I guess she regrets that night but she did all that she could. Laila was just too big. She was what Christy had been, but I'll tell you this. At her best Christy Martin was the chosen one."

I appreciated Jessie's words, but I don't know about that. All I knew was I wasn't going out on my knees.

No Place to Run, No Place to Hide

I can't remember how long it took me to get back into the gym after the Ali fight, but it was a month or two. It wasn't the losing that held me back. It was finding a way to deal with what I'd done.

When I started training again, most people told me Laila was just too big, which was nice, and I appreciated it. At some level, I knew it was basically true. A couple of people even said, "What were you thinking?" What I was thinking when they said that was why didn't you say that before the fight?

It wasn't that I disagreed with their take on things. I was sure I could go back to the proper weight class and dominate again, and I even thought I could win a rematch with Laila if I fought a different fight. I believed I could come back from that loss. What I wasn't so sure about was whether I could come back from knowing that I'd quit in a fight, even if it was a physical mismatch.

A lot of promoters were calling with proposals, because they believed I was ripe to be beaten again by their fighter. But I knew nothing was going to be made for a while. I'd just made more than a half million dollars in nine months, plus I had more than a million in the bank, so there was no reason to rush back until I felt right, which I still didn't.

I wasn't really that focused on boxing. I was training lightly and working with Roland Bryant, the kid I'd signed on to manage, so I was in the gym most days watching him work with Jim. I stayed busy with that and also worked with an amateur boxing team we'd formed, but I was more focused on other things that were bothering me that had nothing to do with boxing.

In nearly 20 years of marriage, Jim and I didn't have that many physical confrontations. Just a few until the day he tried to kill me, but there were almost daily emotional beatdowns, and I was tired of it. I was keeping a diary then, and when I look back on it and read my thoughts, one thing jumps out at me. That's the number of times I wrote about having suicidal thoughts.

Once I wrote that Jim told me he wasn't going to put me on television anymore because I looked fat. Did he really say that to his wife? A wife who was a professional athlete and earned nearly every dollar we'd made since this whole thing started?

I didn't even bother to defend myself when he said it. I was tired of arguing. Tired of being insulted, emotionally abused, and manipulated. Tired of living every day with someone I no longer trusted.

The problem was I also felt too tired to change my circumstances. I didn't fight back like I had when I was younger. I told people close to me I wanted to leave, but I didn't make a move. A couple of times I left for a few days, but I wasn't ready to be alone, I guess, because I always came back.

I don't think being emotionally abused seemed like abuse to me at the time. It took a while to realize what was actually happening. You get uncomfortable when your abuser says that he doesn't want you to see this person or talk to that person, but you go along with it to try to keep the peace. It takes time before you see that a wall has been created between you and the part of the world that used to belong to you alone. By then it's too late. They have you. Certainly, looking back, that's what happened to me.

I was the loneliest person in the world despite having a ton of people around me, because nearly everyone was someone Jim chose. I think women who go to shelters to seek help are much more physically abused than I was. I don't think a lot of people who are emotionally abused see it the same way. In my case, I wasn't even sure it was abuse.

I'd say there were only about 10 times there was actually physical abuse in our 20 years together. When you write down that number, you think, "That's 10 times too many," which is true. But when the abuse is mostly emotional manipulation, you see it differently. You question what you can do to fix things. You start to think he's right about you. You're the problem. Strange as it may sound, it often takes a long time before you realize who the victim really is.

When I ask myself why this happened to me, I always come to the same conclusion. Despite what people saw on the outside the week of a fight, or when I was shooting off my mouth about an opponent, or getting into an altercation at a weigh-in or press conference, I was not a confident person. I was a confident athlete, but an athlete is also a person; and when it came to Christy Martin, I was two people. The fighter and the little girl from Itmann still living in the closet.

If I'd had more confidence, I would have told my dad when I was sexually abused. I would have told my parents as a teenager, I want you to love me, but I need you to love me as I am, a lesbian who wants to love who she wants to love. Even though I fell into my relationship with Jim, when it started to go sideways, I would have bet on myself and left him. Maybe it's not as simple as that, but I believe a lack of confidence in myself outside the athletic arena was the root of my problems. It still is, although I have a much better view of myself now.

My dad always told me I could be anything I wanted to be, but I'd come to believe that wasn't true. I could be anything—including a successful female boxer in a world opposed to that ever happening—as long as it was also what my family wanted and Jim wanted and what I thought the world wanted, which meant that I was never really free to be me. At least not for very long.

So, you compromise. You lie. You hide. You try to fit into a world that isn't your own creation. You accept things that you never thought you'd accept. You replace boxing for love and try to equate financial success with personal happiness. Those compromises only work for a while.

Don't get me wrong. I'm not looking for a pity party for Christy Martin. A lot of things that happened in my life before I was free to be me were great. I wouldn't trade them for a different path, because this is the path I had to walk to be who I am today. All I'm saying is that you don't have to go as far down that road as I did to be free. You can make better choices and, I hope, you can learn from the ones I made that I regret.

You can be stronger than I was. You really can. All you have to do is believe in yourself. Take that first step, and then the second, and the third the same way I believed in myself when I took those three steps up into a boxing ring. I knew there was potential trouble waiting inside those ropes, but I believed I would find a way to handle that trouble. And I usually did. When I didn't, I understood getting knocked down was part of the life I'd chosen. To be successful, all I had to do was get up and fight back.

In boxing I did that all my life, even after I broke down for a few seconds once and took a knee. I got up and fought on. It just took me a whole lot longer to do it outside the ring. In the end, I did that, too, but not without a few more troubles than I expected. But that's life. Trouble comes in some form or another to all of us. It's to be expected, like the dark of night. However dark it gets the sun comes up eventually. You may not be able to hold off the darkness, as I couldn't, but you can have faith that like in that song from *Annie*, tomorrow is only a day away. So is change. You just need the courage to make it happen and understand that you can't make anyone else in your life happy by making yourself miserable, or by trying to substitute everyone else's view of the world for your own.

As I began to sort this all out, it was unclear where my life, both professionally and privately, was headed. About a year after the Ali fight, four huge hurricanes swept across Florida in a six-week span. It was devastating. It was the first time four hurricanes had hit one state in such a short period since 1886.

The first, Hurricane Charley, was the worst. It was supposed to hit the west coast of Florida but took an unexpected right turn and made landfall at Punta Gorda, the place where years ago I dressed for a fight in a janitor's closet.

It landed at around 3:45 p.m. the afternoon of August 13, 2004, rolled up I-4 with 90 mph winds and gusts of 105 recorded at the Orlando International Airport, and slammed into Apopka and the surrounding towns. There were widespread power outages and flooding. It seemed like the whole area had become a landscape of downed trees, roofs with blue tarps where shingles had been, and windows of plywood where glass had been. I've never been to a war zone, but that's what it felt like.

Three weeks later, while the cleanup was still going on, Hurricane Frances hit, and 10 days after that Hurricane Ivan struck the panhandle and the west coast of Florida. Then, on September 25, Hurricane Jeanne hit central Florida. Although the winds weren't as severe, seven inches of rain fell on an area still flooded and battered from Charley. By the time Jeanne arrived, Jim and I were long gone, having moved to my grandmother's old house in Itmann, which I'd bought a few years earlier.

We got tired of living with no power and damage all around us and went to visit my family. Jim decided he'd start remodeling the house, because it needed a lot of work. Like everything else he did, he tore up the place but didn't finish anything.

My mother wasn't talking to me at the time because of our conflicts over my niece and the other issues that had festered for so long between us, so there was a lot of tension in the air. Brittany was just a kid at the time, and my mother wanted me to treat her like she was my little sister, which she wasn't. She was my brother Randy's daughter with his ex-wife, and a growing problem between my mother and me, because it seemed she treated her granddaughter the way she'd never treated me. That hurt me deeply.

Was there jealousy on my part? Yes, sadly, there was. Should I have been more adult about the situation? Yes, but what I saw at the time was my dad and her accepting Brittany as she was while never being able to accept me as I was. That's the most important thing to any child, but especially one carrying the added weight of a sexual identity different from what the world saw as acceptable. A child wants to feel safe and accepted. How can that be so difficult for parents to understand?

My mom missed so many things I was involved in during those years because she was raising someone else's child. Maybe she felt like she had to because no one else would. Maybe she was looking for a do-over after the way things had gone between us. Maybe Brittany was the daughter she always wanted, not the lesbian daughter who threw punches for a living. It's hard to understand anyone's thinking when you can't sit down and have a civil conversation about what's on your mind and in your heart without feeling like you're under attack. So, things got more and more strained. I just felt my parents needed a lesson about the dynamics of a family. When I needed support and reassurance about the most important things about me—who I was and who I chose to love—it wasn't there. My choices always got in the way. With my mom, that's never really changed, unfortunately.

Eventually, my mother never being able to support my choice of partners became too heavy to carry. Outwardly, as a child I had everything I wanted, but I didn't get what I needed, which was unconditional love. The weight of that was just too much, and it fractured the bond between us. When troubled parents approach me now and ask how to deal with the reality of their child being gay, I always say hug them close, tell them you love them, and listen a little deeper. Pay attention to what your kids are trying to tell you. Don't just hear the words they're saying. Really listen, because they may be afraid to tell you what's in their heart.

Try to open your own heart, even if it's painful for you. Hard as it may be, and scared as you may be for them, love them as they are. Don't think I don't understand how hard it must be to learn your child isn't what you expected. But try to understand there's nothing they could do about it. I was who I was by the age of 12. Nothing could change that.

As parents, it doesn't mean you did something wrong if your child loves who they love and not who you thought they should love. They don't need an exorcism. They don't need an intervention. They need affirmation. They need to feel safe and loved by you just as they are. If you make your child feel like you can't accept them if they tell you who they are, that child is being put down and pushed away by the most important person in their life. Think about that for a minute. Your child isn't gay to spite you. Parents need to get over the idea that it's about them. It's not. It's about that child you brought into the world. The one God loaned to you for a while just the way He made them.

I've asked my mom several times if we could just agree to disagree on some things and move on. Just meet me somewhere in the middle and accept some of the responsibility for how things ended up between us. Just accept half, and I'll take on the rest; but in her mind, she's done nothing to make me feel the way I feel, so we stay stuck. It's sad, but we can't seem to get past it.

One thing I do have to add, to be fair, is whatever our differences were, she never resented my success in boxing. I know she was proud of that. She supported me and helped give me the strength to stay with it early in my career when it looked like it wasn't going anywhere. I used to ask her not to brag on me when I'd be interviewed on TV or be off at a big fight, but she did. I always felt that back home you had to downplay things. I never wanted people there to feel that I thought I was better than they were, because I wasn't. Mom was always proud of what I was doing in sports, and she let people know it. In that area of my life, she was always behind me, win or lose, which meant a lot. It just wasn't enough to overcome our other issues.

During the years I was with Jim, there were times I wouldn't talk to my family for months. Some of that was Jim's doing, but a lot of it was our choice. Mom seemed to love Jim more than she loved me, to be honest. In her mind, I guess he was my savior, taking me away from loving women. She just never could understand that was not what was happening in my life. Jim wasn't saving me. He was tearing me down, piece by piece. I would say Jim and my mom always worked together on me, and sometimes they worked against me.

The last straw was one day when I was sitting on the swing that hung over my grandmother's porch. My mom pulled up next door, which was where Brittany's mom lived, to drop her off for a visit. With me sitting right in front of her, she pulled into my driveway, backed out, and drove off without so much as a wave. Not long after that, I told Jim I was going back to Florida.

Many times in life things happen when you least expect them, which is why it's important to always be prepared for the unexpected. When a chance comes, you had best be ready for it because if it passes you by, it's a train that's not likely to come around again. Certainly, that's how I felt the day my phone rang a few months after I got back to Florida. It was Brian Young calling to say he thought Bob Arum was ready to make the only fight I still wanted and the only one that could get me focused again on my career. Arum was ready to promote a fight with one of the few women I truly disliked in boxing—Lucia Rijker.

Although I wasn't fit to fight at that point, there was plenty of time to get ready, and now I had the motivation I'd been lacking since the debacle in Biloxi against Laila. It would probably be a lie to say I would have fought Rijker for nothing, because I'd been a prizefighter for 16 years by then and understood it was a business as well as a sport. But if you think about it, I already had fought her once for nothing, so getting paid to box her would be a bonus.

Despite all my troubles with my fraying relationship with Jim and the off-again on-again one with my family, the one thing that could temporarily pull my thoughts away from my problems was a fight with Rijker. "The coal miner's daughter" finally might get a chance to shut the mouth of the "Dutch destroyer." What could be more meaningful than that?

Once again, boxing was saving me from my troubles. It was giving me a reason to focus on what I still loved above all else, which was athletic competition and the opportunity it always provided me to feel good about myself, even if in the rest of the world I felt worthless or hopeless. Boxing had always been my salvation, and the day Brian called it was again.

Until that call I'd begun to worry that maybe my career was over. A lot of promoters had talked to Jim about putting me in a fight, but nothing had materialized. If I'd gone the distance and lost to Laila, or even if I got knocked out, it would have been different, because size would explain away those outcomes. But I knew that wasn't what happened, and I feared because of that it might mean the end of my career.

Arum was as powerful a promoter as King, the two of them having controlled boxing's biggest events and most popular fighters as blood oath enemies for more than 30 years. Having Arum talking with me about promoting a big fight was like the day King first said, "Give her a contract." It was elevating at a time when I needed that badly.

Lucia had fought only once in the previous year and twice in more than three years and hadn't had a knockout in three and a half years. Her only fight between August 1999 and February 2002 was her scuffle with me at the LA Boxing Club press conference, so basically, she had disappeared from the sport. Then, in 2002, she came back from a two-and-a-half-year layoff and launched a comeback. She started by beating up a woman with a 9-26-1 record. That opponent, Carla Witherspoon, took the fight on eight days' notice after one opponent disappeared and the second came up pregnant. I can't blame Lucia for that, but if she wanted to fight me so badly, why didn't she fight again for 16 months?

You'll have to ask her, but during that layoff I'd fought the two other marquee names in women's boxing, beating St. John easily even though people saw it as a sign of slippage, and then been beaten in four rounds by Ali. I have no idea if it was related, but as I began to show signs of fading, Lucia launched another comeback. Six months after my fight with St. John, she won a decision over 35-year-old Jane Couch, who was another pioneer of women's boxing on the back nine of her career.

Lucia won every round in a lopsided decision, but as with most of her career, there weren't many witnesses to what she'd done. In my opinion, she is the most overhyped myth in the history of women's boxing. She was the killer few people ever saw fight.

While she was boxing Couch, I was preparing for my fight with Laila, and we know how that worked out. At that moment, a Rijker fight was the farthest thing from my mind and, frankly, from the public's until the spring of 2004. By then she'd not only come back again and won a fight in Amsterdam but played a fairly big role in the Academy Award-winning film *Million Dollar Baby* that put her name back on people's radar.

That film won Hilary Swank an Oscar for Best Actress for her role as an underdog amateur fighter who begins to be trained by an old-school trainer played by Clint Eastwood. Initially he has no interest in her but his associate, played by Morgan Freeman, does, and together they begin to improve her in a gym called "The Hit Pit." I wish I'd thought of that name for my own gym in Apopka. It's perfect.

So was that film. Swank's character was a former waitress with a dysfunctional family who, with Eastwood and Freeman's help, fights her way up the rankings because she's a powerful puncher known for knockouts. Finally, she gets a title shot worth $1 million against Billie "The Blue Bear" Osterman, a German ex-prostitute with a reputation as a dirty fighter. Lucia played that role perfectly, ultimately knocking out Swank with an illegal punch after the bell that breaks her neck and leaves her a quadriplegic dependent on a ventilator to breathe.

When her family shows up at her bedside, they don't arrive until they've taken side trips to Disneyland and Universal Studios and immediately begin arguing over whether they can get a big insurance settlement as a result of Swank's injuries. She finally throws them out of her room and, after having a leg amputated, asks Eastwood to help her die. This little waitress from the Ozark Mountains had come to Los Angeles with a lot of baggage but also a dream and had nothing more to live for. It was a story I could relate to.

The public must have connected with it, too, because the film grossed $216.8 million along with seven Academy Award nominations. The movie's success is what got Arum thinking about promoting Rijker. He first tried to match her against Laila, but Rijker was smart enough to see what I refused to see, which was the size difference was too vast a gulf to cross. I was told she refused the fight. She says otherwise. In the end it didn't happen. The reason why didn't matter, because the next person he thought of was me, and on March 18, 2005, I signed a contract that would pay us each $250,000, with the winner getting an additional $750,000.

That was the first (and only) million-dollar payday so far in the history of women's boxing. Arum had timed it perfectly to be in conjunction with the release of *Million Dollar Baby* on DVD, which would be coming out three weeks before the July 30, 2005, date for our fight. Arum understood there would be a lot of publicity surrounding the release, and he had Hilary on board to help promote the fight. Say what you want about Bob Arum: the guy understood timing and how to promote his product.

Arum gave me $100,000 up front plus $10,000 for training expenses. Jim hired some sparring partners, including Lisa. I felt like I'd been reborn. Maybe resurrected is a better word. I'd negotiated with Lucia's people. I'd been sucker punched by her at a press conference. I'd called her out about rumors of steroid use. She'd called me afraid to face her. Now Arum was saying the deal was done. After signing that contract, I felt the same way I did the first time I knocked out an opponent and the crowd went berserk. I was alive!

This was going to be the biggest woman's boxing match that ever happened. In my mind, it was all that was left for me to accomplish in the sport. Rijker was 17-0 with 14 knockouts and seen by some as the woman who would finish me off. I was 45-3-2 with nearly twice as many knockouts (31) as she had fights. This was considered the third women's "superfight," and I'd been the common denominator in all three. But this was the first one with both fighters at their natural weight. I'd moved up three divisions to fight Laila and Mia had done the same to fight me. This time would be different.

I'm sure Lucia thought I was damaged goods, and in some ways she would have been right. I had doubts now about what I could take, and I knew I had to shake them, so I insisted on a tune-up fight, which Arum gave me.

The first time Arum and I spoke was in his office in Las Vegas the day I signed the contract. I wasn't worried about purse parity. I wasn't about to make an argument that I'd built women's boxing, because I didn't see it as a 50-50 purse split. In my eyes I'd be the one walking away with the million. She'd be getting $250,000. Who wouldn't sign that deal?

I started running and training immediately. I got up and ran at crazy early morning hours to tell myself I was out there while she was sleeping. I used to run listening to a song by a rapper named Lloyd Banks, "Born Alone, Die Alone." That seemed like an anthem for my life.

I was struggling a little to make weight, but I had nearly five months to prepare and was confident I'd be in great shape. I wanted to move our camp to Las Vegas instead of staying in Florida, and I tried to find a house to rent out there, because I believed I'd get better sparring, and a Vegas training camp would give a championship feel to the fight. It would have helped my confidence to have someone else cook for me instead of me doing it at the end of a day of workouts and sparring. In my mind it was an investment in winning a million dollars. But it didn't happen because Jim refused, and I didn't insist. I think he just didn't want to spend any of our front money on preparing me for the last big fight of my career. He wanted it in his pocket and, once again, I went along with his decision as if I had no right to make any for myself.

Despite that disappointment, I was in the best shape I could get myself in at that point in my life. I would be 37 years old a month before the fight, and I'd had 51 professional fights once the tune-up happened in April. At that point, there's no way you're the same as you were when you were 27, but I felt confident I was still the best woman in the junior welterweight division.

That didn't prevent me from being nervous before my tune-up fight. I hadn't totally forgotten quitting against Laila, so I was nervous about how I would react. I knew my opponent, Lana Alexander, didn't belong in the same ring with me, but it had been 20 months since I'd last fought, and I was a little unsure of what to expect of myself.

You do different things to psyche yourself up as a fighter. In this case, I wore the same trunks I'd worn for the *Sports Illustrated* cover photo, and I came in to a Gretchen Wilson song, "Here for the Party." It was a big country hit and a way to remind myself why I was there. I was trying to get my mojo back any way I could.

When I didn't stop her in the first round, I started to wonder if I'd lost it as I was sitting in my corner waiting for the second round. When the bell rang, I went out after her and ended up breaking her ribs and stopping her with a body shot. I was glad to have won, but for the first time in my life, I felt something I'd never felt before as an athlete. I felt compassion for my opponent.

It was obvious Lana didn't have the size, the skill, or the experience I had, but that had nothing to do with me. Yet when I started hitting her easily, I actually felt bad for her. Later, I saw her walking through the Isle of Capri Casino down there in Lula, Mississippi, where the fight was staged, and she just looked so sad. I felt like I'd taken advantage of her, and I didn't like that feeling, even though that's what a boxer's job is. Aren't you trying to take advantage of your opponent's weaknesses and mistakes? You can't feel bad about that, but this time it didn't feel quite right, which really meant it didn't feel right to be a boxer any more.

I should have known then that my time had run its course. I'd never felt sympathy for an opponent until that night. I don't know why I did. It wasn't because Laila had shown me I could be on the other side of a beating. I just didn't have the fire any more.

Harsh as it sounds, compassion has no place inside a boxing ring. Respect? Yes. Empathy? Maybe. Compassion? No. Before that fight, if I knocked someone out, I never gave it a second thought. This time it felt different.

Maybe I was just too old to accept the ruthless side of life that boxing demands. It's the law of the jungle. It's you or them. There's nothing in between. But now here I was feeling sorry for someone who would have been very glad to have put me in the condition she was in.

What got me through that was knowing if there was one fighter on Earth I would not feel sympathy for, it was Lucia Rijker. If it had been Lucia on the floor, I wouldn't have felt anything. This was different. I'd fought less-experienced fighters before and stopped them and just walked away. This time I felt bad, which meant the sun was setting on Christy Martin the fighter.

Other than our scuffle in Los Angeles, I'd only seen Lucia once. We did a press conference together to announce the fight, and I told her, "You're like a dog who keeps chasing a car. What do you do now that you caught it?" She didn't have a response.

Late in training I was sparring with Lisa and I leaped in to throw a left hook. I got caught with an uppercut and went down. I'd never been dropped by a woman before. I'd taken a knee against Laila twice, but she didn't knock me down, so this was a little troubling. But I got past it by telling myself it was a warning for me to always pay attention inside those ropes. I took it as a harmless reminder.

Jim had knocked me down twice sparring, and I got dropped once by a liver shot from a guy in sparring and thought I was going to die. I knew I never wanted to get hit with a liver shot again. In about 14 seconds you're OK, but until then it's like your paralyzed. You're clearheaded, but you can't make your body respond to commands. Those are a terrible 14 seconds.

With Lisa this was just a flash knockdown, a careless mistake I knew I wouldn't repeat against Lucia. It didn't make me doubt that I'd beat her. What I began to doubt was that the "Million Dollar Lady" fight would ever come off.

The first sign of trouble came when Arum canceled a highly anticipated fly-weight fight between the longtime WBC champion Pongskalek Wongjongkam and his mandatory challenger, Jorge Arce. That fight lent credibility to the whole card, so when it fell out, I began to worry. Then, just as I was set to break training camp and head to Las Vegas, I got the word two of Arum's other male fighters, Kelly Pavlik and Julio Cesar Chavez Jr., were being moved to other cards. Those were red flags, but I finished my training strong and was anxious to get out there and get that million dollars.

Barely a week before the fight, I finished sparring with Lisa in the morning. It was our last session in Florida before we planned to break camp and head to Las Vegas. My brother and his wife, Sherry, were coming down and were going to fly out with me. I was so excited. It was like the old days with King and Tyson. We were going to fight on Showtime pay-per-view. It was going to be great. Then I walked into my house and heard my phone ringing.

It was Miguel Diaz, my cut man out in Vegas. He just flat out told me, "The fight's off."

I asked him if this was a joke. I should have known better, because Miguel is a very serious guy. His response made clear to me what was happening.

"I'm very professional, Christy," he said. "I don't joke about things like this. She got hurt in training. It's off."

I said, "OK," and hung up. I was stunned. What could I say? Talk about a gut shot. I'd just lost $1 million, and there was nothing I could do about it. Arum's people said Lucia had torn her Achilles and was getting surgery from Dr. Tony Daly, who operated on a lot of big-name athletes on the West Coast. They said the fight would be postponed to a later date, but that meant probably another year. All the momentum would be gone by then. I knew it would never happen.

A few days later I called a woman who worked with Lucia and asked if we were going to do this. She said they'd get back to me. I'm still waiting for that phone call. As far as I know, there was never talk of rescheduling. Lucia never fought again. I believe she understood she couldn't come back if it wasn't to fight me. It was unfinished business. If she fought someone else, the blame for our fight not happening would have shifted to her. She wasn't about to take that on.

Jim didn't have much of a reaction. You'd think he would have at least put his arm around his fighter and said he was sorry, and we'd find someone else, but there was no conversation like that. There really was no conversation at all.

I was supposed to do *Late Night with Conan O'Brien* the week before the fight. Arum's people set it up, but they canceled when the fight fell out.

O'Brien's people called and said they'd still like to have me on, so I flew to New York and did it. Conan asked if I believed Rijker had an Achilles injury. I said, "I think she had a heart attack."

I still believe that. You'll never convince me that fight was going to happen. Some media reports said they weren't selling enough tickets. I know they said she had surgery. I don't know whether she was hurt, but I believe she knew, as the fight got closer, that she couldn't win.

She would have had to knock me out to beat me, and to do that she would have had to take some chances. It wasn't going to be like Laila. At some point I was going to hit her harder than she'd ever been hit, and she understood what that meant. She wasn't going to just walk out and throw a right hand, and I'd go out like a lot of the girls she'd fought.

Unless she hit like a man, the way her myth claimed, she was going to taste some leather, too. I'd only been down once in 51 fights, and it took someone with a 20- or 25-pound weight advantage to do it. Lucia Rijker wasn't going to do that to me.

When that fight fell through, it took the wind out of me. At that point I should have retired. There was no one else to fight who got me excited and no more reason to go on. My heart wasn't in it anymore, and the truth is my heart was my biggest asset.

So, what did I do? What I'd too often done in the past. I didn't listen to myself.

Two months later I took a fight against a former kickboxer named Holly Holm, who would later knock out the MMA star Ronda Rousey and all but end her UFC career. The offer was $50,000 plus $10,000 in training expensive. That $60,000 was a far cry from a million, but it was more than zero, so I took it.

I was in great shape physically but a blank canvas mentally. Instead of fighting in Vegas on pay-per-view, I was fighting off TV in Albuquerque, New Mexico. I didn't have the slightest interest in being there.

Holly was left-handed, and we didn't even bother to get lefthanders to spar with. It was just a payday. I wanted to win, but I didn't care if I did or I didn't. When that starts to happen, it's the beginning of the end for a fighter. The same is true for a person if that happens in life.

I chased Holly all night but couldn't catch her. Even if she had been right-handed, she would have beaten me because all I did was follow her around. Between the fifth and sixth rounds, I was sitting on my stool in the corner and started thinking, "What am I doing here?"

They say after you quit once, it's easier the next time. I thought about it that night sitting on that stool. I would never have believed I would, but I did. I was tired of chasing her but more tired of chasing a life I couldn't make right. Fortunately, I had too much pride and ego to let myself quit again. I pushed myself off that stool and walked out to face her. I didn't quit, but I thought about it, which shows you how far gone I was from what I'd been.

For 10 rounds I followed her like she had me on a leash. Two of the three judges gave her every round. When the final bell rang, I was just glad it was over. Beating me for her was a big thing. If I'd beaten her, it wouldn't have meant anything to me. I just didn't care anymore.

Thirteen months later I lost again, this time by split decision. The fight was in Worley, Idaho. Idaho was beautiful, but nothing else was. I hated Jim. I hated training. I hated what my life had become. I hated myself, too. All I knew was boxing, so I took that fight for $20,000. My career was following a familiar pattern of past champions and old pugs who never could fight. The purses get smaller. The venues get smaller. The crowds get smaller. The people who want to be around you get smaller. Everything around me was shrinking.

There were no bright lights in Worley, Idaho. I was 38 years old, had lost three of my last four fights, and didn't give a damn about boxing anymore. The same was true for my life.

I'd just lost a split decision to a local girl whose trainer fought for the promoter. I thought I got robbed, but so what? The only person it still seemed to matter to was my dad. He used to give me a new $100 bill after I won a fight. He came to me that night with tears in his eyes and a $100 bill in his hand and said, "I can't believe they did that to you."

I could. When that fight was over, I sat in Worley, Idaho, wondering where my life was headed. It was headed to a very bad place.

CHAPTER SEVENTEEN

Sex, Drugs, and Videotapes

Several months after my pursuit of Lucia Rijker and that million-dollar payday ended with her claim of an injury, I got a phone call from one of my boxing guys. There were seven of them who traveled regularly with me almost everywhere I went, and one of my favorites was Jeff Bailey. We called him Elvis because of his fixation with Elvis Presley.

He was a big guy who wore his hair in a pompadour with long sideburns like Elvis and often sported spectacular sunglasses. He even tried to dress like him sometimes, in white jumpsuits and all of that. You couldn't dislike Big Jeff if you tried, but I had a special reason to take a shine to him. He understood me, and he hated Jim, which gave us some things in common. So, when I saw his number pop up on my phone, I was happy to hear from him. In short order I wasn't so happy, even though he was looking out for me.

Jeff told me something had been bothering him for a while, and I was hoping he was going to say Jim had a girlfriend and wanted to leave me. That would have been a relief, because I would have had a justification for walking out that my family could accept, but it wasn't that.

He said Jim had been burying cash in a metal box out by the gazebo in our backyard and having guys from the gym go take money to send to his daughters in Indiana. Jeff said he thought he'd sent about $30,000 in cash out in one summer, and it hadn't stopped there. He said they would take it out in increments of $10,000 or $20,000 so I wouldn't notice it was gone. I'm not even sure it's legal to send cash like that, but it's what was going on from what Jeff told me.

At first, I thought he was crazy. Maybe I didn't pay attention to the business side of boxing the way I should have, but wouldn't I notice if that kind of money was going out of my account? I began to wonder if that money had ever gotten into my account in the first place as it should have because I was the one who earned it. I finally just thought to myself, *"What the hell is wrong with me?"*

I hung up and headed over to confront Jim, who was alone in the gym when I arrived. I started hollering and cursing. He didn't have much of a reaction. He didn't try to deny it, and I got so angry I grabbed a weighted stick, like a thick broom handle that I used to stretch my shoulders, and beat the bejesus out of him with it. You can't even conceive of how mad I was. I totally lost it.

I hit him three or four times. It was the only time he didn't try to fight back. He just tried to ward off the blows until I got exhausted. He never tried to explain where the money went or why he took it. He didn't try to say Jeff was lying either.

I kept asking him, "How could you steal from me? You have a bunch of cars, a $120,000 bracelet, property, those ugly Versace shirts you always want . . . and you're stealing from me? I bled for that money!"

He didn't say anything until I said stealing from me was the last straw. I was done. I was finished with him and our life together.

He kind of smirked and said, "You aren't leaving me. You need me." I was furious, exhausted, and at my wits end, so I turned and walked out. The funny thing is, I guess I knew when I left he was right. I didn't want to believe him, but the truth is I was brainwashed. I was going to walk out to do what? I had no idea. So, I stayed for five more years of misery, both Jim inflicted and self-inflicted. It's ridiculous looking back on it.

Jim stealing from me was the end, though. It wasn't the emotional abuse, the physical abuse, or the lack of feeling between us. Stealing was the breaking point. I'd worked my ass off for that money since I was 21, and the guy who was supposed to love me was robbing me. That I could not justify or blame myself for.

When Jim came home that night, my dad, brother, and nephew were at the house, because they'd been working on our roof. I didn't say anything more about it to anyone, and neither did Jim. Jim's kids had always treated me poorly, even though he was long separated from their mother when we first met. They knew I hadn't broken up his marriage, but I was the same age they were, so I'm sure it was difficult. They resented me, and I accepted that until I found out he was stealing my money to send to them.

That made me feel stupid. Why didn't I know what was going on right under my nose? I wouldn't know to this day if Jeff hadn't told me. I can't prove it, but I wonder now if Jim had had a side deal with King and the other promoters to siphon off some of the money I was supposed to be paid. It would have been easy enough to do, because it wasn't like I sat down and read those contracts. I just agreed to the purse and signed them.

I didn't feel any better when Jeff told me there was also a videotape in the box that he watched. He thought it was a fight tape, but it turned out Jim had been filming me without my knowledge lying naked around our pool, which I did all the time because we had a big yard and no neighbors close enough to see in. What else was he doing that I knew nothing about? Later I'd find out a lot more than I could have imagined.

The confrontations never really stopped after that. I found out he'd also borrowed money from two of our closest friends. He told them he needed it to send to his ex-wife for cancer treatments, because I wouldn't give it to him. It was all a lie, but it was his way of making me look bad while testing them to see how loyal they were to him. They gave him the money and never mentioned it to me until long after I'd recovered from being shot. When it came to Jim Martin, he was a master manipulator.

After I learned about the missing money, I drew up a contract between us that said he'd agree to a divorce but we would continue to live in the house and lead separate lives. I'd agree to work hard on a final comeback with Jim still managing and training me for a couple of fights so we'd both have something after it was over, because by now we were nearly broke. He never signed it, and I didn't pursue it. I didn't stand up too well in those kinds of situations.

After he shot me, the detective who questioned me at the hospital asked why, after all that, I hadn't left him. I had tubes in my lungs, a bullet in my chest, and my calf and ear needed to be sewn back on when she asked. I said, "This is why I didn't leave." By the time he stole my money, I knew one day he was going to kill me.

At first, you stay in that kind of abusive relationship because you don't believe he'll do something like that. Maybe he hits you or psychologically beats you down, but don't all marriages have problems? Then one day you realize you're staying because you know he will do it. So, my advice to anyone is the first time something like that happens to you, physically or emotionally, you need to leave. Anyone who is brazen enough to say threatening words to you means they at least have those thoughts. You don't need to be with someone who thinks and talks like that.

The writer Toni Morrison once said, "When someone shows you who they are, believe them." She's right. It's important you believe an abuser the first time they show who they are, not the last time, because that time is often fatal.

According to the National Coalition Against Domestic Violence (NCADV), one in four women experience severe intimate partner physical violence and/or stalking with outcomes such as severe beatings, PTSD, and constant fearfulness. On a typical day in the United States, there are more than 20,000 calls to domestic abuse hotlines.

When I speak around the country on domestic violence issues, I ask the audience at the beginning to record the time on their clock. At the end of my talk, I ask them how long it's been since I started. I tell them to multiply that by 20, because for every minute I spoke 20 people were abused. That number is unacceptable.

Approximately four and a half million women alive today have been threatened with guns by intimate partners. One million have been shot or shot at. One in three female victims killed by an intimate partner is killed by firearms. The presence of a gun increases the risk of a homicide by 500 percent.

According to Northeastern University criminology professor James Alan Fox, 44.8 percent of women killed during a 10-year study he conducted were killed by an intimate partner. A recent 10-city survey found 20 percent of homicide victims with temporary restraining orders were murdered within two days of the order being obtained. More than 33 percent were murdered within a month.

"Women will often underestimate their risk of being killed," NCADV literature says, and the proof is in their numbers. NCADV statistics say 46 percent of women murdered in the past decade in the United States were killed by a present or former intimate partner. Roughly 57 percent were killed by a gun, 22 percent by a knife. Jim used both on me.

Despite all the warning signs, I didn't believe my abuser until he had me trapped in a dark world where he could even steal from me without any real repercussions. Instead of leaving, once again I stayed. Not long after that, the cocaine started.

My whole life I'd been against using drugs. I tried marijuana in high school, but I didn't like the high. Same with speed. Tried it. Didn't like it. So, I stuck with drinking to excess instead. I'd drink sometimes until I was blotto, but as my life and my career unraveled, so did my resolve.

I was still fighting, but I knew my career was effectively over. The big paydays, the championship fights, the bright lights in Vegas were all gone. All those millions I'd made were gone, too. We were starting to sell off some of our seven cars and my jewelry to stay afloat. The best shot I had of ending up with something to show for all those years of training, fighting, and hiding was to get myself in position for one or two more paydays, which I still thought was possible if I could get off drugs and into fighting shape.

This is the pattern for most fighters. We beat old, faded former champions on the way up to make our name. Then one day we're the sacrificial lamb on the altar of someone else's dream. It's what usually happens. We keep fighting, but there's no real purpose anymore except getting paid, and those paydays get smaller and smaller. So do the arenas, but we keep going back, because boxing is the sport of self-delusion. How else can you pursue it when the odds of success are so long?

Eight months after I lost that fight in Idaho, I won one in Lake Charles, Louisiana, against a girl named Amy Yuratovic. I hit her in the second round with the best right hand I ever threw, and she went down, but unlike most of my career, she got up. I couldn't believe it. I was embarrassed about it, frankly, but I won a six-round decision to improve my record to 47-5-2. It wasn't exactly a comeback fight, but it meant my career was still alive, even if I was dying inside.

That summer we had a fighter in our gym who we all knew was regularly using cocaine. He looked like a million bucks in the gym, but when they turned the lights on in an arena, he wouldn't fight. Jim continued to train him, because in boxing you never know. Anybody can get lucky one night. He didn't, but we kept hoping one night would be his night—because if it's the right night, we'd all benefit. When you're in boxing, you learn to ignore things you wouldn't otherwise.

One night Jim came home with a baggie and dropped it on the table in front of me. He said that fighter announced he was done with cocaine, and there was the proof. I don't know if he really believed that, or if he was tempting me. Maybe he understood he was losing control of me little by little, and drugs might give him another hook to keep me under his thumb.

It's like he threw it in front of me as bait, but maybe it wasn't like that at all. It's one of many questions I'd like to ask him some day, but in the end it doesn't matter. All that matters is I took the bait.

The bag sat there for a day or two, looking at me. I wasn't training much and had only fought once in 18 months since losing in Idaho. I didn't care about myself, and I hated Jim and what my life had become. I was just so tired. What did it matter if I tried cocaine just once?

I was alone the night I finally grabbed that baggie and opened it. I snorted a line, and it was like the first time I knocked someone out and the crowd went crazy. I loved the feeling it gave me. The spiral of my self-destruction had begun to speed up.

At first, I was like most addicts in training. I only did it on Friday nights and weekends. Pretty soon it was Mondays, too. Then it became every day. Maybe it took a month until it had me. Pretty quickly I'd do anything for coke.

I stopped going to the gym. I seldom left my house. I told Jim to get some more. He did. I loved the way being high made me feel. It put me in a good space where I didn't think about the things that were making me unhappy.

I hadn't felt truly happy for so long, and cocaine gave me the illusion of happiness. Suddenly all my doubts and all the pain I was carrying inside were gone. Blown away by blow. I was good. Until I wasn't.

I did coke for three years, from the middle of 2007 until just before Jim shot me in 2010. Not nonstop, but damn close to it. Jim would do it occasionally with me, but mostly it was me, alone in the house.

Once it started, it was his new way to control me. He would hide it and then leave. I'd call him, begging to know where he'd put it. Sometimes he'd tell me. Other times he wouldn't, and I'd ransack the house trying to find it.

Occasionally, I'd go to the gym intending to train, so people would still think of me as a fighter, but I'd be so tired, I'd do coke in the bathroom to get myself going. You can become pretty inventive when you're a drug addict, so one time I asked a fighter I knew had access to drugs if he could get me some coke so I'd have some control over my supply instead of always relying on Jim. He said he could, but he asked how he'd get it to me without Jim knowing.

I told him I'd hand him a boxing glove to try on and tell him I thought it felt great and wanted him to check it out. He'd have the coke in his hand and when he put his hand inside, he'd leave it in the glove. Then I'd take the glove back, put it on, and grab the coke. It worked like a charm that time, but the more I began using, the more paranoid I got, and the more Jim kept watch over me. It wasn't something I tried again.

At some point during my spiral down, Jim hid some cameras around the house that I didn't know about at first. He'd ask me about conversations I'd had when he wasn't home, and I knew he knew what I'd said. It was part of his control game. He wanted me to understand there was nothing I could say or do he wouldn't know about. I kept trying to find the cameras. I was consumed with trying to figure out how he was watching me. But was he really watching me?

It wasn't until after he shot me that I knew for sure I was right. My brother, Randy, found a camera inside a light while he was clearing out my stuff after the police were done with the murder scene. That's when I knew that although I might have become a paranoid drug addict at the time, I wasn't crazy.

Jim also asked me to do things with him in bed I'd never do unless I was high. He had me wear a strap-on a number of times. I never really used it on him, but I can't believe I even wore it. He'd lay out clothes he wanted me to wear with it. I knew he was filming all of what we were doing. I can't say I was innocent about that. I just didn't care about anything but the drugs, so I did what he wanted, and things got worse and worse.

I was also taking pain pills for all the injuries I'd had in boxing and drinking, too. I overdosed so many times I should be dead. I took bottles of pills, was using cocaine so often we were getting it delivered to our house instead of Jim bringing it in. The more I used, the more paranoid I became.

My suicidal thoughts became really common once I started using drugs. I put the gun Jim shot me with to my head plenty of times. My dad's father committed suicide when I was in college, and I remembered asking myself at the time why I didn't see a sign of what was coming or what I could have done differently to help him. Now I found myself thinking I didn't want to leave my parents asking themselves the same questions about me because there is no answer to them. There's only an emptiness inside that you can't fill.

It's exhausting to be watched all the time. It's exhausting to be scared all the time. The anxiety weighs on you, and you just want to stop feeling that way. That's how drugs came into my life. Its how suicide came into my mind.

I so wanted to drown my feelings and slip away, but I have to believe the Lord had something he wanted me to do in this life. If He didn't, I would have been gone a long time ago. Jim wouldn't have had to try to kill me. Eventually the drugs would have done it for him.

Sometimes, when I was alone and sure cameras were watching me, I'd hold a gun to my head to see if Jim would come back. He never did. I guess I was trying to send him a message, but the truth is I didn't have the courage to pull the trigger. Or I wasn't crazy enough. I don't know why I didn't. I'm just grateful I never got that far down.

I had reached the point where I didn't know how to live anymore. I didn't remember how to get up off the canvas, but I wasn't ready to totally quit on myself. Despite the drugs, on some level I understood I was in the fight of my life. I was down on the scorecards, but I refused to take a knee and end it like I did against Laila. I didn't have much fight left in me, but I was not going to take a knee again.

I became so paranoid I'd have my gun in my hand or nearby whenever I got high. I started to think Jim had people outside watching me. I started hearing noises at night. Once when I was high, I went out in the backyard with my gun and heard something scrambling by the back fence. I aimed the gun but didn't pull the trigger. I couldn't make myself do it. I just walked back inside and did another line.

Sometimes I'd be on my computer and all of a sudden it would click that someone was on our home Wi-Fi. I'm sure it was Jim reading what I was writing. It felt like he was watching me all the time. It was like he was getting some satisfaction watching me lose my mind. I believe all this is true, but I also know I'd become pretty paranoid. Cocaine addiction will do that. One of the ways it ruins you is it makes you paranoid. I was both—ruined and paranoid.

At one point, I put flour out around the house by the windows, thinking I'd find the footprints of people he had watching me from outside. That would prove my suspicions correct, but it never worked. I never found any footprints. By the time I'd get out of bed, it would be three or four in the afternoon, and all the flour had blown away or evaporated in the heat and humidity in Florida. You're seldom an early riser when you're up doing coke all night. I never saw a footprint, but I believed people were out there, watching.

We had a fence around the yard made out of slats. One section had come apart a little so you could squeeze through it. I covered the fence post with Vaseline. I thought if someone was sliding through it to spy on me, they'd get Vaseline on them and I might see it and know I wasn't hallucinating. I thought I was a clever detective, but that didn't work either. Maybe no one was there. Cocaine bends your mind, and it certainly twisted mine, but I believe to this day Jim wanted people to see me doing drugs and sexual things with him that made me uncomfortable so he could convince them I was crazy in case I did kill myself or he killed me.

One time I took a bottle of pain pills and drank some beer while I was waiting for someone to bring more coke to the house. I began to get anxious and agitated. Finally, I drove to my gym looking for the coke. I parked out front and started to get scared I was dying.

I didn't have my phone or the gym key, so I walked over to the laundromat across the street. Our gym was in kind of a bad neighborhood, but people there knew me. I found someone and told them I needed help, but they walked away. They'd seen enough drugged-out people to steer clear of who I'd become.

I felt the only way I'd live was if I got home, so I walked back to my car. I must have looked like this high-stepping, crazy white woman trying to imitate Michael Jackson's moon walk because that's what I was doing. I have to laugh now because that image is so ridiculous.

When I got home, Jim was there, and I told him I thought I overdosed. He told me to drink pickle juice. He said it would make me throw up. He didn't want to take me to the hospital and risk a headline that said: "Christy Martin ODs."

I just drifted to the bottom emotionally, and I stayed there for a long time. Once I put the gun to my head in front of Jim, and he said, "You're too chickenshit to pull the trigger." I guess he was right, because I didn't. There was still a piece of me that wanted to survive.

I could blame this all on Jim if I wanted to. It wouldn't take much convincing, because he encouraged my drug use, and he kept the supply coming. I never had to get it myself. But come on. It was Christy Martin's decision to bend over and do that first line. I was alone the first time. I was alone most of the time. Basically, if I was awake in those years, I was high. Who was responsible for that? Me and nobody else. I made those choices.

Jim was the supplier, but nobody made me do it. I was the one who became an addict. Coke made me crazy, but it didn't put itself up my nose. I did that, because I didn't yet have the courage to start my life over on my own.

About a year into my addiction Jim announced he had a fight for me in Houston for the vacant NABF women's middleweight title against a girl named Valerie Mahfood on July 18, 2008. I was in no shape to fight but in no shape to say no either.

I was in Houston the week before the fight and deathly afraid I was going to test positive. It was bad enough that I hadn't put anywhere near 100 percent effort into training, but if I tested positive, it would be so embarrassing to the promoters, who were friends of mine.

I was at the height of my coke days then. My brother, Randy, knew what I was doing by then. He took me to a local CVS and we bought an at-home drug test kit, and I came up clean. I knew coke only stayed in your system for a few days, but I was shocked. It seemed damn near impossible considering how I was living at the time that I wouldn't test positive.

I was six pounds below the middleweight limit and afraid I might be so light they wouldn't let me fight. It wasn't like the Ali fight any more. Commissions were paying more attention to what the women were doing. That was the funny thing about that time in my life. Unlike most people who abuse cocaine in the amounts I did, I never got skinny. At least never too skinny to box for money.

I didn't fight very well, but it was still a close fight. A guy named Claude Jackson was the supervisor. He's passed away now, so I can admit he came to our corner late in the fight and told us the judges had it a draw after six rounds. No one is supposed tell you the scores, which is the oddest thing about boxing. In what other sport do you have to guess what the score is?

The theory is if a fighter knows they're well ahead, they might stop fighting, become real defensive, and it becomes terrible entertainment. I understand that, but it's weird that you're fighting for your life but don't know if you're ahead or behind.

Because we had been tipped off about the score, I realized I had to push myself, and I rocked her with an overhand right in the last round. I thought it might be enough to get the win, but two judges scored it a draw. The third had me winning, 78-74, but that wasn't enough. It was a majority draw, so nobody left with that title belt. I thought I'd won, but at that point in my career, Christy Martin didn't get close decisions any more. That's another thing that happens when you stay too long in boxing. Everything starts to go the other way.

Mahfood was a likable person. After the fight, she even told my dad I'd beaten the hell out of her. When we got back to the hotel bar, my mom broke out some moonshine she'd brought with her from West Virginia. Lisa was there with us. She'd sparred with me before the fight, and this time I was a little more interested in her beyond boxing. I started flirting, but that went nowhere. She told me years later I was terrible at flirting. I certainly wasn't thinking about anything more than that at that point. I didn't need another relationship. I was still stuck in one with Jim.

Even though I didn't care about much of anything but getting wasted, I was devastated after that fight, but not because I didn't win. What bothered me was that the draw made me doubt everything that had happened in my career.

Had I been successful only because I'd had Don King protecting me all those years? I fell into Jim's plan of manipulation, which was to keep me thinking all my success was because of him or Don. They created Christy Martin, not me. Being paranoid all the time didn't help my self-esteem, that's for sure.

I began to wonder if I'd ever accomplished anything on my own. That feeling lingered for quite a while, a fear that maybe I couldn't do it on my own. It was a long time before I saw that wasn't true. For years I didn't give myself and Gogarty the credit we deserved for legitimizing women's boxing. I was well past the end of my career before I came to the realization that a lot of little girls had watched me fight and were inspired by what they saw. Even as I read these words today, I feel a little uneasy saying them, but I've had so many women tell me that I know it's true.

It took many years for me to accept that I was the one who won all those fights. I'm thankful for all the people who helped me realize that I gave a lot of young girls a reason to believe they could do it. Now I had to give myself a reason to believe I could do it again, too, and that wouldn't be so easy.

A Champion Again, But Not for Long

My last great moment inside a boxing ring came the way the first one had—as a complete surprise to me and probably to most of the sports world.

I hadn't fought in 13 months when a Providence, Rhode Island-based promoter named Jimmy Burchfield called out of the blue and offered me a shot at the World Boxing Council women's super-welterweight title. The fight was set for September 9, 2009, in Syracuse, New York. Syracuse is a far cry from Las Vegas, and my purse was only around $15,000, which was a far cry from those Don King paydays, but I was nearly flat broke and a far cry from the fighter I used to be, so I took it.

This was one last chance to wear a championship belt around my waist, so I was eager for the opportunity. There was only one problem. I had barely been inside a gym in a year.

My career had by now become completely sidetracked by my new best friend, Mr. Blow. I was doing cocaine almost daily, and snorting lines of coke is not a way to train for a championship fight. Heck, it's not a way to train for an argument in the kitchen, which I still had with Jim from time to time although far less often than when I was younger. His grip on me was complete by now. If he said, "Go fetch the paper," I would have done it, at least if I thought there'd be a line waiting for me when I got back.

Even though I didn't feel much like a fighter any more, I knew I had to start training like one, if for no better reason than to avoid being completely embarrassed. That didn't mean I stopped snorting coke, nor did it mean I trained in the feverish way I had when I was young and on the way up. But at least my appearances in the gym now weren't viewed as cameos by the rest of my team. I began working as regularly as I could, which was most days, even if I was high when I got there.

I knew I couldn't go into a title fight against a solid opponent like Dakota Stone, who had lost three title shots by decisions in the previous two years, without some sort of tune-up. So Jim and I put together what I hoped would be seen as a homecoming for me in Huntington, West Virginia, six weeks before I was to go to Syracuse.

In an odd way, Huntington was the right spot for me, because it had become the drug abuse capital of a state overwhelmed by the growing opioid crisis that was starting to sweep across America. Welcome home, Christy.

West Virginia was a ripe environment for drug abuse, because of the combination of a crashing coal-based economy, high unemployment, and a lot of people suffering from injuries sustained in the mines that were closing all around us. It was a perfect storm, and Huntington became the epicenter.

This was primarily the result of an influx of various legal painkillers being shipped into the state by some of the biggest distributors in the country. With the high incidence of injuries in the mines, painkillers became first a staple of life in the state and in short order grew into a major cause of drug abuse, not only with prescription painkillers, but also heroin, cocaine, and fentanyl. Just because you ran out of prescriptions didn't mean you weren't still an addict. As I found out, once that happens, you feed the addiction in any way you can.

One analysis cited in a major lawsuit in West Virginia filed against three of the nation's biggest distributors of prescription opioids showed that from 2006 to 2014, about 110 million doses of hydrocodone and oxycodone were shipped to Cabell County and Huntington, which was the county seat. During that nine-year period, there were an average 39.9 hydrocodone and oxycodone doses per person shipped nationally, compared to an average of 72 doses per person to West Virginia and 122 doses per person in Cabell County and Huntington, a city of 47,000 that in recent years has had an overdose rate 10 times the national average. Considering those sad facts and my sad condition, one could say I was back in my element when I went home to face a girl named Cimberly Harris for $1,500 six weeks before the Stone fight.

I actually had a figure of $0 on the contract I signed, which meant I only got paid if the card made money. It barely did. The venue was about two hours from my hometown, but so few people showed up I could have held it in the parking lot behind my high school. I bet I knew 95 percent of the people in the crowd that night.

I was hoping it would be a success, but the only thing that worked right was my ring entrance. We had them shut off all the lights in the building when I came out wearing my dad's coal miner's helmet with the light on. It was the only light you saw as I walked toward the ring. The fans loved it, but they didn't think much of how I fought because I stunk up the place.

I was high all week and ill-prepared but managed to escape with a six-round split decision. I'd copromoted the show with a guy I'd gotten to know in the early days back in Bristol, Tennessee, when it was all about big hopes and dreams and a focus only on my craft. Now I was barely able to focus my pupils. But if there was one thing I could make out, it was this: you see the same people on the way down that you passed on the way up. So it was that night.

As soon as the fight was over, Jim and I left for Canastota, New York, the home of the International Boxing Hall of Fame. I loved that little town and its importance to the sport of boxing. The people at the Hall had always been very warm and inviting to me since I first appeared there after the Gogarty fight in 1996; and because the town is only about 20 miles east of Syracuse, a decision was made to announce the Stone fight there because the Hall was one of the fight's sponsors.

Jim and I decided to finish my training in Canastota rather than go back to the temptations in Florida, but it's a funny thing about temptation. It follows you everywhere.

Although very few things mattered to me in those days, one that did was that WBC belt. It was one of the biggest icons in boxing and still is. For all the craziness and corruption in the sport, a WBC title remains a belt every fighter respects. I wanted one again, but I also wanted to get high to escape the rest of my world, so I was facing an internal fight as well as ones with Stone and Jim.

I managed to stay clean for the final two weeks of training, but Jim and I argued almost every night. We were staying at Graziano's World Famous Inn, a place I wasn't so sure was world famous, but everyone in the area at least knew Graziano's Restaurant as a major boxing hangout during the week of the Hall of Fame induction. Hundreds of the greatest boxers in history had eaten there, and I loved the place. But the owners didn't love hearing nightly foul-mouthed arguments between Jim Martin and his strung-out wife in their hotel, so they finally complained. I tried, without much success, to calm down.

One of the things that had me on edge was that we'd brought along a sparring partner who wasn't worth a damn, but Jim kept paying more attention to him than me. Maybe he didn't believe I could win, so why waste time with me. The fact I wasn't high every day only escalated things until it got pretty nasty. Somehow we got through it, and they got me into the ring, but I wasn't the same. This was not the blood-and-guts Christy Martin everyone was used to.

There was no TV and nothing that made the event feel special. We were off the boxing grid, but somehow I mustered enough energy to win the first six rounds by attacking Dakota's body. She was 5-foot-10, so she was a good target for someone six inches shorter. But when the bell rang for Round 7, I was out of gas. All those sparring sessions with Mr. Blow had hollowed out my 41-year-old body, and it began to ignore my commands.

Stone figured that out and really pressed me. She won some rounds, and I couldn't wait to hear "Round 10," because then it would be over. She attacked me again in that final round, and I fired an overhand right to convince her that wasn't the wisest thing for her to do and broke my hand on her head. I knew it immediately and started to backpedal. I fought that way the rest of the round and was awarded a majority decision, becoming the oldest female fighter to hold a world championship. It was also the longest gap between a debut fight and winning a world title of any boxer, male or female, in the sport's history, a span of exactly 20 years to the day that I drew with Angela Buchanan back in Bristol. As far as symmetry it was a perfect ending to my career, if I'd had the good sense to stop, but I didn't. It was my 49th professional win. Now I wanted 50. I never got it.

A friend pulled my brother aside after the fight and told him I should retire, because if I didn't, Jim would keep sending me up those steps until there was nothing left of me. I told Randy the guy was right, but I kept going because if I wasn't a boxer, who was I? A domestic violence victim? A gay woman in the closet with no marketable skills that I knew of? A drug addict? Who would make my decisions for me? Who would get me high? Who would care about me?

The only thing I was sure of in the aftermath of that fight was I needed to get to a hospital and get my hand fixed. I had it stuffed in a bucket of ice and it was throbbing as our van was getting ready to leave the arena parking lot when someone knocked on the window and I told my friend Dan Lait, who was driving, to stop.

It was pouring rain outside, but I recognized who it was. His name was Emile Griffith, and he once had been one of the greatest fighters in boxing history. Griffith was a Hall of Famer. He won both the welterweight and middleweight titles during his 18-year career and twice was named Fighter of the Year. Now here he was, this great fighter, coming by to say hello. It was such an honor to me that a legend like that would take time to speak to me that I got out of the car, and we stood there, talking in the rain for a long time.

We talked for maybe 30 minutes. My hand was killing me, but I would have stayed there with him for three hours if he wanted—not just because of the great champion he'd been, but because I knew he and I had something in common he had no idea about.

I always admired great fighters, but I admired Emile for more than that. I knew he had faced a lot of questions about his sexuality during his life. Emile was 71 at the time and had been living for years with one of the worst-kept secrets in boxing. Seventeen years earlier he'd been beaten half to death after coming out of a gay bar near the Port Authority in New York late one night and was hospitalized for four months. During that time, his sexuality became a public issue. Like me, he'd been haunted by his sexual identity all his life.

It had long been speculated that Emile was either bisexual or gay dating back to an incident during a weigh-in for a fight in 1962 with one of his biggest rivals, Benny "Kid" Paret. Griffith had worked in a women's hat factory when he was younger and was still designing women's hats, one of the reasons some questioned his sexuality. At the weigh-in, Paret leaned over and whispered the word "maricon" in Griffith's ear, Spanish slang for faggot.

Griffith was enraged and had to be restrained from attacking Paret. Later that night Griffith trapped Paret in a corner of the ring and beat him senseless, in part because Paret's arm got caught in the ropes and he was unable to fall to the floor.

The fight was stopped, and Griffith won a world championship, but 10 days later Paret died after never regaining consciousness. Griffith was never the same fighter and later claimed to have been haunted for 40 years by nightmares of Paret coming back to see him.

His story would eventually become a widely acclaimed documentary film titled *Ring of Fire* and the subject of a best-selling book and two plays. Emile was most likely bisexual, but he never publicly confirmed his sexual identity before he died at the age of 75 in 2013. He did go so far as to tell a *Sports Illustrated* writer in 2005, "I like men and women both but I don't like that word: homosexual, gay or faggot. I don't know what I am. I love men and women the same, but if you ask me which is better . . . I like women."

To me those stories focused too much on his sexuality and not enough on his greatness as a boxer, but that was the world we lived in. I couldn't care less whether Emile Griffith was gay, but I know his life was a great tragedy, because those questions dogged him most of his days and all of his nights. I had a special respect for him because of all the things he'd endured and the homophobia he faced. I never wanted to face that same burden, but in the end, it got us both, I guess.

Now here he stood, a faded old champion like I was, whose pain I understood perhaps better than anyone else could have. The title of that *Sports Illustrated* story about him in 2005 was Shadow Boxer. What Emile didn't know that night was I was a shadow boxer, too.

Winning that title didn't change my life. Boxing couldn't do that for me anymore. I had achieved one last milestone in the sport, but being the oldest champion isn't like being the youngest. World champion or not, the sun had set on Christy Martin's career, and I knew it.

I was lost, miserable, and doing coke every day. Jim was drinking a lot, and I'm sure he was miserable, too. Our life was a wreck, and the only future I could see for us was a bad ending when things took a turn I never imagined.

My mother and I were fighting as usual, this time over whether I was bringing a Christmas gift home for my niece. Jim had told her I wasn't, and he was right. He said she'd told him for me not to come if that was the case.

This time I didn't believe him, so I called her and asked. She said that was exactly what she'd said, and I hung up. We didn't talk for a long time, but that wasn't the worst thing about that Christmas.

Three days before Christmas we were sitting around our house in Apopka, and Jim was taking his blood pressure. The numbers were crazy. I told him to take it again, and it was crazier than the first time. It was going through the roof.

Jim had heart problems and was always monitoring his blood pressure. Once I started abusing cocaine, I started doing the same thing, and there'd be nights when we'd both have skyrocketing blood pressure, but nothing like this.

He was in distress, so I finally called a nurse we knew, and she suggested we get to the hospital in Apopka. As soon as we got there, they said we needed to get him in an ambulance to Orlando, because they weren't equipped to handle the problem they thought he was having.

The doctors in the cardiac unit in Orlando found a serious blockage that would require immediate open-heart surgery. We spent Christmas in the hospital, and the surgery was done the day after. When it was over, Jim didn't wake up.

For the first couple days, they kept saying he'd wake up tomorrow, but it got to the point where no one was sure anymore if he'd ever wake up. I never left the hospital, which meant I stopped getting high. That didn't help my stress, but at that moment I wasn't thinking about drugs as much as I was my growing guilt feelings. My mind kept going back and forth between wanting him to come to and wanting him to never wake up.

I have my problems, but I think I've always been a good person at heart, so I couldn't accept that I was even thinking that way. I started praying for him to wake up. I wanted him to live . . . except for the times I wanted him to die.

One minute I'd think I should just put a pillow over his face like Clint Eastwood had done to Hilary Swank in *Million Dollar Baby*. Next minute I'd hate myself for thinking like that.

Half the time I was worried about what would happen to me if he died, and the other half I thought if he did die, it would be a Christmas present from God. If I was going to revive what was left of my boxing career, I believed I still needed him even though he was the main reason my life had gone so far off the tracks. But if he died, I'd finally be free after nearly 20 years of hell. That's how ambivalent my feelings toward him had become.

Jim was in a coma for 10 days, and after about a week the doctors told me he might never wake up. They didn't know why. They finally told me he might die at any moment or stay in this state for months. I was completely adrift and alone.

I had no one to confide in. I couldn't talk to my family, and I had no friends at the time I felt I could trust with the feelings I was having. I just couldn't come out and tell anyone that part of me hoped he would just fade away. I couldn't even be real with myself at that point about how I felt.

My parents did finally come down to see us, but I barely spoke to them. I just sat there numb, waiting to see if my husband and my captor would wake up.

The doctors finally told me if he didn't wake up after 14 days he probably wouldn't survive. I wrestled with that idea until I fell into a fitful sleep in the hospital. Less than 24 hours later, Jim Martin's eyes opened.

I felt relieved that his kids wouldn't be able to try to hold me responsible for his death. I told myself maybe this was the kind of life-altering experience that would make him act differently, and things would improve between us. It was my last moment of hope for the two of us.

It wasn't long after we got home and he began to get his strength back that I could see his controlling nature had become worse. I had done my best to keep him alive. I made sure he got good care. I was the one who made him take his medications because he'd often forget or just refuse if I wasn't watching over him. I played my role of the concerned wife, but that didn't change a thing.

In addition to his heart problems, Jim also had diabetes and needed regular shots of insulin. I have to admit there were times I'd give him the shot and think to myself, *"Why not jack this up and send him into a diabetic shock and get it over with?"* That's an awful thing to say, but that's the mental state I was in. I never did it, but just having those thoughts troubles me. Who had I become?

While Jim was recuperating, I went right back to doing coke. Despite two fights and Jim's stroke, the coke train barely stopped. The only times were the two weeks before the Stone fight and the two weeks Jim was in a coma.

I thought about leaving him several times, but I felt if I did, it would just confirm the lies he'd told people about me being a terrible person. So, instead, I became his round-the-clock nurse until he was strong enough to go back to the gym. That took a few weeks, and I was skeptical at first when he insisted on going there.

I was in the ring shadowboxing when I saw him trying to bench press 135 pounds. I ran over and hollered at him. He gave me one of his phony smiles, and I wanted to vomit. I took off my gear and walked home alone.

I hated the way he treated me, but now I felt obligated to him. It's a wife's job to take care of her husband, isn't it? It's hard to fully explain how conflicted I was.

One night I was up late, high on coke, and Jim kept staring at me. Then he started singing "You Are My Sunshine" in a low voice, but the look on his face said the opposite. It was mind games all the time now, and my mind was bent.

Later Sherry said I was suffering from Stockholm syndrome. That's when you form an emotional attachment to a captor in a hostage situation, or toward an abuser in a domestic violence or sexual abuse situation. I learned it's considered a mental health disorder by some people, because it creates a thought pattern that interferes with making smart decisions that are in your best interest. That certainly described who I'd become.

That summer I was still getting high, but I was at least talking to my mother again. In August they came to visit, and I asked her to stop speaking to Jim. I told her he was videotaping me 24/7 and stalking me. She says now that conversation never happened. I know it did, but it didn't matter, because by that time she couldn't help me. Nobody could. Jim had manipulated us all.

He'd tell my mom one story and me another, and we'd both believe him. I've never met anyone who could play one side against the other better than Jim Martin. Not even Don King. It's why I began to call him the puppet master. He was pulling the strings and making us all dance.

One afternoon I got in the BMW that King had given me, and I had a problem with the dimmer lights. Jim bought some parts and said he would fix it. He was under the hood and told me to get in and start the car while stepping on the brake. I was so afraid he might kill me that I thought he might be putting a bomb in my car.

Every time he'd say "step on the brake" I was waiting for the car to explode. Yet I did what he told me. He had enough control that I kept stepping on the brake, waiting to die. I know that sounds crazy, because that's exactly what it was.

Eventually I developed a plan in my mind how to protect myself when he finally tried to kill me, but it's giving me too much credit to say I was thinking things through. As the months passed, I knew there was no avoiding what was coming. There was going to be a confrontation, and I was either going to get through it or my life was over. There was no way around it. Jim Martin was going to try to kill me.

If I couldn't change my circumstances at home, I could at least use boxing as a refuge, as I always had. I wanted to try to get that part of my life back, because at least I could control it. I can remember as if it were yesterday what happened next. It was the week before Jim tried to kill me. November 17, 2010. I was walking through my house, high, when I saw my reflection in a mirror and stopped dead in my tracks. I thought, "You really look like an addict." At that moment it hit me. No, you don't. You are an addict.

What was looking back at me wasn't Christy Martin. It wasn't the coal miner's daughter. It wasn't the WBC world superwelterweight women's champion. It was a drug addict. That's what I'd become.

I immediately went and did a line to try and erase that thought, but it wasn't the same any more. By the next day I'd decided things needed to change, and I had to be the one to make the change. I didn't have control of much of my life. But I had control of where I put my nose, and I had control of whether I still wanted to act like a prizefighter. That was the last day I ever used drugs. November 18, 2010. That day I realized if I bent over and did one more line of cocaine, I'd do it until I was dead.

People ask me now how I quit cold turkey like that with my emotions so frayed. That day it was just so clear to me what needed to be done. It had been my choice to start. Now it was my choice to stop. So, I did.

I'd started using because I was miserable. It was a total escape for me, but I could now see there was no escape route there. For those of us who become addicts, we all have some excuse for why it happened, but for most of us the truth is some form of what it was for me. Cocaine helped me hide, but I didn't want to hide any more.

The next day I left for St. Augustine to meet Sherry for the first time in years. Five days later, stone cold sober, I was lying on my bedroom floor with a bullet in my chest, stab wounds all over my body, and blood everywhere. I was finally free, if I didn't die first.

Comeback to Nowhere

Why is this person asking me so many questions? Why do these people keep pushing tubes in my side? Can't they see I'm bleeding? What happened to me?

A lot of questions run through your mind when you've got morphine pumping through your system, a small army of doctors and nurses surrounding you trying to keep you alive, and a lady detective who wants some answers. That was the entirety of my life on November 23, 2010, and for quite a few days after.

Jim was on the run, I was on a gurney, and my family was on its way to Florida just as soon as someone could track down my dad and my brother, who were off in the West Virginia mountains hunting deer together. It's safe to say Christy Martin was in a state of flux.

Rick Cole had saved my life by stopping to pick up an unknown woman covered in blood and taking what was left of me to the hospital in Apopka. He called 9-1-1 on the way and told the police he had someone in his car who said she'd been shot and she'd thrown a blood-covered pink-handled gun on his passenger's seat. By the time we arrived at Florida Hospital, which fortunately was only a few miles from my house, the emergency room people were ready for me, and the cops were on the scene. Unfortunately, the media weren't far behind. In short order the story was not only local news: it was national news from ESPN to CNN.

One thing I remember hearing is someone say, "She's got metal in her back." I was so out of it I didn't understand what they were talking about. I'd forgotten Jim shot me by then, so when a nurse asked if I'd been shot, the first thing I said was, "No."

How do you forget you've been shot? Blinding pain has something to do with it. Shock from all that had happened in the previous hour does, too. Clear thinking is not always your first response to questions. At least it wasn't for me.

They told me later I kept asking the nurses if I was going to die. Only a few hours earlier I'd given up on life, but now there was nothing I wanted more than to live. Maybe the reason why was simply that although I may have been shot, stabbed, and bleeding, I knew I was free of Jim Martin.

It's apparent to me now that because of how far I'd allowed my life to deteriorate, I needed that kind of violent separation from Jim to become "me" again. Our relationship had become like two tectonic plates pushing against each other, the pressure building underground like it does before an earthquake. Relief would only come after a violent eruption, and certainly we'd just had one.

If we had split up before Don King came along, things might have been OK. At that time, the world had never heard of either one of us, so maybe we could have walked away from each other. He didn't have the kind of control over me then that he developed later, and the stakes would have been a lot smaller for me. But we stayed together, and I continued a life of hiding while Jim's power to reveal the truth of that lie grew until I feared it would cost me everything.

I stayed until there was barely any of "me" left. For a long time, I thought things might turn ugly at some point. Killing me seemed like a pretty big jump from emotional abuse or even physical abuse, but the truth is that the abuser is killing you every day in little ways. When I finally came to accept he'd do it, it didn't matter to me anymore. Any escape from the life I was living was acceptable, even the final escape of dying. So, I can't say it came as a surprise that when I finally made the decision to go off and meet Sherry, Jim did what most domestic abusers do in such a situation. He lost it.

I found out later he'd called a lot of our friends and family in the couple of days before it all came crashing down, telling them he couldn't live without me and outing me in every way he could think of, including screenshots of videos with me in compromising sexual situations with him. He said it was because he loved me. The truth is he realized he'd lost control of me. The abuser cannot live with that reality, so he lashes out. Sadly, it's a common response.

What Jim never understood, and the public didn't either, was that the woman I left him for wasn't Sherry. The woman I left him for was me. She just got caught in the backdraft, I'm sorry to say. I didn't leave Jim Martin for Sherry. I left Jim Martin for Christy Salters.

Of course, the why of it wasn't on my mind as I lay in the emergency room with an oxygen mask on my face, IVs in my arm, and two tubes being shoved through the holes in my side to try to reinflate my collapsed lung. It felt like they were shoving a garden hose between my ribs. Inserting those tubes caused one of the worst pains I've ever felt. Worse than those body shots I told you about. I would have preferred Mike Tyson drill me in the ribs all night long to having those tubes being shoved inside me, but either the knife or the bullet had deflated my lung, and they had to fix that and worry about my pain later.

I was in such a precarious state that the doctors in Apopka didn't even bother to stitch up my leg even though the calf was hanging off the bone. They just wrapped it. They figured if they didn't stabilize me first, I'd die, and who would care about my calf.

One thing I did remember was the phone number Sherry made me memorize. I gave it to one of the nurses, and they kept calling her, but I'd told her that if she saw a number she didn't recognize from a 407 area code not to answer, because it would be Jim. The hospital kept dialing until she finally picked up, and I told her Jim had stabbed me and I was in the hospital. I didn't mention being shot. She found that out when she got to Apopka a couple hours later.

She called my mom to tell her what happened and took a lot of pictures on her phone after she arrived, but none of my leg because I told her not to. It was just too gruesome. I kept those photos for quite a while. Don't ask me why. It's not like I needed visual reminders of what happened.

They worked on me for a couple of hours before they let a detective named Tara Evans from the Orange County sheriff's office speak to me. Her transcript says it was around 10:15 that night, less than five hours after I'd been shot.

From time to time she had to stop her questioning for the doctors to tend to me or send me off for a CT scan and things like that. None of what they were doing was helping me give her a totally clear picture of what happened. The fact they had me on morphine had me sort of drifting off from time to time as well, so my answers were confused at times.

I guess she had to get as much information as she could in a hurry in case I died, but some of my answers were wrong, and Jim's lawyers would later try to attack my credibility with them and argue this had been a case of self-defense.

She interviewed me again the next day after they'd taken me to the trauma center at the Orlando Regional Medical Center. Initially, I mistakenly told her I had tried to shoot him after I got the gun from him. The truth was I never got the gun in my hand, but I did tell her that night, "I tried to shoot him but I was too scared of him." Two questions later she asked if I'd shot my husband, and I said, "I didn't." What I meant was that's what was going through my mind while we were wrestling around on the bed and the floor. I was trying to protect myself and get the clip out of the gun. Would I have shot him? Thankfully, I'll never know, but I doubt it.

She asked if he had any wounds, and I told her, "Not from me." Later I said his hand slipped down along the blade while he was cutting me up, but when she asked if I'd stabbed him, I told her clearly that I had not.

There was also some confusion during those interviews whether my gun had been under the mattress or in Jim's pocket. Once I became famous and started wearing a lot of expensive jewelry, I always had a gun with me. I didn't trust anybody from early in life, and my life experiences only enhanced that lack of trust in people. There were very few times after 1996 that I was without a gun if I was going anywhere. My friends used to joke that my pink-handled gun would be the last thing some SOB would ever see.

I'd taken it to Daytona when I met Sherry, but when I got back home, instead of putting it under the mattress as usual, I left it on my nightstand. The migraine I had was pounding, and I just wanted to go to sleep. That's how Jim got it in his pocket, I'm sure.

I told Detective Evans I thought he shot me with my own gun, because that was kind of a running joke between us. It was like a statement we'd make sometimes that became reality.

That first interview created just enough confusion for Jim's lawyer to argue it had been a 50-50 struggle. That's like me claiming my fight with Laila Ali was a 50-50 struggle. I was never once on the offensive in that bedroom. It was Laila all over again, but this time I didn't take a knee. I got dropped by a gun and a knife.

When she asked about our relationship I told her, "To be honest with you, I just kind of dropped out of the world for a while. I was like a recluse. I just stayed off to myself. Our lives were so intertwined, I never left the house." Even in the physical and mental state I was in at the time, I got that part exactly right.

Later that first night the doctors decided I had to be transferred to Orlando, where they had a major trauma center. They had stabilized me but weren't equipped to deal with all my injuries, so they put me on a helicopter and flew me down. That totally freaked me out. I just knew I was going to fall out of that thing.

In the last few days before I was shot, Jim apparently spoke to my mother several times. He sent her some of those embarrassing sexual photos of me, too. While he was talking to her, I was saying goodbye to several of my friends in case he killed me. I'd told them all I was finally leaving Jim. They all told me to stay away from him or come to stay with them. My mom had a different message.

We didn't talk then, but she left me a voice message. She said I needed to "go back to him right now," or he'd ruin everything I'd built. She told me to go back even though I'd told her in August that he was stalking and videotaping me. I was still in shock from the shooting when I spoke to her next, and what I said wasn't kind.

I said, "You might as well have pulled that trigger yourself."

I wish I'd never said that, but I'd be lying if I told you I don't still feel that way. I understand better now what was going on and how Jim manipulated my family, but still she was the only one who told me to go back to a guy who was about to kill me. You can forgive that, but it's impossible to forget. All you can do is try to move on.

In Orlando, they took the tubes out of my side, but my lung collapsed again so they had to put new tubes in. Thankfully, these were smaller and didn't hurt as much. They reinflated it and stitched my calf back on. I have no idea how many stitches that took, but it looked like I had a zipper running up my leg. A damn long zipper.

It's a 12-hour drive from West Virginia to Orlando, so Sherry and my mom talked quite a few times, because they didn't get to Orlando until the next day. Mom told Sherry to be gone before they arrived. My brother told me later that on the drive my mom said they should tell people I wasn't with Sherry. She wanted to put out a story that I was with my sister-in-law, Randy's wife, Sherri. She still wanted to cover up who I was even after Jim tried to murder me. How do you explain that?

The concern wasn't for me as much as it was how the story would come out. She didn't want anyone to think I was with a woman. She'd rather say I was with my sister-in-law, even though she wasn't even in Florida at the time. My mom was still trying to control who I was. I will never understand that. You may not like that your daughter is a lesbian, but at some point, can't you just accept it?

Randy finally got so angry he pulled the car over and hollered at my mom. He told her you can't lie in a murder investigation. He said her daughter might be dying, and this is what she was concerned with?

When they finally arrived at the hospital, things were all right at first, but then I learned that the bank was foreclosing on my house in Apopka. My dad, my brother, and Randy's wife left to go clean out my house. My mom stayed with me. Next thing I knew she was up in Sherry's face, blaming her for Jim shooting me. I've got tubes in me. I'm still leaking blood, and my mom is threatening to get physical with my ex-girlfriend who I'd just spent the weekend with.

When I saw what was happening, I hit the button and security came running in and led her outside. There was a walker by my bed, and somehow I managed to get up and went out and just looked at her like she'd lost her mind. I finally said, "You've got to be kidding me," and wobbled back into my room. I didn't know what else to say.

While all this was going on, Jim was still on the loose. The police had gone to the house and couldn't find him, but they had found a blood trail from my house to his friend Scott Selkirk's, which was a few doors down. They questioned Selkirk and found Jim's blood in his foyer, but he claimed that Jim had run away, and he didn't know where he went.

He said he'd gone up to our house to see if I was still there, but I was gone and, when he turned around, so was Jim. He claimed he then tried to drive to the hospital to see if I was there, but the police had all the roads blocked in our neighborhood. I knew that was bullshit when it came out at trial that he never made any effort to come to see me after that. I was in the hospital for more than a week, and he never came, not that I wanted to see him.

It took the police a week to track Jim down. The manhunt was all over the local news every night. They were using dogs and keeping an eye on Selkirk. As the manhunt was going on, Jim called one of our boxers to come pick him up, and the kid called the cops. Almost instantly a helicopter was over Jim's location. He was hiding behind some bushes next to an old shed on Selkirk's property where he'd been hiding all along.

They found him on November 30, a week after he'd shot me. When the police arrived, Jim was dangling a knife from one hand and bleeding from the knife wound in his palm. It was a police dog who finally found him, and the cop who was with the dog pulled a gun on him and told Jim he'd shoot if he didn't drop the knife.

According to the police, he didn't comply immediately, but he finally did. When they arrested him, he was wearing two diamond rings and a $120,000 bracelet he'd bought for himself in Las Vegas with my money. When they went into the shed, they found Jim's blood and one other thing. They saw someone had carved "I love you babby" in the wall. When they asked if I thought that was Jim, I told them, of course, it was. I knew, because he couldn't spell very well. Jim wasn't book smart; he was a different kind of smart. He was con man smart. He understood how control works.

The police booked him that day and charged him with first-degree attempted murder and aggravated battery with a deadly weapon. He claimed he was only defending himself. After they'd arrested him, I was lying in the hospital still in a lot of pain. The morphine was keeping that under control, but there was no painkiller for the thoughts going through my mind when a nurse came in and told me they'd brought Jim to the same hospital. He was one floor below my room. I couldn't believe it.

They brought him there because of the deep cut on his hand. They later determined it was self-inflicted when he was frantically stabbing me with that bloody buck knife, which can become very slippery. I knew he couldn't get to me, because they had me in a medical lockdown, but it was still an uncomfortable feeling knowing he was there.

I stayed in the hospital for about 10 days and it didn't take long for me to get pretty stubborn about one thing. I refused to use the walker they'd given me. They wanted me to get up and start walking pretty quickly, and I was all right with that, but they said they wouldn't let me if I didn't take the walker with me.

I was furious because it was a symbol to me of weakness and giving in, so I lifted it up and carried it when I was walking down the hall. I wouldn't let it touch the ground. That was my mind-set. I wasn't going to let an injury Jim caused make me rely on a walker. I just decided to be stronger than that. I wasn't going to let him think he could do that to me, even though he wouldn't even know about it. That didn't matter. I knew. That was enough for me.

To be honest, my stay there not only saved my life; it also helped me get off cocaine. After Jim shot me, the hospital was pumping painkillers into me in a controlled way for some time. I'm sure that took the edge off of kicking cocaine. With all that had happened, cocaine was the last thing on my mind. I'm blessed to say it has remained that way for 12 years.

When they told me I could leave, I said I wasn't going until late at night. I didn't want to answer any of the media's questions or see any more television cameras. My family was there when Sherry and I left the hospital together at around one in the morning. I literally had no place to go but one. The next day I went to my gym and trained the best I could.

Sherry and I stayed in a hotel for a few days until she went back home to Charlotte. Now I was alone for the first time in so long I wasn't sure how to act or what to do with myself. So I got into my yellow Corvette and just started driving. I was all by myself, which is where I wanted to be. Jim was in custody, and I was totally free for the first time in 20 years until a car came up behind me and started flashing his lights. It was the father of one of my fighters, so I pulled over.

He asked how I was doing and then he told me he'd gone to visit Jim in jail the day before and given him some money for the commissary so he could buy a toothbrush. I told him to tell Jim to take care of himself. My emotions were so out of whack that when I drove away, I was feeling guilty that he'd shot me and was in jail. Suddenly it was important to me that he was OK. How could I feel like that about someone who had just tried to kill me?

I've read a lot about the cycles of overcoming something like what I went through. One of those cycles is blaming yourself or feeling like somehow you made him do it. I didn't, but that's how I felt at that moment. It wasn't my fault he pulled that trigger, but those were the emotions I was wrestling with for some time after that.

I had to make some decisions for myself for the first time in years, and I was having a hard time doing it. Jim had controlled what I wore, where I went, and even what I watched on television for so long I didn't know how to make a simple decision for myself. I didn't know what I wanted to eat or wear or do. The only thing I was sure of the first night I was free was that I was going back to the gym.

It had been closed since the shooting, so I was in there by myself, limping around, hitting the bags and feeling the way I always did in a gym. I was in the safest place I knew, and I loved being there.

When I walked out of that hospital, I was a changed person. I still had issues and fears and problems, but I adopted the mind-set that people could be on the "Christy Martin is gay train" or not. I didn't care anymore if they were or they weren't. It was very freeing to finally not care what anyone else thought. In many ways Jim killed Christy Martin, but he'd given new life to Christy Salters. I was resurrected from a bloody heap on the floor and happy I was.

I went back to my house once. There was no police tape or anything left, because they were done with it. I couldn't stay there, because my family had moved all my belongings into part of my gym, including my cars and my personal items, but I still felt the need to go back and take a look at the end of that part of my life. I had to break in through a back door, and once I got inside it was an eerie feeling. The best way I can describe it is that it felt like I was in a murder mystery movie where someone is walking through a half-lit house afraid of what they might find.

There were still blood stains on the floor and the carpet. I could see the outline of one of my legs on my bedroom floor. I took a picture of it. It was almost like it was somebody else's leg, and I guess maybe it was.

A couple days before Christmas my friend Donna Westrich invited me to stay in her home down near Ft. Lauderdale. She was going away to see her mother, and I could have the house to myself. I called Sherry to tell her, and she was not happy. She told me either I came to Charlotte for Christmas, or we were done. When I told Donna, she wasn't surprised. Donna didn't like Sherry from Day 1. She told me she was all about the publicity, not me. Donna had worked for Don King for a long time and seen a lot. She thought Sherry was just another hanger on, like so many fighters surround themselves with.

I didn't think that was true, but those words she'd said about Christmas started an internal struggle for me. I could see red flags waving. It felt like I was starting down a familiar road. This was another person who wanted to control me. Yet I still wasn't strong enough to say no.

I came to understand I'd gotten back together with her looking for something that didn't exist. It wasn't so much that I wanted to be with her as it was I wanted to feel the same innocent kind of love I'd felt when we were teenagers in West Virginia. I wanted to relive the past when I needed to move forward.

She was still pretty much the same person she'd been when we were young, but I was nothing like the girl I'd been back then. I'd seen too much and suffered too much to be someone looking up to the town's star athlete and my first female lover and putting her on a pedestal.

When we got back together, I wanted to think I was in love the way I'd been when I was a teenager in Itmann, but I didn't really love her anymore. What I loved was the fact that now I could be who I truly was—a gay woman. That was what I loved about us being together. What it said to the world.

Her need to control me clashed with what I was becoming. To be honest, I became pretty belligerent for a while. I was no longer going to listen to anyone but myself. Everything became a control issue for me, and I was not going to be controlled by anyone for very long. We were together, off and on, for about five years but it was never quite right.

I didn't know all this when I first left the hospital, but I was already having second thoughts about being with Sherry. It was only a few months before we agreed to go our separate ways for the first time, but I asked her to stick with me until I got through one more difficult situation. I asked her to stay until I fought again, and she agreed. It became a volatile truce with lots of ups and downs.

Just after Christmas, I had my personal physician remove the bullet from my back. The only reason it hadn't gone clean through me was that the cement slab under the carpet in my bedroom stopped it. I could feel it poking against my skin.

The prosecutors needed it for evidence, to make sure the ballistics matched my gun. When my doctor lanced my back, the bullet popped right out. I heard it land in a metal cup. The police were right there. They put a cap on the cup and left, but I wanted it back after the trial. I planned to put some small diamonds on it and wear it on a chain around my neck. I fully realized it was a crazy idea, but it would have been a symbol that I had SURVIVED!

It's been more than a decade, and I don't have it yet, but I still want it. It was in evidence for a long time, but Jim has exhausted his appeals, so I assume they don't need it. I don't know what I'll do with it now, but every time I see it, I'll know what it meant. That small piece of lead is what freed me, yet despite the new sense of freedom it gave me, I wasn't finished with Jim Martin quite yet.

Around this same time, Donna introduced me to Gloria Allred, the celebrity lawyer from Los Angeles who specializes in high-profile women's cases. Donna and I didn't tell Sherry I was going to meet with Allred, because I wasn't sure I could trust her. All I knew for sure was that one person I couldn't trust judging people was me. I didn't have a good track record making decisions about people.

I went to south Florida a couple weeks after I was released from the hospital and met with Gloria to listen to her pitch. It was around the same time that Donna offered to let me stay at her home while she was away for Christmas. I ended up hiring Gloria, and one reason was because I knew that Jim hated her. He'd see her on TV and just go off. I wanted to stick it to him a little, which is no reason to hire someone as your lawyer, but there was Jim, still living in my head.

My other reason was that I knew Gloria understood how to get media attention, and I thought that could help me when he went on trial and in my effort to get my career going again. I thought she was on the victim's side, and I thought she could help me make some money off my story, which I really needed. I would come to learn later that Gloria was a lot like Don King. She was good at getting media attention, but mostly for herself, in my opinion.

Not too long after his arrest, Jim was asking for bail. The prosecutors opposed it, and I sat at his bail hearing with Gloria at my side. It was my way of stabbing him back. This would be the first time I'd seen Jim since the struggle in my bedroom. As things turned out, I heard him before I saw him, and it was shocking.

I could hear him walking down the hall because his feet were shackled. You could hear the chains banging along the floor as he walked. Part of me kept thinking they didn't need to do all that to him. It was a crazy moment that was about to get a whole lot crazier. When the door opened, I saw the most remarkable thing. They had Jim in pink handcuffs.

There was some poetic justice in that, but I was astonished. When they put those pink-colored ties on him, he had to really think. I wanted to stand up and holler, "I didn't handcuff you. You handcuffed yourself." Fortunately, I had enough common sense to keep quiet for once.

I was feeling very nervous that he might get bond, because I feared if he got the chance, he'd come after me again. I still feel that fear today. When he tried to get out of jail because of the COVID-19 pandemic in 2021, I was pretty anxious, but his request was denied. So was his bail request. He's been in prison for 10 years now and isn't eligible for parole until 2035, so he'll be 92 if he serves his full sentence. If he was ever released, I'd be looking over my shoulder every night. That's just a fact. Fear and I have something in common. We both die hard.

I had called my old cut man, Miguel Diaz, from the hospital to ask if he'd train me. When he agreed, I asked if he could get me a fight. He said he'd talk to Bob Arum and get back to me. While I waited, I called Don to see if he'd be willing to bring me back. He'd resurrected a lot of fighters, including plenty that he'd had hard times with. I'm not comparing myself to Tyson or Chavez, but he brought back Julio after Julio testified against him in a federal court case over alleged insurance and tax fraud, and he brought Mike back even after Mike beat the shit out of him.

With all the publicity from the shooting, I figured Don would jump at the chance, but he wouldn't even take my call. He's never told me why. We're friends and sometimes promotional allies now, but I was so mad at him at the time, I couldn't even stand to hear his name.

Fortunately, Miguel called back and said Arum wanted me to come to Vegas to meet with him. I couldn't get on a plane fast enough. I negotiated the deal myself with Bob and several of his henchmen in the room, a fact I'm still pretty proud of. Bob agreed to put on a rematch with Dakota Stone on a big pay-per-view show in Madison Square Garden in New York on March 12, 2011, with me on the undercard. Initially, he offered me $30,000, and I said how about $300,000. He went up, and I came down, and we settled on $100,000 and the rights to three minutes of the fight video, which was a big payday for a woman boxer and still is.

I went back to Florida to promote an amateur show in Clermont, a town outside Orlando, before I started training. We didn't get much of a crowd, but Arum had already announced I intended to fight again. As soon as he did, women were lining up to fight me.

One person who showed up that night was a fighter named Chevelle Hallback. She'd turned pro in 1997, when I was at the top of my career, and had been chasing me for a long time. She'd just lost a fight and was looking for a quick turnaround, so she walked in and started accusing me of ducking her all these years. She said I was afraid to fight her. I'm standing there with a bullet hole in my chest, and this girl is accusing me of being afraid of her. I finally had enough and said to her right in front of some reporters, "Are you out of your mind? I just watched a guy shoot me in the chest and lived to tell about it, and you think I'm afraid of you?" That ended the conversation. It also ended any chance she had of ever getting in the ring with me if I had anything to say about it.

People really can come up with some ridiculous notions sometimes. I even had people approach me suggesting I'd set up getting shot to start a comeback. Sherry even asked me once if it had sort of been some kind of setup. I looked at her like she was crazy. Who in their right mind would do that? Hell, who in their wrong mind would come up with that idea? Certainly not me, but that's how twisted things can get sometimes, I guess.

Arum had given me $10,000 up front for training and living expenses, because I needed the money. He also was going to let me train at his Top Rank Gym in Las Vegas, so everything seemed to be falling into place when we headed to New York for a big press conference to announce the card. I should have been excited about that, because I was returning to the big stage at least one more time, but the whole thing turned into an embarrassing moment.

Gloria came with me, and she got up to the podium to introduce me. She went into a long rehash of all that had happened to me as I stood next to her like a mannequin. No one needed to hear that. We were there to announce a fight card, not go over my personal résumé of trials and tribulations.

As she droned on about all that, I could see the crowd wasn't happy. Nobody in that room wanted to hear from her. They just wanted to hear what I had to say about making a comeback. When I finally got to the microphone, I just said, "I'm a fighter. That's all I know how to do. God's given me this opportunity to start over again. Before I left the hospital, I told everyone there I'd be back in the ring. Some believed me. Some didn't. But here I am."

After that was over, I planned to fly back to Florida for a few days before returning to Las Vegas to continue training. It was the first time I'd gone back since the shooting. Just the thought of going back made me so uptight I began hyperventilating on the plane. I was freaking out.

I'd never had a panic attack like that before. I finally told myself to put on my big girl pants and face it. What had happened there happened, and I had to accept that and go back and face those memories. And I did.

When I got back into training, Miguel put me in to spar with a kid, and he told him to bring it to me. He thought if I saw my own blood, it might bother me, and he needed to know that.

With all the trauma, I'd suffered he wanted to test me against a guy who would pressure me, so he could see what I had left . . . if anything. He told me later he wanted to see how I would react to pain and to essentially being legally assaulted.

I wasn't ready for the kind of pressure that kid put on me. He busted up my nose and landed a devastating body shot that broke my ribs. The hospital hadn't told me I'd broken a rib and my scapula at some point during my struggles with Jim and because of what they had to do in the hospital to keep me alive.

I doubled over, and Miguel stopped the sparring session and asked me to do some sit-ups, but I couldn't breathe. I trained a few more days, but my ribs were bothering me so much we went to see a local doctor named Robert Voy, who is well known in athletic circles, and he said there was no way I could fight in March. I had a rib that was snapped in two.

Arum rescheduled the fight for June 4, 2011, in Los Angeles. That would be 21 months, one bullet wound, four stab wounds, and one recovery from cocaine addiction since I'd last been inside a boxing ring. If I could stay healthy, I would finally get a shot at that 50th victory I wanted so badly.

What I would not get, Arum informed me, was $100,000. He'd cut the purse to $25,000, because this fight wasn't part of a pay-per-view show. It would be on a much smaller card, and my fight was now off TV. What he didn't tell me initially was he was also deducting the $10,000 he'd already paid me in training expenses for the fight that didn't happen from that $25,000.

Miguel got the usual 10 percent trainer's fee, but it came off that $25,000 figure even though now I was only going to get $15,000, so there went another $2,500. Now I'm down from $100,000 to $12,500. When you're broke, which I was, that was better than a stick in the eye, but it sort of felt like a stick in the eye, to be honest about it. Welcome back to boxing, Christy Martin.

One Life Ends and So Does Another

I could always lose myself in the gym when preparing for a fight, but without cocaine or Jim around to alter my reality, I could no longer block out the world once I stepped outside the ring. Reality now had to be faced without a crutch or a threat hanging over me to dull my senses. This was more difficult at first than I expected, but I could not deny the realization that things with Sherry were not going the way I'd hoped. As my rematch with Dakota Stone approached on June 4, 2011, Sherry and I decided to split up, but I asked her to stay until after my comeback for a specific and admittedly selfish reason. I didn't want to deal with the public fallout of Sherry not being by my side.

It wasn't that I needed her moral support. I just wasn't ready to face a lot of "where is the woman who made your husband shoot you" questions that would be sure to come if I arrived in Los Angeles alone. She agreed. But while I was trying to focus on the fight, looming in front of me was not only our breakup but also Jim's upcoming trial and my mother's declaration she wouldn't come to the fight if Sherry was there.

My mom never liked Sherry, even before she knew she was a lesbian, and she didn't like her daughter openly living as a gay woman either. It's a tossup which she liked least, but my bet is the latter. Regardless, I was feeling family pressure again, plus the pressure of knowing a lot of the boxing world was watching to see if I had anything left.

I felt good in training but at 43 years old and after nearly 20 years as a prizefighter, I understood how I felt in the gym didn't tell me much about how I'd react in the arena. You only learn that after the first bell tolls.

After my ribs healed, training went well. Despite the pay cut, I recognized that the postponement was a blessing, because I wouldn't have been adequately prepared if I'd come back in March. It would have been too soon after all the trauma, both physical and mental, but by June I felt ready, even though I had a lingering doubt about one thing. Would I have the same kind of resiliency, or had I lost some of the mental toughness that was always so big a part of why I was successful?

Despite those concerns, once I got to the Staples Center on fight night, I was surprisingly relaxed. Even though I hadn't been in the ring in 21 months and inside a truly big venue since I fought Laila eight years earlier, it was like coming home to me until I left the locker room to make that lonely walk through the dark toward the well-lighted boxing ring up ahead.

Instead of being totally focused on my job and on what Stone would bring to the ring, it came into my mind how much I'd overcome and just how far I'd been able to go since the shooting. That was a natural reaction, perhaps, but instead of walking in totally focused the way I usually was, I was looking around, drinking it all in. That's good for posterity, but it's also a good way to end up on your posterior.

As it turned out, I was the one who put Stone on her posterior, dropping her in the fourth round with a left-right combination that ended with my right hand landing squarely on her chin and sending her to the floor for the first time in her career. The crowd went crazy, which lifted me up, even though I knew something the crowd did not. I'd broken my right hand.

Broken hands are part of the trade. They're like cuts on a butcher's hands or burns on a fireman's. Not many fighters avoid them completely, although there are different levels of problems they create. I'd been through it before, so it wasn't like I didn't know how to handle the situation, but in the final round, which was the sixth, I saw an opening and hit Dakota in the head with the same hand, and it hurt like hell.

It was an instinctual reaction to throw it when I saw an opening and my next act was just as instinctual. Because of the pain, I turned my back for a second and stepped away from her before turning back to face her and finish the fight. It was barely a second of weakness with less than a minute to go in the fight. I was ahead by two points on two scorecards and three on the third, so I could only lose if I got knocked out, which was not about to happen.

I intended to coast through those final 51 seconds as I had in the fifth round, avoiding her as much as I could and clinching when possible until I had that 50th win on my record. Avoiding trouble while fighting with an injury is a skill you learn, or you don't last long in boxing, and I knew well how to do it. So, I was shocked when the referee jumped between us and ordered me over to a neutral corner and asked for the doctor to check my hand.

He'd interpreted that one instant of weakness when I turned my back and stepped away from Stone as a signal I'd quit. Quit from a broken hand after all I'd been through? How do you come to that conclusion?

Arum said later I was crying in the ring, but that wasn't true. I didn't cry after I got shot. I damn sure wasn't crying over a broken hand. Was I bitching? Yes. Crying? Absolutely not. I was mad as hell and arguing with the referee and the doctor who was up on the ring apron telling me he was going to stop the fight. I was arguing with anyone who would listen to me, which in the end was nobody. If I'd been a man, I don't believe they would have stopped that fight with 51 seconds left.

I still remember as clearly as if it were yesterday the commission doctor saying to me, "You spoke at our convention a couple years ago and told us the ringside physician has to protect fighters from themselves."

Having my words thrown back in my face just made me angrier, and I hollered back, "Fuck you! I wasn't talking about me!"

Maybe it was an overreaction on the part of the referee and doctor because of all I'd been through, which should have had nothing to do with it. Maybe they really felt I couldn't get through 51 more seconds, which was ridiculous. I really don't know why it was stopped, because other than my hand it wasn't like Stone ever hurt me. The only thing she hurt me with all night was her head, but I'd lost my world title, and my hand was broken in nine places. Nothing would change those realities.

It was another setback, but nothing like what I was about to experience after they took me to Cedars-Sinai Hospital. They had to operate to put my hand back together, and while I was on the operating table, I had a stroke. They say God never gives you more than you can carry, but I think God overestimated my capacity for endurance at that point.

Did I have a stroke because I would eventually have one anyway after all the ways I'd abused my body with drugs? Was it the stress from the murder attempt, the upcoming trial, and the constant turmoil of my personal life? Was it the consequences of living a lie for so long?

Was the stress of my comeback too much for the one thing that had always kept me going, my heart? Or did something just go wrong during surgery that was simply bad luck? At that point it didn't matter. I was flat on my back again.

I'd been admitted to the hospital under an alias, Laura Slone, to avoid the media. Sherry had grabbed my check the same way Jim used to and was at the hospital with me. So was Gloria Allred, as well as my dad, brother, and sister-in-law. I was in ICU because, just like Jim, I didn't wake up after surgery. They told me I kept mumbling, "They're raping me here."

When I finally did awaken, my smile was crooked, I couldn't see straight, and could barely speak. At first, they didn't think it was a stroke, but after a couple of days Sherry said if they didn't get another doctor in to look at me, she was going to call Gloria. They didn't want any part of Gloria Allred on their case, so a neurologist and a cardiologist arrived and soon confirmed our fears.

I stayed in ICU for a week, and when I finally left, I couldn't walk right, talk right, or see right. My words were slurred, and I had double vision, which remains a problem for me at times to this day. I could not believe, after all I'd been through, that this had happened to me.

Despite my condition, I soon found myself in Gloria's office. Waiting for me was a contract to option the rights to my life story for several years for $5,000. She said there were no other people interested, so I signed it. I was broke and in no condition to make decisions like that, and Gloria had to have known it. It wasn't like I'd just had my tonsils out. But I took the check and found out pretty quickly it was a huge mistake.

I began to get calls about selling my life rights, but now they were gone. The woman who had them eventually sold them to someone else and kept the right to be the director if a film was ever made. One lawyer I hired later looked at the paperwork and asked if a kindergartener had signed the thing. All those years ago, when I'd practiced signing my name while I was in college, just in case I ever got famous, I'd never once practiced signing it after a stroke.

I did end up extending that option later and was paid fairly well, but my story has yet to become a movie. At one point Amy Schumer, the actress and comedian who has been nominated for an Emmy, a Tony, and a Grammy, wanted to play me, and it looked like that might happen. She called in 2018 and was pretty excited about the role, so we met in Las Vegas and Atlanta, and it seemed like she was ready to do it.

It was announced in Hollywood trade publications, and she started doing some boxing training to prepare herself, but in the end, she didn't like the person who wanted to direct it, then got pregnant, and the project lost steam. There are still people who say they're interested, but the closest we've come so far has been a documentary on Netflix and a true crime show on *48 Hours*. At this point I look at a film about my life the way I looked at a career in boxing back when I was living in that trailer in Bristol, Tennessee. It's a long shot, but keep trying. You never know what might happen.

Once I was released from the hospital, I was essentially homeless, so that necessitated a change in plans. Instead of breaking up, I went back to Charlotte with Sherry. Even though our relationship didn't work out, I have to give her credit. She took me in twice when I was down and out with no reason to think my career was going to restart. She did it after I was shot, and she did it after the stroke. She was too controlling a person for me to make a new life with, but she didn't have to do those things, and I'm grateful she did.

The only people who knew what happened were Sherry, Gloria, my family, and Miguel. Maybe Arum, too, but I don't know for sure that he did. Sherry wanted to keep it a secret so I could fight again, and I suppose I did as well, but I wonder now if I was even capable of understanding what was going on.

I was basically bedridden for several months. I had no income and nothing in the bank, so Sherry went back to working with special needs people and ex-GIs, helping them find jobs. I helped with it a little but mostly I just laid around trying to figure out what my next move would be.

Once, not too long after I got out of the hospital, I went into the bedroom in Sherry's house, felt lightheaded, and passed out. I was down for the count. Sherry heard a "thunk" and ran in and saw my eyes rolled back in my head. She thought I was dead and called 9-1-1. Being stubborn, I refused to go to the hospital and insisted I was fine. I was many things at that time, but fine wasn't one of them.

The same person who had refused to use a walker after being shot now needed a cane to get around. I'd gone from my cup overflowing with new possibilities to it not even being half full. To say I was depressed would be an almost comical understatement.

I knew my career in boxing was over, but I still wanted that "one more fight" every prizefighter desires. Although I understood my situation, I wasn't ready to accept it. I still was chasing that 50th win, so after a few months I called Miguel back to see if he was willing to keep training me. He said he would, but neither of us knew if I'd even be allowed back in the ring. As 2012 dawned, I had a lot on my mind, but the biggest thing had nothing to do with boxing. Jim's trial was scheduled for April with me as the lead witness, which meant another media circus and the most unnerving week of my life.

As the trial approached, I began to have more nightmares. Sherry told me there were times I'd be screaming in my sleep, kicking her or the wall in the dark. It was always the same dream. It was Jim chasing me around my grandmother's house in Itmann. He'd never catch me, but I never could get away. I'd wake up, and a few days or a few weeks later I'd have the same dream. I'm no dream therapist, but I don't think you need a PhD in psychology to get the meaning. That had been my life for 20 years with Jim and most of my life before that. Running away to try to keep a piece of myself alive.

Jim had been in jail since his arrest, meaning he'd been behind bars for 17 months when the trial began on April 24, 2012. He'd originally been denied bail, because he admitted to stalking me when I'd gone to Daytona to see Sherry. It was a relief to know he couldn't get to me, but now he'd be sitting in the courtroom every day. Because I was the victim, I could have sat there, too, but the prosecutors didn't think that was a great idea. They were afraid I might react to something I heard and that might affect the jury. They had a point. I was at least smart enough to know that would not have been good for me.

Before the trial began, I was afraid Jim was calling my mother. I told her many times not to talk to him, but she always did. I told the prosecutors he might try to call, and she might answer, so they were monitoring his phone from jail. They were never sure whether he did, but I wouldn't have put it past him. He really had my mom snowed.

What they did learn from his calls was nearly as shocking. They intercepted several calls he'd made from jail to a friend. They were trying to sell those sex tapes to media outlets. Jim was in custody and behind bars but still trying to hurt me and my reputation. The prosecutors told me the only reason they didn't sell them was there was no market for them. That's who Jim Martin really was. An abuser to the end.

My mother became an unknowing victim of his manipulation. She couldn't control my sexuality, so she wanted Jim to do it, and he played her. Once she'd convinced herself he'd done what she wanted to have done, she accepted anything else he did. Not trying to murder me of course, but pretty much all the rest of it. So, what we decided was the prosecutors would put her name on the witness list. They never intended to call her, but it meant she couldn't be in the courtroom.

They were afraid she might lose her temper at some of the things she'd hear and have an outburst, and I was afraid she might communicate with Jim in some way, so putting her on the witness list satisfied us both.

This was a time when *Court TV* was a very popular show. They'd show trials live on television, usually salacious ones, or ones with a celebrity involved. My case had both, so they ran it live all four days. I could have watched, but I didn't. What was the point? Jim wasn't going to testify, and I had a good idea what everyone else was going to say.

After all the detectives, medical people, ballistic experts, and several of my friends were done, it was finally time for me. My mind-set was like getting ready for a big fight. My vision was still affected by the stroke, but I was focused on what I had to do. I stared at Jim the entire time I was on that witness stand. I wanted him to feel me in that room.

We didn't do a lot of prep work on my testimony beyond the lawyers telling me not to elaborate too much. The story was pretty cut and dried, but his attorney tried to use what I'd told Detective Evans in the hospital to make it sound like WE shot me. WE stabbed me. Like it was a tag-team match.

At one point he asked me how I could have forgotten I'd been shot after I got to the hospital. Then he said, "Anything else you forgot?"

He'd been arguing without any evidence that I'd shot at Jim, and thus this was a case of self-defense, even though Jim had never made that plea. To claim self-defense, he had to admit to having given me all my injuries, which he refused to do, His lawyer knew he couldn't have it both ways but, like a good lawyer, he was trying.

I finally said, "I didn't point a pink, 9 mm gun at Jim, sir." And that was that.

The defense offered only two witnesses, Selkirk and the boxer Jim had called that led to his arrest. It wasn't much of a defense, but if you ever watched me box, you knew Jim Martin didn't know much about defense.

When his attorney made his closing argument, he pointed out I'd seen a divorce lawyer the week of the assault and claimed I'd gone to see my friends one last time not to say goodbye but to create an alibi for shooting Jim. He forgot to mention the only person who got shot was me.

The best he could do in the end was tell the jury, "Maybe he did it is not beyond a reasonable doubt. Probably he did it is not beyond a reasonable doubt." That was all he could come up with, because it was clear what had happened that evening at 1203 Fox Trail Road in Apopka, Florida. His client had tried to kill me . . . but he couldn't.

The trial had taken less than four days. Now the jury had to make a decision. It was 8:30 a.m. on Friday morning, April 27, when they began to deliberate. As time dragged on, I began to dread the possibility that this might carry over until Monday with no verdict. I wasn't sure I could make it through the weekend without knowing if I was going to have to look over my shoulder for the rest of my life or finally be free.

The prosecutor's main fear was the jury might have trouble understanding how a world championship boxer who was powerful enough to knock out 31 women wasn't able to stand up for herself in her own home. I knew there were many people who felt that way, but I didn't have the mental strength outside the ring to do that.

On the *48 Hours* show they asked one of the prosecutors, Deborah Barra, about that. She told them, "I think it's a remarkable story, because you have a world-famous champion boxer, and she could still be in a domestic violence relationship, because that isn't about physical strength. It is about mental abuse."

As I sat waiting, many thoughts ran through my mind. There was a lot of regret over so many decisions I'd made in my life. Then, just before 2 p.m., my phone rang. It was the loudest I'd ever heard a phone sound.

The voice on the other end said the jury had a verdict. It had barely taken five hours for their decision, whatever it was going to be.

I was happy with the job the two prosecutors, Ryan Vescio and Deb Barra, had done. I knew I'd told the truth, and I had the scars to prove it. I was very confident what would happen until I put down that phone. Then it hit me. What if they didn't believe me? What if he gets away with it? I was suddenly scared to death.

Waiting was the worst part. I thought it would feel like waiting for a decision after a big fight, but it was nothing like that. It wasn't anxiousness. It was pure terror.

When I entered the courtroom, all I could think was if they found him not guilty, I would have to hide for the rest of my life. I kept looking at the attorneys from the state and then at Jim sitting at the defense table, trying to get a sense of what was about to happen.

As the jurors walked in, I watched each one of them as closely as I've ever watched 12 people in my life. I was looking for a sign of what they were about to say, but they were poker-faced. I wasn't ready to die anymore, and I knew as surely as I'd ever known anything in my life that if he got off, that's what would happen. He would finish what he started.

The bailiff handed the judge the decision and then he asked the foreman how they ruled. I heard the only word in the English language I wanted to hear: GUILTY.

It was like someone had taken shackles off my body. I still had enough problems for two people, but I was free to walk my own path now. Free to make my own decisions and finally decide for myself what kind of life I was going to live and with whom I would share it.

One of the first decisions I made was to fire Gloria Allred. I couldn't stand the way she'd talk to me sometimes. She made me feel like I was one of those mistresses she represented in the Tiger Woods fiasco a few years ago. Like I was ignorant or helpless. I hated that.

I really didn't need her anymore anyway. The state of Florida had handled the trial, and it wasn't like there were people offering me all kinds of business deals she could negotiate. We finally had a falling out on the phone, and I fired her. She told me no client had ever fired her before the sentence was announced.

I told her, "Well then, you got a first out of this."

Two months later Jim was sentenced to the minimum mandatory sentence for second-degree attempted murder: 25 years without parole. He got another 10 years for stabbing me, but the judge said he would serve the two sentences concurrently. If he lives, he'll be 92 when he's released. I still fear that day may come. My fear, irrational as it sounds, is that he lives to be 92 and a week, and he uses that week to kill me. I've learned to put that thought mostly out of my mind . . . at least until 2035. His release date, last time I checked, was November 23, 2035. That's exactly 25 years to the day that he shot me. That's a little chilling, to be frank.

Before the sentencing several people gave victim impact statements. One of them was my friend Stacy Adams. The story she told made me feel ashamed of myself.

She said she never saw me have a single friendship of my own. "If Jim was not part of the relationship, there was no relationship," she said, but that wasn't the sad part. The sad part came when she told the judge she'd stopped working out at my gym after Jim accused her of being a lesbian in front of a room full of people.

"Christy was there," Stacy told the court that day. "She didn't say a word (in her defense). We didn't speak again for nine years. Not until Jim tried to kill her. Christy had become disposable, like everyone else in his life."

What hurt was knowing how weak I'd become that I would not stand up for a friend when Jim belittled her. It's not a moment I'm proud of. To not be strong enough to stand up for your friend is a sad state of affairs.

Stacy and I are friends again, thankfully. She helps me with my social media efforts, which is something I know next to nothing about. It's a blessing she didn't just walk away from me for good, but I would not have blamed her if she had.

Finally, it was my turn to speak, and I went after him. I wanted him to look at me. I didn't want him to ignore me one more time. I finally said, "Look at me, Jim! Look at me!"

Then I poured out my heart.

"From the beginning I financially supported you, your family, and all your significant others," I told him. "The only repayment I asked for many times was for you to let me go, not harm me physically, emotionally, or professionally. How was I repaid for taking care of you all those years? Blackmailed, addicted to coke, you sharing what I thought were private sex acts. But what really stands above all these things was you leaving me for dead on the bedroom floor. You coloring your hair and taking a shower, leaving me there. Dead. Stabbed. Shot. Bleeding.

"You *shot me*! You shot me with my own gun. Basically, point-blank and guess what, motherfucker? I walked out. I walked out by the grace of God."

The room was so quiet when I finally stopped talking, you could have heard a rat pissing on cotton, as my dad would say. I walked off the witness stand and instead of just leaving down the aisle between the prosecution's table and the defense table, I swerved over and walked right toward Jim. The prosecutors told me later they didn't know what was going to happen. It wasn't something I planned. Frankly, even if I'd thought about what I was about to do beforehand, you never know if you'll have the nerve to do it.

I just walked up and stared at him. I could feel Ryan's eyes getting wide at the prosecutor's table. I made Jim look at me and then I said, "I hope you burn in hell, motherfucker!"

Then I walked out. I didn't look at Deborah or Ryan over at the prosecutor's table. I didn't look at my friends or family. That was just for me.

Later Deb Barra told me, "I was like holy shit! In 115 trials I'd done, the victim had never done that. Everybody was stunned."

The prosecutors had coffee mugs made up with the scale of justice on them. Underneath it said "State vs. Martin 4/23/12. Under that line they added one more. It read, "I hope you burn in hell motherf***er!"

Later a counselor told me that as long as I was talking about attacking Jim, I wasn't healing, and that was true. It took some time to realize that, but you're still his victim when that's how you're thinking.

Somebody once said, "Living well is the best revenge." Easy for whoever said that to say, but they were right. Living well, loving well, and letting yourself be yourself really is the best revenge, even for a fighter.

There were a couple of statements of support for Jim, and one stunned the prosecutors. They had no idea who the woman was who had submitted a letter on Jim's behalf, so they asked me. It was one of Dad's sisters, Linda Salters Turner. My own aunt. My dad has never spoken to her since. Neither have I.

Jim made a statement to the court before he was sentenced, but I didn't stay to listen. I'd heard his lies for more than 20 years. I didn't need to hear any more, but later I was told he said, "I controlled nothing. I mean nothing in our life, outside boxing."

He claimed he was scared of me and that I once threw battery acid on him. That made me laugh, because that was one of the threats he used to make. That he'd throw acid on my face and leave a scar that would never go away.

At some point he said he realized now he should have entered a plea of not guilty by way of self-defense. Deb Barra told me she didn't think he could bring himself to do that, because he would have lost his "man" card. That's how inflated an abuser's ego can become. A few years ago, he even tried to sell his prison ID card on eBay. Unbelievable. Or maybe not so unbelievable.

What truly was unbelievable was that he also said during his statement to the court, "Christy was my hero in the gym and more so outside the gym. I worshipped the ground Christy walked on."

The last thing he added was, "I did not attack Christy."

Almost all the outward scars from the stabbings are gone except for the long one on my leg. Sherry wanted me to have plastic surgery to remove it, but I wanted a reminder of what I'd survived. Sometimes I think people are looking at it when I'm in shorts or a skirt. They may not be, but maybe I want them to so they know what I had to survive. Or maybe it's just a reminder for me of the cost to become the person I always wanted to be. The price was high. It was worth it.

CHAPTER TWENTY-ONE

Necessary Endings,
New Beginnings

Six weeks after Jim was sentenced, I lost my last professional fight. It hardly came as a surprise. My time had passed, as it does for all athletes. What's interesting is even when you see it coming, you don't expect it to be on *this* night.

Fittingly, considering how I'd lived so much of my life, I lied one last time to get into a boxing ring. I told no one involved but Miguel that 14 months earlier I'd had a stroke. The promoter was Roy Engelbrecht, a guy from California who was promoting Mia St. John, the former *Playboy* model I'd beaten 10 years earlier at the Silverdome outside Detroit. He made the fight, and I agreed, even though I never got paid for our first fight. Maybe Mia was bad karma for me, but all I could focus on was getting a paycheck and avoiding too much medical scrutiny. The less I said, the better.

The California State Athletic Commission didn't have a clue about what I'd gone through at Cedars-Sinai the year before, and I wasn't about to volunteer any information. When they asked about my hand, I told them it had been surgically repaired and healed fine. Nobody ever questioned Christy Martin's heart, so why would they?

All the people in my life who could have told me to stop were at the fight that night watching the curtain come down. I don't know that I would have listened to anyone, because that wasn't something I was doing much of at that point, but nobody tried to talk me out of it. Maybe they all felt the way I did, which was that even as dissipated as I'd become as a fighter, there was no way Mia St. John could beat me.

I didn't train fully and certainly wasn't capable of pushing myself at 44 the way I had at 24. Because of all I'd been through, Miguel decided not to let me spar. I hadn't sparred much in years anyway, and he believed at this point I knew how to fight and my style wasn't going to change, so we focused on my conditioning.

It wouldn't have mattered if I'd sparred a thousand rounds. Nothing would have changed what was coming. In the middle of the fight, Mia hit me, and I felt it in a way that wasn't normal. I noticed it hurt, which isn't how you react if you're a professional boxer. It hurt because I wasn't really a fighter anymore.

I still wanted to win, but most of the reason I was at the Table Mountain Casino outside of Fresno, California, on August 14, 2012, was the check. It was the opposite of how it had been when I was at my best. I couldn't see that in the moment, but I realize it now. It's just the truth of the matter.

Late in the final round, I put my hands down and just let her hit me. I knew I'd lost. I knew there would be no more boxing for me, so this was my defiant way of saying, "You can't hurt me!" I'm not sure if I was saying it to Mia or the world.

I lost a unanimous 10-round decision that was close on the scorecards but not in reality. I could make no excuses. I didn't deserve to win, and I couldn't go on boxing if I couldn't beat someone like Mia. If I'd lost to an up-and-coming hot prospect, it would have been different. Losing to someone I knew wasn't better than me was hard to accept, but I had no choice. In the boxing ring, you learn hard truths about yourself, and the truth was, I was finished.

After they announced the decision, I took the microphone from the ring announcer and said, "You've seen the coal miner's daughter for the last time. Thank you!" Then I walked off toward the locker room knowing there was one last thing in my career that had to be done.

A few days after that fight I went back to Las Vegas to see Dr. Margaret Goodman. She was one of Nevada's ringside physicians and someone who really cared about the fighters. That's why I chose her.

I told her I'd had a stroke after the second Stone fight. I don't think she believed me at first but after she got the paperwork from Cedars-Sinai she told me, "You know you can never fight again."

She told me that as my doctor she couldn't tell anyone because that information was confidential, but she was firm about my future. One way or another, she would make sure I never was allowed to box again.

That was exactly the reason I'd gone to see her. I knew the history of fighters. We keep fighting even when there's no logical reason to do it anymore. It's part of the mind-set that makes a champion in the first place. We defy the odds, and I had certainly defied more than most people. Knowing that, I wanted to make sure I would never fight again even when the inevitable happened and a promoter who thought he could make some money off my name called and offered me another payday. I'd already gotten that 50th win I'd been chasing the day I walked out of the courtroom in Orlando with Jim Martin on his way to becoming Florida Correctional Institution's prisoner number 78664. It was time to move on.

My life was far from settled at that point. My boxing career was over, but I had no idea what I was going to do next. I was still struggling to sort out my relationship with Sherry. We'd said we were finished after my fight with Mia, and I went back to Las Vegas for a little while, but before long I was back in Charlotte with her.

I once told a counselor I felt I owed her, because she'd taken care of me when I couldn't give her anything back. My counselor asked me a simple question that made me rethink how I viewed my life.

"Do you really?"

The truth was we stayed together off and on for most of the next five years, because we each thought we could get things out of the other that we couldn't find anywhere else. You can analyze a relationship to death, but the bottom line is we were both holding on for reasons that had little to do with the other person. I'm sure of that. Call it codependent. Call it using each other. Call it what you want, but we weren't together for the right reasons, or for the long haul.

By the time I was recovering from the stroke, I realized I wasn't in love with her. I was in love with what the two of us being together symbolized to me. I was letting the world see the real me, not the fighting me, or the hiding me. I was in love with living an authentic life for the first time, not who I was living it with.

Things were very rocky most of the time after I began to heal emotionally. I was a bundle of conflicting feelings, and they were all leaking out. I think we knew there was nothing there, and two years later I moved back home to West Virginia to work on getting my teaching certificate renewed.

I felt like a total failure. After all I'd accomplished in boxing, I was back where I started. I had no money, no job, and no idea what the future would hold. In my mind Sherry had become as controlling a personality in my life as Jim had been, always talking about protecting me. Protecting me from what? I wasn't going down that road again, but I had to admit to myself that although they may have both had controlling personalities and all that comes with that, I was the common denominator in those relationships. Did my personality leave me gravitating toward controlling people like my mother? Was I the problem?

Eventually she and I decided to try one last time. I earned my teaching certificate on March 28, 2014, from West Virginia University and found a job in a big high school in Charlotte. I never really wanted a full-time teaching job, so I started part-time to make myself get out of bed. I worked a day or two a week, and pretty soon it became a few more, and I began to like Charlotte and that part of my life.

Charlotte is a pretty progressive city. It was nothing to see two girls in the high school holding hands without anyone batting an eye. That really warmed my heart to see those young women free to be together and other people in school not caring.

At one point we moved to Flagler Beach, Florida, near where I'd agreed to marry Jim, thinking a change of scenery might solve our problems. I'd always loved the beach, but the beach couldn't do that for me. By early 2017, I was back in Charlotte alone. We were done.

I sold the one building in Florida I still owned, which was my gym, to pay off our debts, and on June 1, 2017, I finally got my own place for the first time since living in that trailer behind the grandstands at Bristol Motor Speedway nearly 25 years earlier. I became a permanent substitute at Vance High School so I could pay my bills, and I was a single woman dating who I wanted when I wanted. I wasn't "with" anyone, and that's the freedom I needed.

At first, I was just Christy Salters a teacher, but there was a janitor at the high school who once had been IBF bantamweight champion, a guy named Kelvin Seabrooks. He was a nice guy who knew who I was, or at least who I used to be. He told some people, and that led to an important moment in my life.

A senior doing a project on domestic violence approached me and asked if she could interview me. Her first question was, "How has being a victim of domestic violence changed your life?"

That question opened my eyes.

I sat straight up and looked at her for a minute. Then I said, "Honey, I'm not a victim. I'm a survivor. Victims are the ones who die, or can't get over the trauma that happened. I may still be struggling to get over it, but I'm no victim."

It was the first time I'd thought about my life in that way. That's when I realized one of the reasons God let me live was to spread that message to women suffering like I had. You do not have to be a victim. There's a way out, and you don't have to go as far down the rabbit hole as I did to find it.

I began to think more and more about domestic violence and how to spread a message of hope, not hopelessness. If you stay in the frame of mind that you're a victim, that's exactly what you remain. When you make yourself step out of that and see yourself as a survivor, you're on the way back up. The moment you do that for the first time, even if it's only for a few minutes, your abuser has failed.

Maybe you took a knee on life for a long time the way I did, because you had to, or you didn't think you had a choice. But that first moment you see yourself as a survivor, you're back on your feet.

It's not easy to stand up for yourself if you're still in an abusive relationship. Maybe you slide back, or fall down again, but you know you can get up, because you did, so you rise again. Eventually you realize that looking for someone else to save you won't work. You have to act to save yourself.

There are people who can help you along the journey. Friends, family if you're lucky, counselors. But the only one who can save you is you. All those years I'd suffered in hiding, I was OK with being a victim of my abusers. I can see that now. I accepted it as a part of my life, a sacrifice I had to make for good things to happen. One thing: seeing yourself as a victim means you're not responsible for anything. That's how you begin to think. A victim isn't responsible for their situation. A survivor is.

In a crazy way, you think being victimized is the easy way out. I could hide behind other people's control over me and blame them for what happened. Jim made all my decisions. I convinced myself I couldn't be who I wanted to be, not because I lacked the courage to stand up for myself, but because I had to hide it for the good of my career and my family. As long as I allowed others to control me, I didn't have to face the fear of what might happen if I let the world see the real me.

Until you can get beyond thinking of yourself as someone's victim, you can't become a survivor. When I heard the word victim that day, I instantly refused to accept it. I'm a lot of things but no victim. I accomplished a lot in my life inside the boxing ring. I won a lot of titles. But my greatest achievement is being a domestic violence survivor.

It can be a hard road to walk at first, and it can be a long one, as mine was. I'm still on it to this day, but it's the right road for all of us to follow, because it's the only one that will lead you back to yourself. It's the road to freedom, and I was finally on it. This young student helped me see what was next in my life. I had to find a way to use my story to help others.

How would I accomplish that? Once again, boxing lifted me up.

I'd promoted a small boxing show the previous year in Charlotte and began to work harder at it. I put on three more local shows and on February 28, 2017, filed the necessary paperwork to form a foundation dedicated to helping anyone suffering from emotional or physical abuse, children as well as adults. That's how Christy's Champs was born.

We work with local shelters and do all we can to support those trying to overcome domestic violence and live a life free from threats, blackmail, shame, fear, and physical and mental intimidation. We bring kids who have been victims of domestic violence or lived in families where it happened and now are in shelters to a boxing gym once or twice a week. They take a boxing class, but we're also buying computers so they can do their homework. We forget sometimes there are people who don't have access to the kinds of things most of us take for granted.

We have a hotline people can call, and at each of my promotions we try to partner with someone working on domestic violence issues in the local community. From that young student's question, my eyes were opened to what the purpose of my life needed to be. We called the foundation Christy's Champs because that's what we hope every survivor can become—the champion of their own life.

Around the time I began regular substitute teaching, I started going around to local boxing gyms in Charlotte and began thinking about becoming a real promoter. I financed my first show on some of the money I made selling my gym. It was October 19, 2016, and I've now done 25 shows in North Carolina, South Carolina, and Florida.

That first show lost $20,000, because I didn't know what I was doing. Like learning to box, you need to learn how to promote boxing. Heck, I put my first fight card on a Wednesday night. Who goes out on Wednesday night to watch boxing? Nobody, as I learned the hard way.

Some people wonder why I'm still in boxing after all the heartache and the pain, but the truth is boxing didn't bring me any of that. Boxing was my savior.

Promoting small shows is a grind, but I enjoy it. I'm always looking for a kid with that special gift. The spark that excites a crowd. A kid who wants to fight like hell the way I did. When I was fighting and people met me, it was like I was your neighbor. I was like Mr. Rogers until that bell rang. Then I was Freddy Krueger. That's the kind of kid I'm looking for.

Will I ever find that fighter? I know I won't if I don't keep looking, so I'm always searching for that special one who has talent and heart, because without heart talent doesn't mean anything.

I've actually worked with Don King a few times since I retired. I've brought him some fighters and been event coordinator on a couple of his shows. We've talked about copromoting, and I hope we will. Don's 90 now, but nobody knows more about how to promote a boxing match than he does.

I'm not teaching anymore. My life now revolves around boxing, my work with domestic violence survivors, and one other thing that's a big part of my life. Like most of the good things I've experienced, it came to me through boxing.

After I got shot, a lot of people reached out to me. One was a former opponent, Lisa Holewyne. She was the woman I boxed the last time I ever fought for Don, and it was one of my best wins, because I wasn't trying to knock her out. I was trying to outbox her, and I did well.

Later Lisa was one of my sparring partners for a few fights, and we developed a professional respect for each other. But it never went beyond that. There was no real relationship there, but I did remember how she'd acted once when she was in my training camp, and I wasn't feeling well.

Usually, the sparring partners stay in a hotel, but this time Jim said Lisa could stay at our house. The second day of sparring I was so sick I had to stop training, and I went home and went to bed. Jim went out, and Lisa came to see how I was doing.

She brought me some tea and honey and asked if I had a thermometer. I had no idea where it was, so she put her cheek against my forehead and said I felt like I was burning up. She touched my face as if she had real concern for me beyond just being someone worried that I wouldn't be able to train the next day. I remember thinking here was a person who barely knew me and was showing me real kindness. I hadn't felt like someone was there for me like that for a long time.

There wasn't any attraction between us. It wasn't a sexual thing. It was just that I'd forgotten someone could just be kind to me, the person. Not to Christy Martin, the fighter, or Christy Martin, the moneymaker. Just Christy, the person. I'd forgotten what that felt like.

After that camp was over, she went back to Texas, and I stayed in Florida training with Jim. We didn't have much contact with each other until I started promoting these small shows in North Carolina. She'd called after the shooting to see how I was doing; and when I heard her mom had passed, I sent her a sympathy card that she still has. But we didn't see each other until 2017, when she finally came to watch one of my promotions.

She was supposed to come in April but broke her ankle and couldn't travel, and I told her that if she didn't want to come, she could have just said she was busy. She finally made it to a show on July 29, 2017, at a place called Center Stage in Charlotte. She's been center stage in my life ever since.

The night before the show she came back to my house, and we started flirting. The next morning, I knew I was falling in love, which was the last place I expected to be.

The day after the fights, my parents were at my house because they'd come down for the show. Lisa went off to pick up some food, and after she left my mom asked why she was there, and I just blurted out, "She's my girlfriend."

My mom had been fine with her when she left to get food, but Lisa found herself in the deep freeze when she came home and had no idea why. I was heading to Vegas a few days later; Lisa met me there, and we've been a couple ever since.

For a while she flew back and forth between Charlotte and Austin, where she has a thriving construction business. What struck me was how different our relationship was from the ones I'd had with Jim and Sherry. I had nothing to give Lisa. My career was over. My cars and real estate were long gone. All I had to offer was me, and that seemed to be all she wanted. She didn't need anything from me. Maybe because she had been a successful boxer and track athlete herself, there was never any resentment about me being Christy Martin, whatever that meant to the public.

By November, we'd decided to get married, but I wanted her to understand what she was getting herself into. So I called home the day before Thanksgiving to tell my parents. It was November 22, 2017.

I put my mother on speaker so Lisa could hear our conversation. I didn't tell her Lisa was there. There I was, a 49-year-old woman with big news. When I said Lisa and I were getting married in Austin the Saturday after Thanksgiving she hollered, "No! Don't do it. I'm telling you, don't you do it!"

I was pretty calm because I wasn't seeking anyone's approval anymore. Instead, I told her what I wished I'd said years ago. I said I'd spent most of my life trying to make everyone else happy, and I ended up shot, stabbed, and miserable, so I intended to spend the time I had left trying to make me happy, and I hung up. Lisa was shocked.

Within about five minutes my mother called back. I didn't want to talk to her, so I let it go to voice mail. She said she'd spoken to my dad, my brother, and my niece Brittany, and they all approved, so I should do it. Later my brother, Randy, told me he'd told her, "As long as Sis is happy, it's OK."

I was a little angry at the time, but looking back I have to admit that that second phone call was a big step for my mother to take. It couldn't have been easy for her to make that call, but she did it. She came as far as I guess she could on something that has tormented the two of us nearly all my life. It was a start. We still have a long way to go, but you have to start somewhere.

Same-sex marriage was legal in Texas, but there is a waiting period of a few days after you applied for the license. We waited the required 72 hours, and then the two of us went before a justice of the peace and were married. No one else was there.

I was 100 percent sure I wanted to spend the rest of my life with Lisa, and five years later nothing has changed. I was surer of that than anything in my life, including my decision to give over my life to boxing.

We did the Charlotte-to-Austin arrangement for almost a year. I continued to substitute teach and work on my domestic violence outreach and my boxing promotions, but finally we just wanted to be together, so I moved to Austin. That was hard for me, because I'd gotten to the point where I felt at home in Charlotte, and I loved the beaches in Florida, which are not too easy to get to from Texas. I was comfortable in Charlotte, but I was more comfortable with Lisa. Despite all the headaches a promoter has to put up with, I still love boxing, too, but it isn't my first love anymore. Lisa is.

When I finally went public with who I was, I didn't exactly sneak quietly out of the closet. It was *bang*, and I was out. Literally, a bang to be honest. Today I go to boxing events and people ask, "Hey, where's your wife?" We were back in West Virginia not long after we were married, walking down the street in Mullens holding hands. This local guy drives by in a big pickup, hits the brakes, and starts backing up. Before we could panic, he hollers out the window, "Hey, Sis. What's up?" He was a friend of my family. I introduced him to my wife. It was like everything had changed.

My fear is it may not be quite as changed as we would like to think, though. You can see that in the antigay actions being taken by some politicians. And there are still too many people who have trouble with it and make trouble for other people who just want to be free to love who they love. That's pretty sad, and it makes me wonder.

I'm sure there's a young girl in a little town somewhere who doesn't believe she has the luxury or the freedom to walk down the street holding her girlfriend's hand. Hopefully the next generation sees people like us and believes it's OK to be who we are. After all, who's really against love?

People still know me best as the first big female star in boxing. In 2014, I became the first woman boxer elected to the Nevada Boxing Hall of Fame, and three years ago I was among the first three women boxers inducted into the International Boxing Hall of Fame. Coincidentally, Lucia Rijker was also elected, so who knows? Maybe we'll fight yet, although at our age I think we'll just shake hands.

The induction was put off a couple of years because of the COVID-19 pandemic, so I'm still waiting to see my plaque on the wall next to all those great champions I admire so much. But it's amazing just to think it will happen. It was always just so incredible to me to be around such great fighters. They took me in like I was their sister or their daughter. I was so terrified of Marvin Hagler, who many feel is the greatest middleweight champion ever, that the first time I saw him at the Hall of Fame in 1996, he walked into the room, and I walked out. I was in awe.

At the end of that weekend, we were standing in line waiting to be introduced, and he walked over and said, "You have a really good left hook." I nearly passed out.

That's the kind of respect I always wanted. It's the kind of respect I have for boxing, the Hall of Fame, and the legends who are in there. It's hard to believe I've joined those fighters, and I'm so honored to be among them. But because of all that's happened in my life, I wonder sometimes what people would be saying to me if I were still that 21-year-old gay girl from Nowhere, West Virginia, hiding in the closet society created for people like me. I'm not totally convinced they'd be so quick to say, "Be who you are," but I can hope, can't I? After all, hope is what will keep you going, so believe in hope. I know I do.

I've written this book from my scars, not my wounds. Scars are a sign of healing. Wounds signal bleeding . . . or brooding resentments. Both signal pain, but only one is a sign that most of the pain is gone, and it's time to live again. That's where I am today.

I'm not pain free or without painful memories. I usually don't open my blinds until sunlight for fear someone might be looking in the window, and Lisa has woken up more than a few times from me throwing punches in my sleep because Jim is "chasing" me. Sometimes flashbacks come when I least expect them, like the time Lisa was chopping some vegetables with a big sharp knife. I had my back to her, and it freaked me out. But I'm healing every day and happy to be alive.

I get asked a lot, "How did you go from victim to survivor to happy?" I tell everyone the same thing. It was incredibly hard, but also incredibly easy. I just kept getting up.

That's the difference between champions and everyone else. The first American heavyweight champion to wear boxing gloves rather than fight bare knuckles was a guy named John L. Sullivan. In 1892, he defended his title against a guy named James J. Corbett, who is considered the father of modern boxing because of his scientific approach to the sport. He ended up knocking John L. out in the 21st round. When he was later asked what made him a champion he said, "You become a champion by fighting one more round.

"When things are tough, you fight one more round. When your arms are so tired that you can hardly lift your hands to come on guard, fight one more round. When your feet are so tired you have to shuffle back to the center of the ring, fight one more round. When your nose is bleeding and your eyes are black and you are so tired that you wish your opponent would crack you one on the jaw and put you to sleep, fight one more round remembering that the man who always fights one more round is never whipped."

That is a champion's code for life, and I don't think it only applies to boxers. If you are being abused by some sort of predator, and you're hurt and scared, remember what James J. Corbett said. The man or woman who fights one more round for themselves is never whipped. That is what got me through all my trials and all my failures.

I'm not here to bs you. I'm not going to try to tell you it's easy to overcome sexual abuse or domestic abuse or societal prejudice. It's not. I'm here to say your life is worth fighting for. When life is bleakest, you may even have to take a knee for a moment to rest, but you have to find a way to get up. I took a knee once and still regret it, but what I don't regret is I did get up. I had no idea where I was headed or how I would get there, but I knew one thing for sure. Don't stay down.

So whatever you're facing, I know you can do it if you're willing to fight one more round. Why am I so sure of that?

Because I did it with a bullet in my chest.

You may be surprised where you end up once you stand up, but wherever that is, I'm sure of one thing. You'll end up with your hand raised. You'll be one of Christy's Champs.

INDEX

abortion, 48–51

abuse: drug, 226; emotional, 202, 216, 236; physical, 216, 236; sex, drugs, videotapes relating to, 217–18, 254; of women, 1, 6, 13. *See also* domestic abuse; sexual abuse, by cousin; sexual abuse, by husband

abuser, Martin, J., as, 1–2, 6–13, 39, 65, 122–23, 217, 234

abusive marriage, 149

abusive relationship, leaving of, 217

Achilles heel surgery, of Rijker, 212

Acuna, Marcela, Martin, C., sparring with, 148, 152

Adams, Stacy, 257

aftermath: of Gogarty and Martin, C., fight, 117, 121, 133; of murder attempt, of Martin, C., 242

aggressiveness, 17, 21, 43; in boxing, 57, 158, 159–60

Alexander, Lana, 210–11

Ali, Laila, 185, 207; as daughter of Ali, M., 182, 190, 191; Mayweather, R., training of, 190

Ali, Laila, Martin, C., fight with, 184–85, 201, 204, 207, 238; broken records with, 192; brutality of, 197–98; confidence lost during, 194; knee taken during, 197–98; losing during, 198–99; in Mississippi Coast Coliseum, 192; purse relating to, 191; turning point after, 190–98; weight difference relating to, 190, 191–93, 195

Ali, Muhammad, 161, 174, 182, 190, 191

Allred, Gloria, 244, 246, 251–52; firing of, 256–57

All-Star catcher, in Little League, 19, 21

All-Star team, in basketball, 26

America Presents, 179

Anani, Sumya, Martin, C., fight with, 152; brutality during, 153–56; disappointment with, 156; head-butting during, 153; majority decision with, 154

anger: in ring, 158, 165–66; with sexual abuse, 30, 32

Apopka, 204, 255; gym in, 188, 208, 264; home in, 124, 181, 230, 239; hospital in, 230, 235, 237

appeals, of Martin, J., 244

appearances, on television and radio, 121–22

Arce, Jorge, 212

art, in boxing, 159

Arum, Bob, 186, 245–47, 251, 253; King, D., rival of, 131, 149; as promoter, 41, 212; Rijker and, 149–51, 178, 206–12

athletes, 21, 27, 28, 85; confidence as, 202; gay women as, 1, 5, 22, 39, 78, 149. *See also specific athletes*

attack, 2; of Martin, C., by Rijker, 176–79; in sports, 21, 31, 105, 177, 197, 228–29

attitude toward women, of Martin, J., 67–69

background, 16–17, 21, 27, 29, 32, 36

Bailey, Jeff, 108, 178, 196, 215

Barkley, Charles, 173–74

Barr, Roseanne, 128

Barra, Deborah, 175, 256, 258, 259

Basilio, Carmen, 133–34

basketball, 50, 60, 61, 62; on All-Star Team, 26; on boys' team, 17, 21, 22, 105; in college, 36–39, 46, 53, 57, 59, 63; with Dad, 17–19, 21; on girls' team, 23; with Lusk, 33–34

bedridden, after stroke, 253

"The Bite Fight," Tyson-Holyfield rematch as, 143

ABOUT THE AUTHORS

Christy Martin is the most successful female fighter in boxing history and widely regarded as the woman who legitimized women's participation in boxing and other combat sports. When she began her career, women's boxing was banned in most countries around the world and many states in the United States. She became an international sensation after turning pro at 21 following a brief time fighting in Toughman contests in West Virginia.

Discovered by legendary promoter Don King, Christy went undefeated for nearly a decade, won the WBC world junior welterweight championship, and became the first female fighter to box on national television, at Madison Square Garden, on premium cable (Showtime), on pay-per-view, and to sign for a $1 million purse. She remains the only female fighter to appear on the cover of *Sports Illustrated*. She retired in 2012 after a comeback fight following a stroke with a 49-7-3 record and 31 knockouts. In 2016 she became the first female boxer inducted into the Nevada Boxing Hall of Fame, and in 2020 was among the first three women fighters enshrined in the International Boxing Hall of Fame.

She is currently CEO of Christy Martin Promotions, a boxing promotional company. She also runs Christy's Champs, a foundation offering support to all domestic abuse victims and bringing child victims of domestic violence to boxing gyms in search of improving their self-esteem. She is a frequent speaker on domestic violence, having survived a hellish 20-year cycle of physical and emotional abuse at the hands of her husband before he shot and nearly killed her in 2010.

Today she is happily married to a former opponent, Lisa Holewyne, and resides in Austin, Texas.

Ron Borges has attended more than 1,000 world championship fights around the world. He covered boxing, pro football, golf, baseball, hockey, and four Olympic Games for 25 years at the *Boston Globe*. He then became the lead sports columnist at the *Boston Herald*, where he also continued to cover prizefighting.

He has been named Massachusetts Sportswriter of the Year five times, was selected one of America's top 10 sports columnists by the Associated Press sports editors multiple times, and his work has been anthologized in *Best Sports Stories* more than a dozen times. He is also the author of *Present at the Creation*, the autobiography of Upton Bell, son of legendary NFL commissioner Bert Bell and a longtime NFL executive. In 2022, he was enshrined in the International Boxing Hall of Fame.